EXTERNALITY AND INSTITUTIONS

EXTERNALITY
AND
INSTITUTIONS

ANDREAS A. PAPANDREOU

CLARENDON PRESS · OXFORD

Oxford University Press, Great Clarendon Street, Oxford OX2 6DP

Oxford New York
Athens Auckland Bangkok Bogota Bombay
Buenos Aires Calcutta Cape Town Dar es Salaam
Delhi Florence Hong Kong Istanbul Karachi
Kuala Lumpur Madras Madrid Melbourne
Mexico City Nairobi Paris Singapore
Taipei Tokyo Toronto Warsaw

and associated companies in
Berlin Ibadan

Oxford is a registered trade mark of Oxford University Press

Published in the United States by
Oxford University Press Inc., New York

First published 1994
First published in paperback 1998

British Library Cataloguing in Publication Data
Data available
ISBN 0 19 828775 5 (hbk)
ISBN 0 19 829307 0 (pbk)

Library of Congress Cataloging in Publication Data
Papandreou, Andreas A.
Externality and Institutions / Andreas Papandreou.
p. cm.
Includes bibliographical references.
1. Externalities (Economics). I. Title.
HB846.3.P36 1994 330.1—dc20 93-48886
ISBN 0 19 828775 5 (hbk)
ISBN 0 19 829307 0 (pbk)

Printed in Great Britain
on acid-free paper by
Bookcraft (Bath) Ltd
Midsomer Norton, Avon

ACKNOWLEDGEMENTS

THIS book, which draws on my thesis with the title 'Ideas of Externality', was completed during my stay as a research fellow (1992–3) at the Stockholm Environment Institute. I thank the entire staff of the institute for providing a stimulating and friendly environment. Special thanks are due to the director of the Stockholm Environment Institute, Michael Chadwick. I am also grateful to my colleague Gordon McGranahan, who read over many parts of my book giving me valuable advice.

I have had the great fortune of Amartya Sen's advice as a thesis supervisor and during the completion of this book. He has been a constant source of inspiration and guidance, for which I thank him warmly.

I am grateful to Warren Samuels who has kindly offered extensive and valuable comments, and to Petros Ioannou with whom I had lively and constructive debates on many of the issues I cover in this book. Many people have contributed to my efforts in various ways, and I would like to thank them: Wilfred Beckerman, Kostas Gatsios, Zoe Georganta, Vaggi Kastanidou, Louis Lefeber, Richard Lissak, Peter Mathews, Nick Papandreou, George Trepeklis.

Finally, I would like to thank my family, whose love and support has always been there.

A.P.

To Maniani

CONTENTS

LIST OF FIGURES

1

Introduction

More than a century ago Alfred Marshall had an idea which he felt identified a systematic blemish on the proverbial invisible hand. He called this idea 'external economy'. Naturally it attracted attention, not only because of Marshall's stature, but because it raised the ever-contentious issue of governmental management of the economy. Not too long afterwards Sir John Clapham called Marshall's idea an 'empty box'; a category that was empty because nothing in the real world corresponded to it. This was but one incident in a long, often-heated, and largely unsettled battle over the significance of what came to be known as 'externality'.

Over the years economists have filled the 'empty box' called externality with various possible associations with real-world phenomena (synergies among firms, pollution, congestion, envy, etc.). But more important, the box has been filled with ideas of what the contents of the box should be (including the idea that it should be empty), ideas that try to provide a clear-cut rationale for why some activities should be allowed entry and others not.

Stated this way this noetic turf war sounds trivial, but in fact it has had a central role in shaping our understanding of economic inefficiency, and the many concepts associated with the malfunctioning of the market (public goods, non-convexity, information deficiencies, missing markets, poorly defined property rights, etc.). And this is not a mere exercise in taxonomy, it is critical in organizing our panoply of analytical skills, in helping us identify fundamental causes of allocational inefficiency and suggesting theoretical and practical means of dealing with these. The externality debate has influenced our perception of the role of governing authorities. More recently it has become central to our appraisal of the ecology–economy connection. It has also had an important role in the development of new sub-disciplines such as Law and Economics and Neoinstitutional Economics.

Given the importance of externality in economic theory, and

the effort put into characterizing externality, it is surprising how hazy a concept it has remained. Extending the empty-box metaphor, not only has there not been consensus on what externality should signify, but the box seems to be semi-opaque, preventing a clear understanding of what the different ideas are. The present intuitive notion of externality as activities that take place outside market transactions, belies the difficulties that arise the minute one tries to give analytical content to this intuition, treating it as a separate category of market failure. This has not prevented a flourishing 'theory of externalities' that has undoubtedly contributed greatly, and will continue to contribute, to our understanding of resource misallocation with corresponding insights into policy mechanisms for correcting such misallocations. None the less, this intuitive understanding of externality, though apparently compelling, is also misleading. Accordingly, the standard theoretical apparatus of dividing the world into those activities that are 'internal' to the market, and those that are 'external' (like environmental degradation or under-provision for education), and seeking means of 'correcting' or extending the market so that the activities in question are 'internalized', or properly priced, confronts some serious limitations.

Some of these limitations can be sensed by pointing to pervasiveness of externalities. It is becoming clear that the number, significance, and complexity of what we perceive as 'external' interdependencies among agents in the (global) economy, have been growing rapidly. This concern over the 'quantity' of externality is no doubt important. If a large-enough proportion of economic activity turns out to be somehow outside the functioning of the market system, the standard approach of trying to 'correct' the existing institutional structure to incorporate these 'missed' activities would be put in question. If so much important activity is taking place outside the institutions that are meant to guide resource allocation, then surely attempts at 'marginal' adjustments would be deficient. We would have to take one step back in the conceptualization of the resource-allocation problem. Rather than looking at how the signalling devices (prices) of existing institutions fail to do their work, it would be more appropriate to ask how institutions need to be formed so that many important economic activities are explicitly guided by the institutional structure. In a sense, one needs to move from the question of optimal prices to the prior question of optimal institutions. Instead of seeking ways of correcting certain prices in the system, we would seek to form a better overall 'voting' system, which would result in improved 'prices'.

In fact, I argue that the methodological focus on institutions is critical even if externalities are not pervasive. An understanding of the ideas of externality raises with far greater clarity and force the kinds of issues alluded to when contemplating the pervasiveness of externalities, as well as other methodological issues. It is my contention that a better understanding of the ideas behind externality will go a long way in addressing some of the limitations of the standard applications of externality, and more generally, limitations of the neoclassical conception of economic inefficiency.

This is a book about ideas of externality and some of the ways that these have influenced and should continue to influence economics. It critically surveys the different approaches to the characterization and use of the concept of externality in the large and varied literature on the subject. Their reach and relevance are compared. An attempt is made to clarify the plural concepts that underlie the apparently homogeneous notion of externality.

Finally, I argue that much of the difficulty that surrounds attempts to understand externality derives from the inadequate treatment of the role of institutions in the economy. A richer understanding of the economic function of institutions proves to be critical to understanding certain limitations of mainstream economic theory, as well as the means to overcome them. The importance of institutions for economic analysis is not a novel idea. Many economists have recognized this, and institutional economists (broadly defined) have been stressing the need to place institutions at the centre of economic analysis for some time, and their analysis has generated a wealth of insights. Despite these important advances, there are implications of incorporating institutions endogenously in economic models that affect core concepts of economic analysis (that have been at the heart of the externality debate), like economic inefficiency and causality of market failure, that still have not been adequately addressed in mainstream or institutional economics.

My hope is not simply to add an idea to the 'externality box', or reshuffle the contents. My aim is to make the box as transparent as is possible.

Different ways of characterizing externality have been critically reviewed here. The view that externality corresponds to non-marketability is one of them, and has become increasingly dominant in the literature. That view does indeed have considerable cogency, but it suffers from two major problems. First, what is or is not outside the market depends on the institutional arrangements which govern the extent of the market. The presence of substantial externalities themselves provide incentive for creating markets where none existed. This suggests the need to investigate underlying economic mechanisms that lead to the formation of alternative institutions. Rather than emphasizing the separateness of non-marketable activity, it is important to view all economic activity, as well as the extent of the market, within a broad and evolving institutional context.

Second, in studying the relation between the presence of externalities and the resulting inoptimality of outcomes, one has to contrast the actual outcome with some alternative which could have actually been used. As some have argued, if a relation that is not made 'internal' to some market process cannot be 'internalized' in any institutional relationship, there is no alternative to leaving that connection unattended. The inoptimality connection has to be, on this view, conditional on actual possibilities of market and other institutional arrangements. The use of the idea of 'non-marketability' as a pointer to inoptimality of outcomes relies therefore on the counterfactual possibility of whether some alternative institutional procedure could have 'internalized' the relation in question.

The concept of non-marketability and its inoptimality implications are, therefore, less simple than they may first appear. In particular they call for supplementation and modification by institutional analysis. While institutional analysis is neglected in some treatments of externality, others have tended to treat the institutional possibilities in rather stylized form, implicitly assuming that any relation which is not 'internalized' by some actual market *could not have been* 'internalized' by any alternative arrangement (e.g. potential markets which for some reason did not actually develop). The institutional approach I have tried to pursue takes the possibility of institutional developments extremely seriously (as Coaseans do), without reading the actual non-existence of some market as proof that it could not have existed. The tendency to assume that what is observed is typically optimal is thus resisted, without downplaying the focus on institutional questions that Coaseans have brought to bear on the older neoclassical literature on resource allocation.

PLAN OF BOOK

The book is divided into two parts. Part I takes on the task of critically surveying the many approaches to the characterization and use of the concept of externality in the literature. The aim is to uncover the many concepts and motivations that underlie the illusive notion of externality, and to investigate the relevance of these. Chapter 2 begins this task by providing a history of the notion of externality. The focus is on how economists have characterized externality or what they thought it was. Figuratively speaking, it provides a family tree of the many meanings and names associated with externality.

A standard characterization of externality identifies externality as being present when the actions of one agent directly affect the environment of another agent, i.e. the effect is not transmitted through prices. In Chapter 3 I critically scrutinize one of the more rigorous characterizations of externality given by Baumol and Oates (1975) that is representative of this kind of approach to externality. I try to show the inherent difficulty that these kinds of characterizations have in meaningfully identifying a class of phenomena or activities to call 'externality', and more importantly raise the question of whether it is analytically useful to make a distinction of 'external' and 'internal' activity on these lines.

Chapter 4 moves to another representative set of characterizations of externality in the literature, in particular those of Bator (1958), Arrow (1970), and Heller and Starrett (1976). The latter two offer more analytical or abstract characterizations of externality, which make some kind of identification of externality with missing markets. Rather than looking for some phenomena to identify as externality, these authors are more concerned with understanding market failure and what causes it. I argue that these 'missing market' characterizations are also inadequate in providing a classificatory structure of market failure. On a more positive note I argue that these various attempts to characterize or 'locate' externality have had a profound effect on the way market failure and the various causes of market failure are perceived in economics, but that an adherence to a 'missing market' view of externality will ultimately obscure or sidetrack these important methodological developments. I suggest that this function of the notion of externality may be the more important contribution of the notion of externality.

It becomes increasingly clear that the difficulty in understanding externality results from the inadequate treatment of the role of institutions in the economy. The transformation of views on fundamental concepts like market failure, causality of failure, efficiency, non-convexity, etc., are concomitant with the groping awareness of the role of institutions and organizational costs (transaction costs). More specifically, the costs of organizing economic activity (forming institutions), known in the literature as transaction costs, need to be made an integral part of economic analysis. Rather than treating institutions as given at the outset of modelling resource allocation, models need to be devised that treat institutions endogenously.

A term that has been closely associated with externality, and market failure more generally, is non-convexity. Chapter 5 elucidates the relationship between non-convexity in production (although the insights can be extended to the space of utilities and organizational activity) and 'externality'. The notion of non-convexity is often discussed in mathematical treatments of the subject and it is sometimes difficult for the reader to figure out the precise relationship between non-convexity, missing markets, lack of property rights, and more generally market failure. Non-convexity is often seen as a more fundamental cause of failure than externality because it is perceived as being independent of how institutions are defined. While there is an element of truth to this view, it needs to be emphasized that the very existence and form of non-convexity in production sets is in fact largely dependent on how institutions are defined. An important element in comprehending the role of non-convexity is to understand how it depends on the way property rights, markets and firms, or agents, are defined. For instance, property rights may be defined over resources, over activities, or over the exchange value of some goods or activities (as when an individual is entitled to the fruits of her labour or some portion thereof). A change in the space of property rights will alter the shape or very existence of non-convexity of the production space. A clearer understanding of the relationship between the way entitlements are defined and non-convexity itself is an important ingredient in an analysis of market failure.

We often talk about this or that cause of market failure. Much of the literature on externality is about investigating the causality of failure. Chapter 6 delves into the question of what it means to say that something 'caused' a market system to fail. It has been questioned whether 'externality' or 'missing markets' can be usefully looked at as causes of market failure. A number of economists have suggested that all market failure can be explained in terms of transaction costs or, more specifically, lack of information. I criticize this view and offer a methodological discussion on what may be considered relevant ways of imputing causes of market failure.

Much of Part I involves a kind of extended anatomy of market failure through the guise of the peculiar concept of externality. Effort is put into uncovering the inadequacies of existing approaches to externality along with the several ways of classifying market failure, but also suggesting the kinds of issues that economic theory should be more sensitive to. Having raised doubt about the existing characterization of externality (as well as the accompanying distinctions of market failure) a natural question becomes: Is there a constructive role for some concept of externality? If so, what is it? Since my argument is (in part) that there is no clear understanding of what externality is or what the word 'externality' stands for, we need to zero in on what motivated economists to attach some meanings to the word 'externality' and why the antonyms 'external' and 'internal' have had such a grasp on the imagination of economists. I argue that two very different meanings of the word 'external' have driven the notion and confusion of the two has been conducive to confusion in the literature. By getting to the heart of the motivations and meanings associated with 'externality' one is in a position to evaluate whether there is room for constructive use of the term. In fact, I argue that the appellation 'externality' is not a very good term to signify some specific category of economic phenomena, or some cause of market failure. More important, however,

than being able to clearly identify some category of phenomena
to be labelled 'externality', or find a name for some important
cause of market failure, is to attempt to clarify and answer the
questions, and pursue the motivations, that made the search for
'externality' so compelling. To take Quine's words and to twist
them somewhat by putting them in a different context: 'To define
an expression is, paradoxically speaking, to explain how to get
along without it' (Quine 1987: 44). In a sense it is my hope that
we can learn to get along without the word 'externality' by better
understanding the concerns and motivations that underlie the
many attempts to characterize the term. In Chapter 7 I suggest
what these concerns are and sketch the kind of implications they
may have for the notion of market failure and efficiency in economics. In particular, I suggest that market failure needs to be
placed in a broader perspective of institutional failure, where
markets (or the market system) are seen as being less effective in
attaining some social welfare objective relative to some alternative institutions. I also suggest what is meant by institutional
failure.

Having established that a central function of the notion of
externality has been to place at centre stage the need for a richer
understanding of institutions and their role in resource allocation,
Part II confronts this issue squarely. The 'Institutional' school of
thought, by making institutions central to its analysis, is able to
offer important insights into the function of institutions, and the
reappraisal of notions such as market failure, optimality, causality of failure, etc. Specifically, I am interested in bringing out
more fully the implications of incorporating organizational costs
into economic models. Chapter 8 reviews some of the existing
theories of how institutions are formed. I criticize theories that
treat efficiency as the driving force behind institution-formation
for presuming that private gains in institution-formation will be
aligned with social gains. In the externality literature it is often
presumed that existing market institutions are efficient; my discussion argues against this presumption. Some related issues are
also discussed.

Once institutions are treated as endogenous in models and are
not taken as given at the outset, a major policy question becomes
how to form efficient institutions. In Chapter 9, I criticize one of
the fashionable theories of optimal institution-formation in the

Law and Economics literature that Posner (1983) has developed, known as Wealth-Maximization. When this principle is used to establish entitlements on a small scale, it can in some instances lead to institutions like slavery, which would find scant defence by most standard theories of ethics. If the principle of wealth-maximization is used to structure entitlements on a large scale it is unclear in what way the resulting entitlements can be considered efficient. On a larger scale, the very objective of wealth-maximization is incoherent. The question of how to form optimal institutions remains open.

In Chapter 10, I look more closely at the alternative notion of optimality that derives from fully incorporating organizational costs in economic models. While there has been much criticism of the notion of optimality in traditional welfare economics for not incorporating organizational costs, the alternative of a transaction cost constrained notion of optimality is far from clear. Chapter 10 examines what appears to be a serious defect of such a notion; that once organizational costs have been made endogenous, and governing or enforcement mechanisms are also treated endogenously, we seem to arrive at the odd conclusion that the institutions that exist are the only ones possible. The form that the deterministic nature of these models takes is such that there is no room for policy intervention. If the world in which we live is the only one that can exist, optimality becomes a moot question. I argue that in order to give more content to this alternative notion of optimality one must find ways of introducing reasonable counterfactuals into economic models.

PART I
EXTERNALITY

2

A History of the Notion of Externality

1. INTRODUCTION

At least one hundred years have passed since 'external economies' entered into economists' vocabulary.[1] The concept has been used widely, but no precise and agreed-upon meaning of the term seems yet to have emerged. This might not be of much concern if it were just marginal differences of interpretation that were under discussion. But this is not the case, as the differences in meanings attributed to this notion are often fundamental in nature. Despite concerted attempts over the years by very prominent economists to zero in on the basic notion of externality, the claims regarding the true nature of externality have not converged. This is all the more striking given both the wide use of the notion, and the steadily growing volume of work done in the area known broadly as the 'theory of externalities'.

In this chapter I will try to convey how economists over the years characterized externality, and what they thought it was. I will not focus on the substantive debates over policy and theory and the many 'results' of the externality literature, except to the extent that they are essential in sketching the several meanings attached to the notion of externality. I will try to trace some of the origins, and in chronological order, the several associations and meanings attached to the words 'external economy' and later 'externality'; a kind of etymology.

Any history is necessarily an interpretative history, but I will try as much as possible to convey the senses that the authors themselves attached to the notion. In general, I will not be offering my own position on the merits or demerits of different views, though I may indicate some reservations from time to time, or point out some flaw, especially if little space is required to develop some point.

[1] The first use of the term of which I am aware is in Marshall (1890).

2. BIRTH OF 'EXTERNAL ECONOMIES'

Marshall wrote in his *Principles of Economics* (1920: 266):

We may divide the economies arising from an increase in the scale of production of any kind of goods, into two classes—firstly, those dependent on the general development of the industry; and, secondly, those dependent on the resources of the individual houses of business engaged in it, on their organization and the efficiency of their management. We may call the former *external economies*, and the latter *internal economies*.[2]

Marshall was concerned with explaining, in a static framework, the long-run decrease in costs associated with an expansion of a particular industry in a way that would be consistent with increasing or horizontal marginal costs faced by individual ('representative') firms within the industry. He was trying to reconcile the possibility of a competitive industrial structure with his observation that firms and industry often operated under increasing returns in the real world. Typically, increasing returns to scale are incompatible with a highly atomized industrial structure. By introducing the distinction between 'external' and the 'internal' economies the competitive model could be salvaged despite the presence of economies of scale. As firms entered and the industry expanded, certain economies would be set in motion that were associated with the scale of the industry. To potential entrant firms, the gains associated with the increased scale would accrue only in small part to them, because the benefit would be spread out to all existing firms. These gains would be in large part external to the firm, yet internal to the industry. They would lead to a downward shift of the marginal-cost curve faced by each firm. So while the individual marginal-cost curve would be upward-sloping (presumably due to diseconomies related to the entrepreneurial function) and thus be limited in its size, the industry would operate under a 'forward-falling' supply curve traced by the shifting aggregate marginal-cost curves.

This way Marshall was able to dodge, as it were, the problem of monopoly that loomed large when increasing returns were pre-

---

[2] Although this quote is taken from the 8th edn. of 1920, the distinction is traceable to the 1st edn. of 1890.

sent. But while avoiding inefficiency associated with monopoly, external economies provided an alternative source of inefficiency. Marshall, along with Pigou who helped refine and develop Marshall's ideas, argued that competitive industries enjoying external economies, or downward-sloping supply curves, would produce less than optimal levels of output. The market forces could not be relied upon for optimal resource allocation, and government subsidization of these industries would be required to bring about the expanded optimal level of output. A symmetrical argument for increasing cost industries, or industries with upward-sloping supply curves, meant that they would over-expand and taxes would therefore be required to reduce output. Appropriately, revenues from increasing cost industries could provide the subsidies to decreasing cost industries. In Pigou's terminology, and in both cases, marginal social product diverges from marginal private product.

3. PRE-WAR CONTROVERSY

The Marshall–Pigou analysis had flaws, which became clear only with some thirty or so years of vigorous debate involving Young, Clapham, Robertson, Robinson, Knight, Sraffa, and Viner;[3] Schumpeter (1954: 1048) refers to this debate as a 'striking instance of the slowness and roundaboutness of analytical advance'.

3.1. Empty Boxes

Clapham (1922) attacked Pigou on the value of sorting of industries into 'boxes' of diminishing and increasing returns. A debate ensued about the reality of external economies: whether such things exist or whether they are 'empty boxes'. The actual causes of external economies and diseconomies to which Marshall had referred were vague. He talked about an external economy as the 'general development of industry' associated with the entrance of a new firm. Not only were the economies and diseconomies

---

[3] Most of these articles can be found repr. in Stigler and Boulding (1953). Young (1913) is not included.

vague, but it seemed that it was exceptionally difficult to categorize industries in the real world to fit neatly into these categories. What is the use of such categories if one cannot associate real-world phenomena with them? No practical value could come of them. Pigou rebutted by acknowledging the practical difficulties involved but defending the importance of the analytical understanding afforded by such categories.

3.2. Congested Roads

The real difficult problems were elsewhere. Allyn Young (1913) first questioned the proposition that the inclined-supply curves were a cause of divergence of competitive equilibrium from a social optimum. The issues resurfaced when Knight (1924) emphasized that decreasing returns are not a cause for alarm. He argued that Pigou's example of external diseconomies resulting from the congestion of the better of two roads, as drivers decide at the margin which road to use, is in essence a case of the free use of a scarce resource.

An illustration will help illuminate the controversy. Consider the case of deep-sea fishing. Fishing within a limited area is subject to diminishing returns, as new vessels that enter the fishing ground eventually reduce the catch per boat. As output expands, each firm perceives an increase in the average cost of fish. The full cost of the increased output resulting from the marginal firm is above the cost perceived by that firm. The marginal firm only perceives the cost it bears directly. It does not take into account the (external) costs incurred by all other intramarginal firms as a result of its activity.

Diagrammatically this can be seen as an increasing average-cost curve and a more steeply increasing marginal-cost curve lying above it (see Fig. 2.1). For expositional reasons assume that the upward-rising marginal-cost curve is the result of adding increments of a variable factor that has an infinitely elastic supply to a factor that has a fixed supply (the sea). This allows us to treat the area between the marginal-cost curve and the average-cost curve as a rent to scarce sea. In a competitive economy with open access to a scarce resource the industry will tend to produce an output above the optimal level.

With open access to the sea the average-cost curve faced by

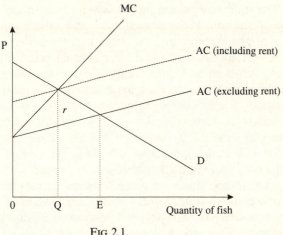

FIG 2.1.

fishing firms is one that excludes rent on the scarce resource (fishing ground). If the sea in question were to be privately owned, and not treated as a free good, the area would be rented out at a positive price. Maximization of rent on the scarce resource would ensure that no firm was imposing costs on intramarginal firms greater than the gains accruing from the additional output. The average-cost curve including rents would be equal to the marginal-cost curve. Fishing firms would be making zero profits, the owners of the scarce sea would be maximizing rents, and, assuming competitive conditions in all markets, an optimal allocation of resources would arise. In effect entrants would be confronted with all costs that they impose on the industry through the increased price of the scarce factors.

As long as increased costs associated with increasing scale of industry simply reflect rising rents on scarce resources, then there is no problem of a competitive industry over-expanding, the rising-supply curve is both a marginal curve excluding rent and an average curve including rent. On the other hand, if there are effects that somehow go unpriced, as when the sea is treated as a free resource, then the industry will produce more than is optimal. The rising-supply curve is an average curve excluding rent on some input.[4]

[4] Gordon (1954) and Cheung (1970) offer good graphic discussions of the process of rent-dissipation from open-access resources.

The traffic-congestion debate is analogous to the fishing-industry illustration. Pigou argued that where there were two roads, one of good quality and the other not, the better road would be over-utilized. Each marginal vehicle would perceive only that cost that accrues to itself, not taking into account the increased costs (external diseconomies) it adds to all intramarginal vehicles as a result of congestion. Pigou constructed a curve marginal to the average-cost curve and showed how the optimal level of traffic could be attained by levying a toll on all vehicles equal to the difference, at the optimal flow, between the average and the marginal cost. In Figure 2.1 this would correspond to r.

Knight saw this divergence between private and social net products as an instance of wasteful exploitation of a scarce natural resource. If the congested road were privately owned then the price of use would be bid up as vehicles increased. Optimality would be attained as scarce factors were appropriately priced. In Fig. 2.1, r would represent the price of using the road that drivers would face in competitive equilibrium. Knight and Pigou were looking at the problem from two sides of the same coin. Pigou's tolls were making the drivers face the marginal cost excluding rent, while Knight's rents confronted drivers with average costs including rents. Both approaches lead to the correct competitive upward-sloping supply curve.[5] An important aspect of Knight's contribution was that the presence of external diseconomies was shown to be dependent on the institution of private property, or more generally, that institutions mattered.[6]

4. PECUNIARY AND TECHNOLOGICAL EXTERNAL ECONOMIES AND DISECONOMIES

As indicated from Knight's analysis, the Marshall–Pigou position was flawed in treating all upward-sloping supply curves as indicative of inefficiency. Viner (1931) separated Marshall's external economies and diseconomies into two categories, pecuniary and

[5] The neatness of this result depended on the assumption that increments of a variable factor in infinite supply were being added to a factor in finite supply. For a look at the complications that arise when both factors are in finite supply, see Mishan (1969).

[6] Later it became clear that taxes and ownership rights could be seen as alternative institutions (or property rights) dealing with the matter.

technological. Any external economies or diseconomies which were simply the outcome of changing factor prices were labelled 'pecuniary'. Not only were these not a cause of inefficiency, they were an essential feature of the efficient functioning of the price system. In the case of pecuniary diseconomies, the rising supply price is an indication of any interdependent economic system where production functions are characterized by constant returns to scale, where factor supplies are imperfectly elastic, and where factor proportions differ from one product to another. The increasing factor prices resulting from the expansion of an industry simply reflect the efficient functioning of the price system as demand for scarce resources increases. These rents or transfer costs ensure that scarce factors are used to the point at which their marginal-value product is equal in all uses in the industry.

Technological economies and diseconomies, on the other hand, are a source of inefficiency, precisely because the change in costs resulting from a firm's entry into an industry is a change in the coefficients of production, and is not reflected in prices. The upward-sloping supply curve associated with technological external diseconomies underestimates the costs of expansion, as when the average cost excluding rent determined output, when rents were not being imputed in the fishing industry.

The downward-sloping supply curves, which were Marshall's central concern, could be related either to pecuniary or technological external economies. However, the situation is not symmetrical with diseconomies, because in order for pecuniary external economies to exist (falling factor prices in response to higher demand) there have to be either increasing internal returns or technological external economies elsewhere in the economy. If the forward-falling supply curve brought about by falling factor prices was a result of inputs being supplied by a firm with increasing internal economies, the monopoly problems that Marshall so wanted to avoid would seep in through the back door. On the other hand, the downward-sloping supply curve could be due to inputs being supplied by an industry enjoying technological external economies, in which case it would be the latter industry that was underproducing, and required subsidization, and not the former.

While Viner's pecuniary–technological distinction has played an important role in dispelling confusion, it has come into relative disuse, since pecuniary economies are simply price changes brought about by changing demand and supply, and there does not seem to be a need for a new term for simple market interdependence. Since the only kind of external economy that seems to differ from market interaction is the technological kind, it has been felt that 'external' can refer to these without the prefix 'technological'. There are authors, however, who have argued that there are certain kinds of pecuniary economies and diseconomies that can be associated with suboptimality of competitive equilibria. I shall come to them later.

By dropping the prefix 'technological' there is a danger of associating 'external' with inefficiency, when in fact it is a particular kind of action whose effects are felt by others as well as the initiator that leads to inefficiency. Nor could they simply be labelled technological economies since this may simply imply what we know as increasing returns to scale at the firm level. An increase in scale of operation may affect the technological coefficients of production of the initiator and thereby be internal technological economies. Also, there may be pecuniary internal economies that result from the lowering of factor prices purchased by the firm in question, e.g. advantages in buying due to scale (note these require indivisibilities elsewhere in the economy, either in production technology or transaction technology).

4.1. What Remains of Marshall's External Economies?

As the dust settled, the question became what remained of Marshall's external economies? Were they numerous and important? Marshall's external economies and diseconomies were attempts to confront a specific problem and that is why they focused on firms' interdependent production sets within an industry and not across industries. He was also concerned to present these in a static framework (technical irreversible economies would not be portrayed as a forward-falling supply curve, but as shifts of the curve). While it is not too difficult to find reversible external diseconomies within an industry, it is difficult to come up with examples of reversible external economies confined to an industry. An example of the latter might be the formation of a pool of skilled labour. As new firms move into an industry, and if there is some local concentration, all firms may benefit from the formation of a larger skilled labour force and more informed labour-market; labour turnover and training costs will decline.[7] Another example might be that of the trade-journal case where economies are attained by increased information about market conditions. With a large-enough industry, publishing information becomes feasible and the increased information disseminated reduces production costs.[8]

Ellis and Fellner (1943: 262) emphasize the narrow scope of external economies and diseconomies, and, importantly, reiterate the institutional nature of external diseconomies:

Where there are *genuine* diseconomies ignored by the competitive producer—smoke nuisance, wasteful exploitation of resources, etc.—these results follow not from the atomistic character of production, but from technical or institutional circumstances as a consequence of which scarce goods are treated as though they were free; and the divorce of scarcity from effective ownership may be equally complete for atomistic, oligopolistic, and monopolistic private enterprise.

They consider these to be marginal phenomena and, it is important to note, they confine institutional explanation to external diseconomies; external economies seem to be another fruit. As such, the industry structure is relevant for their existence; a monopolist is likely to be able to predict dynamic economies.

'The departure of the economist's *free* competition from the ideal of social costs is in fact negligible for external economies and non-existent for the cost-increasing forces' (Ellis and Fellner 1943: 263). Interestingly, lack of private ownership of some good, or treatment of a scarce good as free, is not considered a cause of failure of a competitive economy.

5. THE BROADENING SCOPE OF EXTERNAL ECONOMIES AND DISECONOMIES BY EXAMPLES

After the initial turmoil external economies had created, there was a period of respite. While a consensus had seemingly formed,

---

[7] Although these must be seen as transaction-cost economies. If there were no organizational costs, turnover would not be a problem. The training gains must be linked to turnover problems.

[8] Needless to say, transaction-cost economies are implied here as well.

external economies and diseconomies were undergoing changes by small degrees. Examples were proliferating in the literature that seemed to fall naturally into the category of 'external' activity and seemed to be accepted as such by the community, and yet these appendages were reshaping the notion. While external economies, and their opposite, had been confined to intra-industry interaction, examples were offered of inter-industry interaction. External economies infiltrated consumption as well.[9] In 1947, in his famous *Foundations of Economic Analysis*, Samuelson makes the connection between 'external' and consumption. In some reference to Veblen-like motivations in individuals, he says that certain modifications may be required in the standard conclusions of welfare economics, 'to allow for certain "external" consumption economies not dissimilar analytically to the external technological economies and diseconomies of the Marshall–Pigou type' (1947: 224).

More ambitiously, every inefficiency started to look like an external economy or diseconomy. Baumol (1952: 72) states that:

Divergence between marginal social and private cost means ultimately that an individual's marginal activity involves undesirable effects on the community without his remuneration being thereupon decreased or vice versa. . . . Indeed the terms external economies or diseconomies are often used loosely as synonyms for divergences between marginal, private and social cost, and where the meaning is clear from the context it will be convenient to continue the practice here (Baumol 1952: 72–3).

For Pigou, external economies and diseconomies were a distinct subset of divergencies of marginal social and private products. Yet by the 1950s this general category, which always included the smaller one (external economies and diseconomies), had taken its name. Furthermore, divergence of social and private costs expanded beyond Pigou's initial category[10] to incorporate every source of market inefficiency.

One other point I want to mention with reference to the broadening scope of externality, is that Lange (1936) had associated external economies with centrally administered economic

----

[9] Note two potential meanings of external when used in association with consumption: (*a*) external preferences, implying that an individual places value on another's welfare, and (*b*) one's utility is affected by another's decision variable.

[10] Pigou did not treat all causes of market failure as divergencies of private and social cost. Obstacle to movements, imperfect knowledge, and imperfect divisibility were not associated with divergence. See Pigou (1962: 174).

systems, and they were not unique to market economies. The strong identification of external economies with specifically market systems came later, yet there remained proponents of Lange's initial stand (see e.g. Nove (1983) and Montias (1976)).

6. 'UNPAID FACTORS' AND 'ATMOSPHERES'

While there were those that used external economies and diseconomies in so loose a fashion as to entail almost any market inefficiency, others clung on to more narrow conceptions, or broadened the notion less dramatically. Yet for a while there remained a tendency in sections of the debate to couple external economies with increasing returns to scale, or a falling supply curve, and vice versa, although it had become quite clear that the inefficiency had little to do with the slope of the supply curve as such, but with the divergence of the 'perceived' or 'effective' supply curve from the actual or correct one. It was perfectly conceivable that external economies could be present in an industry with decreasing returns. It was the initial preoccupation with the shape of the supply curve that seemed to preserve the association of external economies with downward-sloping (or diseconomies with upward-sloping), as well as the confining of external economies and diseconomies to intra-industry, as opposed to inter-industry, interaction.[11]

In 1952 Meade offered a treatment of externalities which further helped distinguish the terms 'external economies and diseconomies' from 'increasing and decreasing returns', as well as to give it a notational representation that has become standard. His stated purpose was to distinguish between two types of external economies and diseconomies, called 'unpaid factors of production' and 'creation of atmospheres'. The fruitful story of apples and bees (not to be confused with the birds' version) was utilized to illustrate the nature of the first type.

The story is that the apple blossoms provided nectar for the bees, thereby improving production of honey. Likewise, the bees

[11] Marshall himself considered external economies across industries, 'the economies of production on a large scale can seldom be allocated exactly to any one industry: they are in great measure attached to groups, often large groups, of correlated industries' (1919: 188).

fertilized the apple trees, thereby enhancing apple production. These two factor inputs (nectar and fertilization) went 'unpaid' for. When keeping apple production constant and, as a result, nectar, the honey-producer would find decreasing returns to scale when increasing all other factors of production (similarly for apple production when honey production was fixed). If all factors, including 'unpaid factors of production', were variable, then the combined returns to scale of both industries were constant. The apple industry and honey-producing industry, when taken separately (each taking the other's production as given), produced under decreasing returns to scale, while if taken together produced under constant returns to scale.

'Creation of atmosphere' was distinct from 'unpaid factors' because it was presumably not dependent on the number or scale of industries present. As an example Meade suggested that rainfall in a given district may increase farmers' output, and that the availability of rainfall would be the same regardless of the number of farms in some region.[12] Rainfall was a given, an 'atmosphere', and seemingly uncontrollable by any industry, whereas nectar was an unpaid factor of production. But Meade offered a further point of distinction. If the 'atmosphere' can be varied, for example by a lumber industry's deforestation,[13] then the combined production of lumber and externally affected farm goods would be characterized by increasing returns to scale. That is, if lumber production had constant returns to scale and farm goods also produced under constant returns to scale for a given level of rainfall, then when rainfall was varied by increases in lumber production, the social-production function of lumber and farm goods would present increasing returns to scale.

If the combined- or social-production function was non-convex then, according to Meade, there was an adding-up problem in using a Pigouvian tax-subsidy scheme, that does not present itself in the case of constant returns to scale, as with the apple–honey illustration. Presumably when there are constant returns to scale in combined production, then revenues from taxes on industries with external diseconomies will match expenditures on subsidies

[12] The words used to describe 'atmosphere' come very close to one of the features used later in the formal definition of public goods, i.e. non-rivalrous in consumption.

[13] Interestingly this ex. comes from Sidgwick (1883).

of industries with external economies (i.e. budget would balance). This will not be the case with non-convex external economies and diseconomies.[14]

While the distinction between 'unpaid factors of production' and 'atmospheres' is convenient, whether it is clear-cut is questionable. If rainfall is somehow controllable, as in the case of deforestation, then there is no reason not to treat it as an unpaid factor of production; the fact that it accrues to many farmers or many industries does not change this aspect. If rainfall is not controllable then there is no economic problem. The fact that the combined-production set may be non-convex does not seem to provide a reason for alternative labels for external economies and diseconomies. The apple–honey example could also turn out to lead to increasing returns to scale in combined production. There is nothing special about 'unpaid factors' that precludes it.

Meade's 1952 paper consolidated a certain widening of the scope of external effects. Inter-industry economies and diseconomies were included. Economies could result from changes in input use as well as from output changes. 'It may be the employment of one *factor* in one industry which confers an indirect benefit or the reverse upon producers in the other industry' (Meade: 65.) The term 'indirect' is used to distinguish from direct market interaction.[15] Furthermore, economies could be spread over a large group of industries. Finally, his notational representation of external economies and diseconomies has become a staple.

'External economies exist whenever we have production functions of the form

$$x_1 = F_1(l_1, c_1, l_2, c_2, x_2)$$
$$x_2 = F_2(l_2, c_2, l_1, c_1, x_1)$$

where F_1 and F_2 are not necessarily homogeneous of the first degree' (Meade 1952: 67); x_i is output of industry i, c_i is capital used in industry i, and l_i is labour used in industry i.

---

[14] Actually, for a tax-subsidy competitive equilibrium that is Pareto-optimal, all that is needed is that the taxes and subsidies must be offset by the sum of all lump-sum taxes on consumers which must be imposed so that the consumer is able to just afford the goods consumed in that allocation.

[15] The terms 'direct' and 'indirect' have since been used interchangeably in characterizations of external economies. Sometimes, as here, they are described as 'indirect' to emphasize the unintended nature or the fact that they are not part of the goal towards which actions are directed. Alternatively, they are described as 'direct' to point out their unmediated nature; no exchange preceding the action.

7. PUBLIC GOODS AND EXTERNALITIES

The central challenge for policy response to external economies remained the Pigouvian tax-bounty and it was felt that this procedure, when needed, would restore the resilience of the competitive markets. A new angle on external economies and diseconomies was brought into the literature when Samuelson (1954, 1955, 1958) wrote his seminal papers on public goods, affecting both the notion of externality as well as the sense that the market mechanism could ultimately be relied upon.

In two very influential papers, Samuelson (1954; 1955) brings to economists' attention a 'theory of optimal public expenditure'. As he points out, economists, with the exception of Wicksell (1896), Lindahl (1919), Musgrave (1939), and Bowen (1943), had neglected this area, focusing exclusively on the theory of taxation. The Walrasian model of a private-ownership competitive general equilibrium can be seen as an extreme polar case, which if formulated stringently could leave no role for the government. Even if room for government was made by relaxing certain assumptions, the decentralized function of the competitive price system could be preserved with taxes 'correcting' the parametric prices.

One could form another extreme or antipodal model of a 'collective consumption good' (public good) provision by the government. Public goods are distinguished from private goods in that the consumption of the good by one agent does not subtract from another's consumption of that good.[16] Or as Samuelson (1955) put it 'each man's consumption of [the public good] . . . is related to the total . . . by a condition of *equality* rather than of summation' (p. 350). Examples are defence, education, law-enforcement, courts, television broadcasts, etc. (Most goods will not fall into either pure category of private or public, but will lie somewhere in between.) Now in addition to the standard welfare conditions that have to be satisfied for the competitive economy to be optimal, an economy with public goods as well as private goods would have to satisfy the condition that the provision of

---

[16] A 'true-blue' public good also requires that it is not possible to limit the consumption of the good to any particular group or person. This condition is known as non-excludability.

public goods should reach the point where the marginal rate of transformation equals the sum over the individuals of the marginal rates of substitution between the public and private goods.[17]

Unlike the situation with models of private goods, agents have an incentive to give false signals concerning their preferences. Agents' stated demand for a public good has a minimal effect on the total supplied and by understating their demand they can aspire to enjoy the public good without paying the costs of provision. An alternative voting system to the competitive private-market system has to be found if optimality is to be attained. The provision of public goods, which forms an essential part of government activity, poses a serious threat even to the theoretical decentralized pricing system. By not revealing one's true preferences (not treating prices as parametric),

any one person can hope to snatch some selfish benefit in a way not possible under the self-policing competitive pricing of private goods; and the 'external economies' or 'jointness of demand' intrinsic to the very concept of collective goods and governmental activities makes it impossible for the grand ensemble of optimizing equations to have that special pattern of zeros which makes *laissez faire* competition even *theoretically* possible as an analogue computer. (Samuelson 1954: 389)

Samuelson (1958) believed that since the real world represented some mix of the two antipodal models of pure private and public goods, it could be possible for a theorist to form 'some kind of mixed model which takes account of all external, indirect, joint-consumption effects' (1958: 335).

I shall not write down such a mathematical model. But if I did do so, would we not find—as Pigou and Sidgwick so long ago warned us is true of all external economies and diseconomies—that the social optimum could not be achieved without somebody's taking into account all direct and indirect utilities and costs in all social decisions? (1958: 335)

Of course Sidgwick (1883)[18] did not know what 'external economies' were when he gave us his warnings (they had not been invented yet), and Pigou was warning us of a far broader

---

[17] 'So much for the involved optimizing equations that an omniscient calculating machine could theoretically solve if fed the postulated functions. No such machine now exists' (Samuelson 1954: 338).

[18] Sidgwick invented the ex. of a lighthouse as a public good.

category than what Pigou meant by 'external economies'. But Samuelson was using the expression 'external economies' to describe all the diverse phenomena to which Pigou ascribed divergence of private and social net product, and more. What had once been a very specific phenomenon was now approaching universality. Could it be that all market inefficiencies were instances of somebody not 'taking into account' some effects, 'externalities'?[19]

If external economies have egos, they were greatly boosted by Samuelson. For the purposes of our historical account let us recount the new clothing in which external economies were dressed. 'External effects' or 'externalities' are now associated with the nature, or definition, of goods. External effects impart 'publicness' to goods. The pure public good is a polar case of external effects. The 'ideal' decentralized function of the competitive market is seriously impaired by public goods. 'Externality' is intrinsic to government activity.

Interestingly increasing returns also come into the picture again. Samuelson points out that 'when you try to analyse why public utilities are public utilities and why certain activities may fall into either the category of public or private enterprise, you will usually find that some significant deviation from strict constant returns to scale is involved' (1958: 335). While this is not a firm statement that non-convexity is behind all 'externalities', it takes it in that direction.

8. DO PECUNIARY EXTERNAL ECONOMIES MATTER?

At the same time that Samuelson was broadening sharply the concept of external economies, Scitovsky (1954) was knocking it back into place in certain respects, though stretching it in other ways. Little did he know when stating that 'definitions of external economies are few and unsatisfactory' that defining externality would become the rage for years to come. And although there are now many characterizations, his verdict on their merit is largely still applicable. But when he made this statement, explicit

---

[19] It seems that it was during this period of broadening horizons for the notion of external economy that it acquired this new name of 'externality'.

definitions of external economies were rare, so let us peruse this early definition:

> It is agreed that [external economies] mean services (and disservices) rendered free (without compensation) by one producer to another; but there is no agreement on the nature and form of these services or on the reasons for their being free. It is also agreed that external economies are a cause for divergence between private profit and social benefit and thus for the failure of perfect competition to lead to an optimum situation; but for this there are many reasons, and it is nowhere made clear how many and which of these reasons are subsumed under the heading of 'external economies'. Nor do examples help to clarify the concept. The literature contains many examples of external economies; but they are as varied and dissimilar as are discussions of the subject. Some give the impression that external economies are exceptional and unimportant; others suggest that they are important and ubiquitous. (Scitovsky 1954: 70)

From here he goes on to argue that because of the separation of different branches of economics, the notion of externality has different relevance and meaning in different contexts. Two contexts are important: (1) equilibrium theory, and (2) industrialization in underdeveloped economies. In the first context he points out that Meade's definition is good. In a static general-equilibrium model with perfect competition and perfect divisibility the economy settles into an equilibrium that is Pareto-optimal unless there are 'direct interdependencies',[20] i.e. some interactions among agents of the economy not transmitted through the market mechanism. Four direct, 'non-market' interdependencies are distinguished: (*a*) 'individual person's satisfaction . . . may depend on the satisfaction of other persons'; (*b*) on activities of producers (smoke, noise); (*c*) producers output may be influenced by others, e.g. innovations; and (*d*) 'the output of the individual producer may depend . . . on the activities of other firms'.

While Scitovsky felt the first to be important, and the second and third not, because they had been dealt with respectively by zoning laws and patent laws, the fourth was the only category entitled to the name of 'external economies', and instances of such phenomena, he felt, were exceptional.[21] In a historical sense

---

[20] Recall Meade's (1952) use of 'indirect' for external economies.

[21] 'Instances of this are the oil well whose output depends on the number and operation of other wells on the same oil field; the fisherman whose catch depends

he was correct; Marshall and Pigou reserved the term 'external economies' for a distinct phenomenon among the many sources of inefficiency.[22] By so confining the use of the term it can be seen easily why ubiquity of external economies may be curtailed. I shall not question the value of Scitovsky's classification, for now I confine myself to recording his position.

In the context of industrial development, Scitovsky tried to breathe life into the seemingly redundant category of pecuniary external economies by giving it a new *raison d'être*. The gist is that in a dynamic world in which many of the conditions of the static, perfectly competitive, general-equilibrium model do not hold, pecuniary as well as technological economies may have a substantial bearing on the optimality of economic interaction. His definition of this second concept of externality is simply that 'external economies are invoked whenever the profits of one producer are affected by the actions of other producers' (1954: 75). Standing alone, this is simply general economic interdependence, pecuniary and technological. A close reading of Scitovsky's arguments shows that they primarily include a simple statement that under highly imperfect conditions, firms' private profits may be a poor guide to social profitability, or that prices are a poor guide to economic activity under imperfect conditions.

An example of this second concept of external economies might go something like this. There are two firms with complementary outputs such as steel production and railway construction. The railway industry would produce more if steel were cheaper, generating a higher demand for rail transportation, and further enhancing demand for steel. Steel would be cheaper if there was a higher demand for it, because it enjoys increasing returns to scale. The demand for steel, however, never materializes because at the present prices of steel, railway construction is expensive and so transportation is expensive and does not generate potential increases in demand issuing from lower prices. If only the railway industry somehow knew the potential price

on the operations of other fishermen on the same waters; and the firm that uses a public road (or other publicly-owned utility) and is partly crowded out of it by other firms using the same road' (Scitovsky 1954: 74).

[22] Scitovsky was extending it a bit by including interaction among different industries, as with decreasing economies from use of common resources such as public roads.

reductions in steel that would spring from higher demand, then maybe the process would get going. But at the given prices, and without the knowledge of the steel industry's production function, the virtuous cycle never gets off the ground.

For such an example Scitovsky would have to invoke non-convexity which seems to be the real force behind 'pecuniary external economies'. In fact if the steel industry had increasing returns to scale it could be a cause of failure even in a static model (without mention of external economies). As long as the market demand kept the industry in the range of increasing returns it would not even come into existence under competitive conditions. Pecuniary economies must be dependent on other 'technological economies' or non-convexities in the economy; they do not seem to warrant a separate status from market interaction. Certain aspects of Scitovsky's arguments were revived a good twenty years later, and offer some stature to pecuniary externalities to this day.[23] These will be discussed later in section 14.4.

In a sense it is as if Scitovsky wanted to revitalize the original senses of 'external economies' that Marshall had ushered into economics, by narrowing the ambit to a confined set of phenomena with regard to the 'technological' type, and reinvigorating the 'pecuniary' type. With regard to the technological type, one might think it a matter of taste when deciding what to include under the heading of 'external'; as far as the pecuniary type is concerned, however, it does not seem to be a successful rehabilitation of Marshall's inefficiencies caused by changing factor prices, since the inefficiency must be sought elsewhere.

There is one example that Scitovsky used which has been largely neglected in the externality literature, and harks back to the single defence of pecuniary external economy that Pigou persisted in making.[24] A more general account of it may be given here. In short, questions concerning the distribution of economic activity among nations may be determined largely through

[23] In fact this rehabilitation was based on a comment made by Arrow which Scitovsky included in a footnote, to the effect that failure of the kind discussed with the two complementary firms could be seen as signalling problems due to lack of future markets.

[24] This can be found in Pigou (1924: 194–5). As Pigou revised his position on what is now known as pecuniary externality, his only defence narrowed to the question of foreign trade. See also Ellis and Fellner (1943: 250–3).

market transaction, and there may be good reason to expect that well-functioning market interaction may be suitable to international interests but may not converge with strict national welfare. Imagine that nations are represented by individuals in a general-equilibrium model. If the economy is perfectly competitive we know from the two Welfare Theorems that, provided certain conditions are satisfied, the price interaction will be able to sustain any social welfare function. When stepping outside the individual and taking the view of a government with a monopoly of power (or a supranational government if individuals are nations), this provides a strong rationale for the market, since with income transfers all Pareto-optimal points can be attained. However, when taking the agent's (nation's) viewpoint there is little reason to view the price system as optimal unless the agent knows what distributional policy the government has and finds that it best represents her interests. If not, the agent will naturally be displeased with the pecuniary economies and diseconomies accruing to her,[25] yet due to the negligible impact she can have on prices in a competitive environment, there will be nothing she can do about it. A nation state, unlike individuals in the model, may be in the privileged position of not treating all prices as parametric; it may often have good reason to support policies which seem inefficient from the cosmopolitan vantage point. Pecuniary interaction is not a problem for optimality, so long as the unit of account for welfare evaluation is the entire economy within which such interaction takes place. If the unit of account under concern is not the global economy, but the national economy, then national-welfare optimization may diverge from international-welfare maximization, and thus pecuniary economies and diseconomies (or normal market interaction) may be of interest.

9. EXTERNALITY AS MARKET FAILURE

Four years after Scitovsky's paper, Bator (1958) provided us with the broadest explicit[26] characterization of external economies to

---

[25] Even though they reflect price changes that are optimal from the viewpoint of the economy as a whole.

[26] I say 'broadest explicit' since one may consider Samuelson's identification of externality with publicness and failure as an earlier version of this characteriza-

date. 'I think it more natural and useful to broaden rather than restrict, to let "externality" denote any situation where some Paretian costs and benefits remain *external to* decentralized cost-revenue calculations in terms of prices' (1958: 362). Bator wanted to classify the kinds and causes of market failure. He was not looking at a specific problem, such as rising-supply curves, public expenditure, or even external economies as such. His context was the general-equilibrium static model of 'perfect (though limited) information and foresight', which differentiated his approach to external economies from many preceding ones that looked at it from a partial-equilibrium perspective. In this context it seemed that all departures from Pareto-optimality could be interpreted as some action (or potential action) not being transmitted through prices, or 'direct interaction'. Pecuniary interaction was by definition not a cause of failure, since failure had to be traced to 'direct interaction' somewhere in the system.

If it was the problem of under-investment in skill-formation of labour, the problem could be seen as the investor's inability to 'effectively control' the fruits of her investment. If it was the inefficiency implicit in increasing returns, it was the firm's inability to price-discriminate and thereby capture the 'unaccounted'-for consumer surplus or potential gains (potential interaction) present in the situation. If it was strategic behaviour brought on by too few agents, it was the inability to account for all the gains of trade. If it was noise-pollution, it was the lack of property rights over air that prevented the actors from exploiting the gains associated with noise reduction. In short, wherever there was failure, someone was not taking something into account, or there was 'direct interaction'.

Bator asserted that 'ownership', interpreted broadly enough, could be treated as a cause of all static failure. Where there was non-market interaction or 'direct interaction', the ownership of some resource was somehow not defined in the most effective way. Some activity was 'escaping' control, or ownership. However, while Bator accepted a broad use of externality, he felt that the notion of ownership should be less encroaching. He reserved lack of private ownership, or inability to establish private property, as one of several causes of 'direct interaction' or

tion. Bator himself believes he is recapitulating the Ellis–Fellner type of characterization, but it is not clear that they meant externality to be so broad.

market failure. If cause of failure was to be the organizing principle of classification, then three polar types of causes were present: (1) Ownership Externalities: these were essentially Meade's 'unpaid factors'. The distinguishing feature of this category was that the problem resides with the institutional arrangement, 'the feasibility of keeping tab'. (2) Technical Externalities: problems arising from indivisibility that lead to non-convexity of production sets. (3) Public-Good Externalities: the public nature of goods was treated as a separate cause from 'unpaid factors'. Bator pointed out that these were often hard to separate, or that they blended into each other, but none the less felt they were distinct enough to warrant three polar causes. It is interesting to note that with this taxonomy there seem to be two notions of externality. One is a description of failure, or indirect cause ('direct interaction'), and the other is an ultimate cause of the direct interaction. So market failure is externality (also described as 'direct interaction' or 'unowned activity'), and the ultimate cause of market failure is also an externality, e.g. increasing returns to scale.

I do not intend to provide a view of this characterization now, that will come later, but wish to offer a rough sketch of the metamorphosis of 'external economies'. Externality has already come a long way from Marshall's first penning of the term. Then, 'external' referred to the action of a firm that was unnoticed or unexploitable by the firm yet fully exhausted within the bounds of the industry to which the firm belonged. It was one of many causes of failure (although for Marshall, and initially Pigou, an important one). Now, for Bator, 'external' did not even explicitly refer to an actor of the system, but to the system itself. The action was external to the decentralized price system. All failure was caused by these 'external' actions or interactions.

Since Bator's contribution, it seems that an important question in the minds of economists is how to clarify where externality stands in relationship to market failure. (This had always been an implicit issue, but with Bator's rigorous treatment, the classification of causes of market failure drew greater attention.) Is it an equivalent category with market failure as Bator presents it, or narrower, or maybe even broader?

10. GENERAL INTERDEPENDENCE AND PARETO-RELEVANT AND -IRRELEVANT EXTERNALITY

Some eight years after Scitovsky had noted the deficiency in definitions of external economies, Buchanan and Stubblebine (1962: 199) reiterated, 'Despite [their] importance . . . rigorous definitions of the concept itself are not readily available in the literature.' The appendage of 'rigorous' had become necessary because definitions had already started to abound. Given the growing use of the term 'externality' and its increasing importance in economics, Buchanan and Stubblebine felt that a more 'operational and usable' definition was needed. The following definition is given:

We define an external effect, an *externality*, to be present when,

$$U^A = U^A(X_1, X_2, ..., X_m, Y_1)$$

This states that the utility of an individual, A, is dependent upon the 'activities', $(X_1, X_2, ..., X_m)$, that are exclusively under his own control or authority, but also upon another single activity, Y_1, which is, by definition, under the control of the second individual, B, who is presumed to be of the same social group. (Buchanan and Stubblebine 1962: 200)

The similarity to Meade's characterization can be seen (especially in the notational form which has become the standard way of expressing externality). On the other hand the characterization attempts to be much more general, moving beyond production to activities in general. It tries to pinpoint that which transforms activity in general to 'external' activity.

The real difficulty with this characterization is in how one defines 'exclusive control', which seems to be the feature separating externality from non-externality. While the act of eating seems a natural candidate for an activity under an agent's exclusive control, one could easily argue that it is contingent upon the availability of food. This availability is likely to be dependent upon the activity of others, so the act of eating is to some degree controlled by others (through exchange, production, force). On Robinson Crusoe's island there would be no definitional problem since all activities are under his exclusive control, but in a world of more than two agents in close proximity, the absolute notion of exclusive control begins to fade. Is there any activity over which an agent has exclusive control? A lot must depend on how one defines activity, that is, an activity may be defined in such a way that no one except the actor can influence the action.[27]

If the slightest interdependence is taken as absence of exclusive control, then Buchanan and Stubblebine's definition essentially equates externality with general interdependence.[28] It is not clear whether this is what Buchanan and Stubblebine meant; most authors did not interpret their definition in such broad terms. But at least we have potentially the first characterization of externality as general interdependence, which is the broadest characterization to date and even broader than Bator's, since it straddles market failure. If a characterization narrower than general interdependence is sought, then either some more specific definition of exclusive control is needed, or an alternative basis for distinguishing external from non-external activity is needed.

Note that 'external' here seems to denote any activity that is 'external' to agents. It has the Marshallian focus on agent but has been stretched to include all interaction among humans.

Buchanan and Stubblebine introduced a few new classificatory terms, some of which have had a lasting influence in the literature. The first distinction they made was between potentially relevant and irrelevant externalities. A potentially irrelevant external activity is one for which the affected agents have no incentive to alter the generator's behaviour. In short, this happens when in equilibrium the affected party is satiated, i.e. has achieved a maximum utility over all other possible values of the external activity. For example, if I am concerned about you getting a balanced diet, then when you have a balanced diet in equilibrium, I have no incentive to alter your behaviour.

From the group of potentially relevant externalities Buchanan and Stubblebine form another subdivision that gives rise to the distinction between Pareto-relevant and -irrelevant externalities. Accordingly, the desire to modify another's behaviour does not provide a good rationale for actual modification unless the ensuing change can be done in such a way that the party affected by

[27] If one defines activities broadly, e.g. A's consumption of good k, then it is likely that there will be no exclusive control. On the other hand if one were to define them narrowly, e.g. A's consumption of the morsel of good k she is presently holding to her mouth, and A is far enough away from anyone for them to interfere, exclusive control over some activities may be established.

[28] Warren Samuels (1972), interprets Buchanan and Stubblebine's definition in this very broad way.

the externality gains without the acting party being made worse off. Only then would the potentially relevant externality also be Pareto-relevant. If it happens that no gains are possible to one party without making the other worse off, then the externality is Pareto-irrelevant.[29] It is important to note that while the externality may be Pareto-irrelevant, that is, the activity level in question may be Pareto-optimal, the externality still exists. In other words externality is not defined, as with Bator, with respect to inefficiency alone; it has a separate existence that does not rely solely on consequences. Of course, if externality were viewed as general interdependence *per se*, it would be a trivial recognition that externality existed even in a Pareto-efficient economy, since general interdependence is a feature of any economy. This sense of a category of activity having a separate existence, independent of whether or not it is efficient, and not being broad enough to encompass all interdependence, has been at the core of the intuitive notion of externality for many economists since Buchanan and Stubblebine (and may have been so prior to them as well).

The policy implication of this analysis is that government should intervene when Pareto-relevant externalities remain after all possible negotiations have taken place. That is, if the gains from trade have already been squeezed out of the situation by the agents in question, there is no reason to intervene. 'The observation of external effects, taken alone, cannot provide a basis for judgement concerning the desirability of some modification in an existing state of affairs. There is not a *prima facie* case for intervention in all cases where an externality is observed to exist' (Buchanan and Stubblebine 1962: 208–9).

Finally, Buchanan and Stubblebine go on to relate their analysis to the Pigouvian discussion of divergence of marginal social and private cost. They point out that if trade is possible between

[29] Buchanan and Stubblebine say that in such cases, an *internal* economy just offsets the *external* economy, i.e. if an agent is generating some external economy, in order to provide the Pareto-optimal amount, there must be some internal economy that 'compensates' her and makes such a provision selfishly optimal as well as socially. Many economists have presumed Pareto-relevance to refer to potential gains after transaction costs have been taken into account (see Dahlman 1979). This is a logical extension of Buchanan and Stubblebine's concept, but it is not what they meant. Even if transaction costs were prohibitively high, it 'does not invalidate the point that potential "gains from trade" are available' (Buchanan and Stubblebine 1962: 205). This latter point distinguished Pareto-relevancy.

the externality interacting parties, the imposition of unilateral taxes (in the case of a diseconomy) on the externality-generating party equal to the marginal social cost will lead to an inefficient allocation of resources. The reason for this is that after the imposition of the tax the parties will have an incentive to move away from the Pareto-optimal equilibrium prior to taxes.

Buchanan and Stubblebine argue that, if there is to be taxation, it has to be a bilateral tax-subsidy scheme so that not only the generator's behaviour be modified, but also the behaviour of the receiver. If this is the case, they argue, there will remain no incentive to move away from the Pareto-optimal equilibrium. However, this seems an elaborate scheme if indeed the involved parties are able to attain Pareto-optimality through trade to begin with. It is pointed out that this analysis is consistent with the arguments in Coase (1960).

11. COASE AND PIGOU: ENTER TRANSACTION COSTS

At this point I will backtrack a couple of years from Buchanan and Stubblebine's 1962 contribution to the notion of externality, and discuss Coase's (1960) well-known article 'The Problem of Social Cost'. I do this partly to emphasize that Coase made no explicit connection between what he was discussing and the concept of externality, and partly because the influence of this article on the externality literature has been too great not to afford it some separate space.

Though I may be culpable of oversight, I believe there isn't a single reference to the word 'externality' or external economy throughout his article. The reason is probably simple. It was not Coase's intention to clear up the confusion surrounding the notion of externality. Rather, he was dealing with a specific problem: what to do in those situations in which the 'actions of business firms . . . have harmful effects on others' (Coase 1960: 1). More generally, the question was, what policy should be adopted in cases where the action of some agent harms another? Prime examples in his article are the case of straying cattle that destroy crops on neighbouring land, the 'confectioner the noise and vibrations from whose machinery disturbed a doctor in his work' (1960: 2), and the running of trains on a railway in which the sparks emitted by trains damaged crops along the lines. There are many more examples as well.

Coase wanted to contest the position that, in cases of divergence of social and private cost, as in the example of a firm emitting smoke and thereby harming some nearby productive activity, the generator of harmful activity should be liable for the consequences, and usually by the imposition of taxes. Coase attributed this position to Pigou and his followers. Besides the elaborate discussion of examples and interpretation of Pigou's position, the distilled theoretical points that Coase makes are as follows: First, if there are no costs in transacting, government intervention should be limited to establishing rights to the activities in question, since irrespective of the allocation of rights the allocation of resources will be efficient in the sense of Pareto. This is known as the Coase Theorem.[30] It would be wrong to unilaterally tax the perpetrator in such a case because it would move the economy away from the Pareto-optimal allocation. Secondly, if transaction costs are present, and hinder the interacting parties from trading with each other, then a social arrangement should be selected that maximizes the total social product. This means that both the liability for the damages (whether the factory emitting smoke must pay the laundry service, or the factory is afforded the right to emit, or intermediate rights are established), and the means by which liability is enforced (taxation, quantity restrictions, rights of use, forms of enforcement), should depend upon the overall impact that such measures will have on the total social product. This includes the possibility that no correcting action whatsoever should be taken since the costs of such intervention may outweigh the gains.[31] A derivative point is that there is no a

[30] There had been some question and controversy as to whether Coase believed that the efficient output of the harm-generating activity resulting from different legal rules would be invariant. If the change in legal rules has a non-trivial effect on the agents' income, then the evaluation of the harm done will be different under different legal rules, and thus the level that is Pareto-optimal will vary according to the rule selected. The correct proposition is that the allocation will be Pareto-optimal irrespective of legal rule, although this does not mean that the output will necessarily be the same. This is the accepted version of the Coase Theorem today.

[31] It is noteworthy that this important insight had been made by Sidgwick: 'It does not follow that whenever *laissez faire* falls short government interference is expedient, since the inevitable drawbacks of the latter may, in any particular case, be worse than the shortcomings of private enterprise' (1901: 414).

priori reason why the generator of harm should be the one to pay.[32]

Pigou was generally portrayed as advocating state intervention in the form of taxation, at least in the kinds of examples discussed by Coase. More generally Coase attributes to him a kind of *naïveté* in not recognizing alternative institutional ways of dealing with those situations necessary for the selection of appropriate policy according to the theoretical points made above. Coase was more at loggerheads with what he termed the Pigouvian tradition, which was 'a fairly well-defined oral tradition', and in fact, about Pigou's written position he says: 'Not being clear, it was never clearly wrong' (1960: 39). Pigou actually had quite a sophisticated view of the import of alternative institutions, though he did not take explicit account of the costs of government intervention.

Coase has had a lasting impact by centring economists' attention on the costs of alternative institutions in organizing economic activity, and the importance of these costs in evaluating the efficiency of the system. He criticized welfare economics in its treatment of harmful effects for not incorporating in its evaluation of corrective measures the possible harm or cost issuing from intervention. He also felt that by comparing the *laissez-faire* system to an ideal, comparison between actual or feasible alternatives that bore little relation to an ideal would be obscured. Since an ideal is not attainable it would be better to compare all feasible real-world alternatives and pick the one that leads to the best outcome, however defined. Finally, he felt that welfare economics had a 'faulty concept of a factor of production. This is usually thought of as a physical entity which the businessman acquires and uses (an acre of land, a ton of fertilizer) instead of as a right to perform certain (physical) actions' (1960: 43–4). Once factors of production are seen as rights, one can see the right to pollute or to harm as a factor of production, and all ownership of factors of production will entail the denial of certain uses by others. 'The cost of exercising a right (of using a factor of production) is always the loss which is suffered elsewhere in consequence of the exercise of that right—the inability to cross

[32] Philosophically one might go as far as arguing that the generator of harm can never be established in one acting agent, since the 'passive' agent is necessary to define an action as harmful, and therefore is equally a generator.

land, to park a car, to build a house, to enjoy a view, to have peace and quiet or to breathe clean air' (1960: 44).

Coase's article generated a lot of debate. There was disagreement over interpretations of what Coase said as well as to the validity of the various propositions. Many of the articles in the externality literature of the 1960s were devoted to clearing up the points he raised. The points to which I refer above are generally accepted today as the valid arguments in Coase's paper, although some may still question whether these points represent what he really meant.

11.1. Illustration of Complications that Transaction Costs Introduce

I now want to present a partial-equilibrium illustration to indicate the kinds of difficulties that transaction costs were beginning to pose for questions of policy as well as for the very notion of Pareto-efficiency. The example is taken from Mishan (1971). Consider the spillover of aircraft noise. Assume that the government does not impede any agreements among the affected parties. Assume that the magnitude and incidence of transaction costs will depend upon the existing legal rights established over the act of 'noise-making'. Mishan suggests the following list of costs in determining overall transaction costs for the two groups of noise makers and noise absorbers: 'a) identifying the members of the group; b) persuading them to make, or to accept, a joint offer; c) reaching agreement within the group on all matters incidental to its negotiation with the other group; and d) negotiating with the other group' (Mishan 1971: 21).

Consider a very simple diagrammatic exposition of two polar extremes of right distributions. Figs. 2.2 and 2.3, show the marginal-cost and benefit curves (of the victims and perpetrators respectively) associated with different levels of aircraft flying overhead and the jointly produced noise, as well as the respective transaction costs faced by the group unprotected by law.[33] In Fig. 2.2, the noise-makers are prohibited from making any noise

[33] It is very often assumed that those unprotected by law bear the transaction costs of bribing the rightful 'owner' of the resource or act in question. A more sophisticated model would allow for the possibility that the rightful owner may find it worthwhile to seek out prospective bribees.

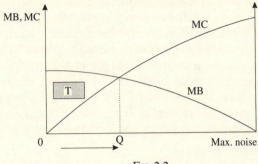

Fig 2.2.

so that the initial endowment of noise is at zero. In Fig. 2.3 the noise-makers have the right to unlimited production of noise so that the initial endowment is at the maximum noise-level. The marginal costs (to the noise-victims) and benefits (to the noise-makers) associated with the contested activity differ under the alternative regimes to account for wealth effects. When the noise-makers are prohibited from making noise the potential victims require relatively larger amounts of money to forego their right to a noise-free environment, then they would be willing to pay to reduce noise if the initial right structure allowed noise. Furthermore, the magnitude and incidence of transaction costs will differ as the structure of rights changes. One possible trans-action-cost structure is shown in Fig. 2.2, where the little shaded

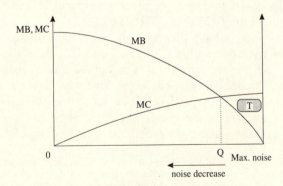

Fig 2.3.

box indicates that the transaction costs are small relative to the net benefits of bargaining for a new noise-distribution, and that the transaction costs face the noise-makers. In Fig. 2.3, the transaction costs are again low, but the incidence is on the noise-absorbers.

As the diagrams are drawn, it can be seen that the wealth-effects of alternative distributions of rights change the optimal quantity of the harm-generating activity. The following scenarios can therefore be envisioned:

1. Under either right-regime a 'net potential Pareto-improvement' emerges, i.e. the benefits of an output change through mutual agreement outweigh the costs of a change, or gains accruing to the bearer of transaction costs are greater than losses elicited through transaction efforts. Under both law-regimes 'optimal' levels of noise-pollution are emitted, although they differ in quantity. There are distributional implications.
2. Net potential Pareto-improvements do not take place under either legal rule. This could be due to too-high transaction costs or possibly non-convex transaction costs. How does one compare the two regimes? What can be said about Pareto-optimality?
3. Moving from one legal regime to another may imply additional transaction costs to those associated with the given rules already being established. Does this offer a leaning towards the status quo? Note that the non-existence of a rule is effectively equivalent to the noise-maker having a right to unlimited noise creation.
4. The actual establishment of a legal rule or a change of legal rule will generally entail non-Pareto-movements. If there is knowledge about the levels of transaction costs associated with alternative legal rules, then one might try to pick the rule that minimizes transaction costs. This would be a kind of Kaldor–Hicks compensation rule for right assignment. One could try to maximize the social benefits net of transaction costs. Would this be Pareto-optimal? What kind of efficiency would this represent?

Most of these problems have been at the heart of the Law and Economics literature, and many advances have been made in understanding the issues. More generally the problems associated with inclusion of transaction costs in economic models has been an underlying feature of the externality literature since the early 1960s and the illustration given above offers but a slight indication of the rumblings underfoot.

12. INTERLUDE

Coase's article (1960) represents a kind of junction or turning-point, reflecting a growing awareness of the import of institutions in issues of resource allocation. While economic analysis was being affected more generally, the need to incorporate institutional costs into the analysis came into sharp focus with the question of externality. More and more, externality was associated with that hazy borderline between the world of institutions and the beyond. An understanding of externality was linked increasingly to a better appreciation of the import of organizational costs, and vice versa. Organizational costs were having a strong impact on the notion of efficiency and market failure. This new impetus of change in economic analysis shaped the evolving notion of externality, and was shaped by it.

To appreciate the new meanings attributed to externality, but also the growing confusion, it is important to consider the contexts from which the question of externality was being approached. This of course is true for the entire history of the notion, but with the increased compartmentalization of enquiry in economics, the context becomes increasingly important (especially as the very vocabulary begins to be differentiated across spheres of enquiry).[34]

For purposes of greater clarity I will break down the remaining history of the notion into three different but substantially overlapping contexts of enquiry:

    1. Phenomenological approach: A rising concern over environmental issues was crucial to the revived attention that exter-

---

[34] One substantial difference in the meaning of words used should be noted: 'market' is used by some to refer to any kind of private exchange, e.g. barter. Even such activity as marriage may be considered 'market' exchange (see Becker 1975). Among general-equilibrium theorists, 'market' has a much more restricted meaning. This difference in vocabulary has played a substantial role in the confusion surrounding the notion of externality.

nality has received since the early 1960s. The direct association of externality with pollution enhanced the sense that externality was a distinct category of some phenomena. The most common characterizations were attempts to spell out directly what class of events or phenomena externality entailed.

2. General-equilibrium approach: Many economists considered the problem of externality from a general-equilibrium approach. This has generated the notion of externality as missing markets. The endeavour is to offer a more rigorous analytical classification of market failure. Externality is seen primarily as a cause of failure, a subset of market failure. Arrow's (1970) and Heller and Starrett's (1976) analysis come under this heading.

3. Institutional approach: This label is used to cover a number of diverse approaches in economics which have the common feature of focusing on the formation of institutions. The two contexts above, irrespective of their differences, tend to treat the institutional framework as given. Alternatively, a growing number of economists and social scientists turning their attention to the formation of institutions found it necessary to form models wherein the institutional framework was at least partially endogenous. It is precisely because of the lack of a rigorous set of tools to deal with such questions that this group is characterized by diversity of approaches, models, and vocabulary that often confound analytical clarity. However, by focusing on formation of institutions they offer insights into the notion of externality that are difficult to derive from more conventional models. Under this heading I will consider characterizations of externality by Buchanan and Tullock (1962), Demsetz (1967), Samuels (1972), Zerbe (1976), and Bromley (1989).

These three contexts of discourse do not in any way represent three distinct views of externality. There is much diversity within each category as well as much in common between different categories. This classification should be seen simply as a heuristic device used to grasp the many connotations of the hero of this story, externality.

13. PHENOMENOLOGICAL APPROACH

Despite the broadening scope of the notion of externality in the post-war years, and while it was central to the question of government intervention, it remained a complexity for the theoretical economist to grapple with, and somewhat removed from the policy-makers' immediate concerns. The growing attention afforded to environmental problems in the early 1960s gave a new relevance to the notion of externality. Here at last, it seemed for many, was an example of an externality that really made an impact. It was no longer an elusive borderline entity, an 'empty box'. When associated with a specific phenomenon, like pollution, it acquired a more distinct persona than it had enjoyed as a theoretical construct.

There was something very distinct about environmental spillovers that separated it from other human activities scrutinized by the economist. It was this kind of narrowing of focus that prompted Baumol and Oates (1975) to look for an alternative characterization of externality other than the very broad ones given by Bator (1958) and Buchanan and Stubblebine (1962). They did not want to include such phenomena as increasing returns, as this 'problem is ultimately quite different from that of the more conventional externalities that constitute the primary threat to the environment and to the quality of life more generally' (Baumol and Oates 1975: 16). They also felt that many characterizations put too much emphasis on what externalities do, rather than what they are. Environmental problems revived the sense that externality was a distinct, almost tangible, phenomenon.

Baumol and Oates offered the following alternative definition:

Condition 1. An externality is present whenever some individual's (say A's) utility or production relationships include real (non-monetary) variables, whose values are chosen by others (persons, corporations, government) without particular attention to the effects on A's welfare. (1975: 17)

Condition 2. The decision maker, whose activity affects others' utility levels or enters their production functions, does not receive (pay) in compensation for this activity an amount equal in value to this resulting (marginal) benefits or costs to others. (1975: 18)

The use of two conditions was related to their desire to separate the notion of externality from some general category of inefficiency, or the consequences associated with the notion. They stressed that externality existed, and that whether it 'caused' or was associated with market failure was a different matter. Condition 1 determined existence, while the optional condition 2 reflected association of externality with inefficiency. Furthermore, they did not want just a separation of existence from consequences, since that could be done by calling externality general interdependence, and inefficiency a specific category of interdependence.[35] Externality must be a narrower category than general interdependence. This explains such clauses as 'real (nonmonetary) variables' and 'without particular attention to',[36] which are restrictive. But they also felt that the particular way that the utility and production function was represented reflected more than just a distinction between agents in isolation and agents that were interdependent. It represented some kind of distinction between market and non-market interdependence, but they did not want to refer to the existence of an institution as a point of distinction. They seemed to be looking for a characterization of externality that would make it somehow identifiable without reference to institutions. It often looks as if the distinction between 'external' and 'internal' has to do with the degree of control an agent has over a decision, but it is never quite clear how this distinction can be made, short of general interdependence *vis-à-vis* total independence.

When Marshall used the pair external–internal he referred to a very specific phenomenon and clearly a subset of general interdependence. Baumol and Oates looked for a more general category, but still not too broad. This sense that externality was a subset of general interdependence that could be somehow identified in a utility or production function, and that had an existence that was not contingent on the institutional framework, has been the most enduring sense of externality, and the likely cause of so many

---

[35] In some sense this is what Buchanan and Stubblebine (1962) did.

[36] Mishan (1981) had stressed that he believed externality should refer to 'unintentional' acts; that the 'external' act is some unintended by-product of an intended action.

attempts to find the ultimate distinguishing feature of externality from other phenomena.[37]

Meade's (1973: 15) focus on environmental issues, also suggests that 'an external economy (diseconomy) is an event which confers an appreciable benefit (inflicts an appreciable damage) on some person or persons who were not fully consenting parties in reaching the decision or decisions which led directly or indirectly to the event in question'. This is a far broader notion than that which Baumol and Oates were trying to establish. Taken at face value, it seems to omit only unconsented acts, which surely comprise the vast majority of human activity. On the other hand by adding the clause 'appreciable', it might exclude the myriad of actions taken daily that alone have an imperceptible effect and yet in aggregate comprise the most important components of an agent's circumstances. Meade offers an interesting discussion on the senses of 'consented' acts and 'appreciable' in order to narrow the purview of the concept.

Characterizations like Meade's and Baumol and Oates's have a certain immediacy. They conjure up pictures of specific acts or events that can be categorized directly, and both also attempt to name externalities without reference to institutions or an institutional framework. It seems to me that both these attributes derive from the sense that externality is a distinct phenomenon much like pollution which must somehow be objectively, and without reference to institutions, categorizable. It also may be linked to the need to offer a more policy-oriented understanding, as if to say to a government official, 'Look, there is an externality' while pointing a finger. On close inspection, however, these characterizations do not always yield a clearly identifiable class of events. This becomes more apparent when one considers the more analytical characterizations offered from a general-equilibrium framework.

---

[37] Even those of Arrow's (1970) and Heller and Starrett's (1976), which I discuss shortly, which explicitly link externalities to the institution of the market, ultimately presume (at least implicitly) some underlying phenomena or kinds of interdependence as being behind externality.

14. GENERAL-EQUILIBRIUM APPROACH

14.1. Missing Markets

Eighty years after external economies entered the economist's vocabulary Arrow (1970: 59) says that 'surprisingly enough, nowhere in the literature does there appear to be a clear general definition of [public goods] or the more general [concept] of "externality"'. Arrow himself does not offer an explicit definition of externality but he does say that market failure can be seen as synonymous with the non-existence of markets, and externality can be viewed as one underlying cause of non-existence of markets. The context from which he approaches the notion is the general-equilibrium model. Like Bator he was interested in offering a classification of market failure on the basis of causal factors of failure. Unlike Bator externality is not treated as equivalent to market failure nor broken down into so many causes of failure, but is one among other identifiable causes of market failure.

To illustrate Arrow's missing market notion of externality I will present a simplified model. Consider a two-person two-commodity exchange economy. Assume that each individual has an initial endowment of a private y-good which can be exchanged at a parametric price for a 'public' x-good. The y-good is conventional so that each agent cares only about her own consumption of the y-good. The x-good might be cigarettes or cars, where smoking bothers the neighbour and the car generates envy, or it could be healthy food generating good feelings in an altruist. The standard way for expressing the two individuals' externality-infested utility functions would be

$$u_1(x_1, x_2, y_1)$$
$$u_2(x_1, x_2, y_2)$$
(2.1)

Where x_2 in u_1 represents the fact that individual 1 is affected by individual 2's consumption of x. In this standard model there are only two markets and while Mr 1 can control his own consumption of x and y, he has no way of indicating his preference for Ms 2's consumption of x which affects him. Likewise there is no market for Ms 2 to signal her enjoyment of (or displeasure from) Mr 1's consumption of x. It is this inability to pay for the benefits (or receive money for costs) that prevents the two-market

competitive equilibrium from reaching a Pareto-optimal allocation, and the reason for this failure is that markets are missing.
In particular, two additional markets are needed: one for Mr 1's
consumption of x as it affects others, and another for Ms 2's
consumption of x as it affects others. This can be attained by
appropriately 'naming' these goods for which separate markets
can be created: effectively 'privatizing' the 'public' good.

The two individuals' utility functions can now be expressed as

$$u_1(x_{11}, x_{12}, y_1) \atop u_2(x_{21}, x_{22}, y_2).$$
(2.2)

The subscript $i = 1, 2$ in u_i tells us whose utility is involved (as
before) and the subscript $i = 1, 2$ in x_{ik} tells us in whose utility
function the good enters, while $k = 1, 2$ tells us who is actually
'consuming' ('producing') the good. For example, x_{21} could
denote Ms 2's envy over Mr 1's consumption of sports cars. This
is now a 'named' good[38] that Ms 2 can pay for through a newly
established market. If there are ten people envious of my sports
cars then I would be the producer of ten different commodities
each with its own market. With externalities redefined as 'conventional' private goods all the formal achievements of competitive
private ownership economies follow.

Individuals 1 and 2 would maximize their utility functions in
(2.2) subject to the following budget constraints:

$$p_x x_{11} + p_{12} x_{12} + p_y y_1 \le p_y \bar{y}_1 + (p_x + p_{21})\bar{x}_1 + p_{21} x_{21} \atop p_{21} x_{21} + p_x x_{22} + p_y y_2 \le p_y \bar{y}_2 + (p_x + p_{12})\bar{x}_2 + p_{12} x_{12}}$$
(2.3)

where the i in p_{ik} tells you the price that i pays for the good x
that k consumes. Furthermore in this example we have

$$x_{ik} = x_k \text{ (or } x_{kk}) \text{ for all } i \text{ and } k.$$
(2.4)

Since k cannot simultaneously consume different amounts of x,
all those affected by her consumption will be affected by a uni-
form quantity.[39] So the budget constraints can be rewritten as

$$p_x x_{11} + p_{12} x_{12} + p_y y_1 \le p_y \bar{y}_1 + (p_x + p_{21})\bar{x}_1 + p_{21} x_{11} \atop p_{21} x_{21} + p_x x_{22} + p_y y_2 \le p_y \bar{y}_2 + (p_x + p_{12})\bar{x}_2 + p_{12} x_{22}}$$
(2.5)

---

[38] 'Mr 1's consumption of sports cars' is the named good which can be 'purchased' in the 'Mr 1's consumption of sports cars' market by anyone.

[39] In fact this is why a 'private' price is needed for goods with subscript ik
where $i \ne k$. While 'producers' of this good cannot vary the quantities they sell
they can vary the price they charge as is standard in joint products.

The first-order conditions of the two Lagrangeans will be

$$\frac{\partial u_1}{\partial x_{11}} = \lambda(p_x - p_{21}) \quad \text{and} \quad \frac{\partial u_2}{\partial x_{22}} = \mu(p_x - p_{12}) \qquad (2.6a)$$

$$\frac{\partial u_1}{\partial x_{12}} = \lambda p_{12} \quad \text{and} \quad \frac{\partial u_2}{\partial x_{21}} = \mu p_{21} \qquad (2.6b)$$

$$\frac{\partial u_1}{\partial y_1} = \lambda p_y \quad \text{and} \quad \frac{\partial u_2}{\partial y_2} = \mu p_y. \qquad (2.6c)$$

Observe that equations in (2.6a) reveal that with the full set of markets for the 'named' goods, individual i pays the net price of what she pays for good x and what others pay her for consuming x.

From (2.6a) and (2.6b) one obtains

$$\frac{1}{\lambda}\frac{\partial u_1}{\partial x_{11}} = p_x - p_{21} \quad \text{and} \quad \frac{1}{\mu}\frac{\partial u_2}{\partial x_{22}} = p_x - p_{12} \qquad (2.7)$$

and using (2.6c) one gets

$$\frac{\dfrac{\partial u_1}{\partial x_{11}}}{\dfrac{\partial u_1}{\partial y_1}} + \frac{\dfrac{\partial u_2}{\partial x_{21}}}{\dfrac{\partial u_2}{\partial y_2}} = \frac{p_x}{p_y} = \frac{\dfrac{\partial u_1}{\partial x_{12}}}{\dfrac{\partial u_1}{\partial y_1}} + \frac{\dfrac{\partial u_2}{\partial x_{22}}}{\dfrac{\partial u_2}{\partial y_2}} \qquad (2.8)$$

One can easily check that this competitive equilibrium is Pareto-optimal by maximizing:

$$a_1 u_1(x_{11}, x_{12}, y_1) + a_2 u_2(x_{21}, x_{22}, y_2)$$
$$\text{subject to} \qquad x_{11} + x_{22} = \bar{x} \qquad (2.9)$$
$$y_1 + y_2 = \bar{y}$$

and recalling (2.4) so that a change in x_{11} implies (and equals) a change in x_{21}.

In looking at the first-order conditions associated with utility maximization in this model we get the Samuelsonian (1954) conditions of Pareto-optimality in the presence of public goods. This further reveals an essential equivalence of externality and public goods. With public prices for private goods and private prices for public goods, all interdependencies are dealt with efficiently by the market system. Externalities are a problem only when some market is missing.

Externality can now be seen as simply the non-existence of markets, and the failure associated with externality has a clear analytical description within the general-equilibrium model. Once it is established that non-existence characterizes the problem, the question becomes: why do markets fail to come into existence? Coase had already formulated the answer (there are costs of forming institutions). Markets may not come into existence because the costs of forming markets may obstruct that from happening. Either property rights may be too costly or the construction of a market may be too costly. Failure is related to the fact that some costs prevent markets from coming into existence. Arrow emphasizes the importance of transaction costs, and even asserts that the notion of market failure has to be modified so that failure becomes a relative notion dependent on the existence of institutions that can allocate more efficiently, rather than comparing the market to a utopian transaction costless model. However, he does not really develop this notion, nor does he integrate it into his analysis of externality.

An interpretational question arises. Is it assumed that externalities have an independent status from the existence of markets? Do we say, 'markets for externalities', or is it presumed that if a market exists then externality no longer exists? Arrow himself seems to take the former position, that there are some underlying causal factors or phenomena that prevent markets from coming into existence. Even if markets are formed, these underlying phenomena are still present; externality exists despite it not having negative welfare consequences for the economy, it's markets *for* externalities rather than markets *or* externalities. Furthermore, Arrow asserts that not all instances of non-existence of markets are caused by externality. Externality entails a subset of non-existence of markets.

14.2. Non-convexity

Arrow's convention of treating externalities as missing markets seemed to imply that any failure attributed to externalities could be interpreted as some market missing. Starrett (1972) dispelled this notion. In the case of detrimental interaction among agents even if a market existed for the 'named' good, the non-convexity in the expanded production space would effectively prevent the existence of an equilibrium price for the 'named' good.[40] Missing markets did not provide a complete description of market failure. This further heightened the sense that externalities had a status that was at least somewhat independent of institutions.

14.3. Externality as Failure of Markets to Form

Arrow (1970) had indicated the importance of uncovering the causes behind the non-existence of markets. Heller and Starrett (1976) turned their attention more squarely to this issue. If there were activities for which no markets existed, what was the reason that markets did not form? The question was to discern in what ways transaction costs obstructed the formation of markets. Also, failure was not associated simply with the non-existence of markets since if transaction costs are high it may be more efficient that no market exchange takes place. It was therefore important to discern cases where markets were not coming into existence when in fact their presence would entail efficiency gains.

Heller and Starrett suggested that the culprit was non-convexity in transaction costs. Referring to an article by Foley (1970), they pointed out that if transaction costs were convex, and assuming that property rights had already been defined, one could expect that only those markets that should come into existence on efficiency grounds would do so. If the transaction costs involved in forming some market were too high, it would be inefficient for that market to exist anyway, and non-existence would not signal inefficiency of the system. If there were substantial set-up costs in some market, the private economy would lack the incentives to form a market, and the non-existence of this market would signal inefficiency.[41]

This analysis gave rise to a new characterization of externality. Externality is 'a situation in which the private economy lacks sufficient incentives to create a potential market in some good and the nonexistence of this market results in losses in Pareto efficiency. It is general enough to include both pecuniary and nonpecuniary externalities' (Heller and Starrett 1976: 10).

---

[40] I deal with the issue of non-convexity in some depth in Chapter 5.
[41] Cornes and Sandler (1986) argue that there could be failure of the private-incentive system even if transaction costs are convex.

14.4. Pecuniary Externalities Revived Again

The missing-market view of externality has brought with it another revival, this time more enduring, of the relevance of pecuniary externalities along the lines of one of Scitovsky's original arguments. Heller and Starrett (1976) used as an example the case of two complementary industries, steel and railway. Both industries exhibit increasing returns to scale up to a point. If enough demand is generated for their goods then they will be viable, but they both require each other's demand to come into being. This problem would be obviated if future markets were complete. The railway industry could register its demand for steel and given the increased demand that the steel industry perceived, it could produce and offer a price which would make the railway industry viable, etc. This missing future market view seems to offer a place for pecuniary externalities as a cause of market failure.

Laffont (1988) offers some other reasons to rehabilitate pecuniary externalities. He argues that outside the Arrow–Debreu framework prices may play additional roles than just equating demand and supply. It may be that actions of agents alter the information content of prices, and thus the expectations of others, and so affect their expected utility. Though this argument is not spelled out fully, it could be argued that it is subject to the same kind of weakness that Scitovsky's original argument had, i.e. being a restatement of the simple fact that in an imperfect world, prices may not convey the right signals. Laffont also talks about 'distributional' externalities as pecuniary effects that accompany redistributions of income that lead to the coming into existence of some firm with initially increasing returns to scale.[42]

15. INSTITUTIONAL CONTEXT

15.1. The Calculus of Consent

Many of the meanings attributed to externality, and its relative import for resource allocation, seemed to derive from the context

---

[42] Note that pecuniary externalities have often been called distributional externalities.

within which economists were approaching the notion. No matter how the contexts differed they tended to have one feature in common—that the institutional framework was a given. While the institutional element in externality had become apparent, there was no investigation into how institutions were formed, or should be formed, and what this might mean for externality. In their influential book *The Calculus of Consent*, Buchanan and Tullock (1962) offered a substantially different context from which externality would acquire additional meanings. Rather than taking the institutional framework as given, institutions were to be an endogenous element emerging from a kind of social contract among agents in a pre constitutional setting.

This book was an important contribution to what is today known as the field of public choice, often described as the application of economics to political science.[43] In contrast to the organic view of the state which seemed at least implicit in most economic analysis, Buchanan and Tullock presented a contractarian theory of the state. They present an argument as to what the state should be. Agents are supposed to decide what activities should be private and what activities should be subject to collective choice, and what kind of collective-choice rule should be used. To avoid the infinite regress implicit in questioning how agents decide how agents should decide, it is presumed that agents begin in a kind of Rawlsian veil of ignorance, wherein decisions about the constitution are taken under the rule of unanimity. This affords some normative weight to the emerging constitution. What state or government functions should exist will be an outcome of such a hypothetical process. Traditional explanations of the division of public and private domain consider the question from the vantage point of an omniscient person that tries to correct the existing market system, or tries to form some voting rule that will maximize a social welfare function. Buchanan and Tullock, on the other hand, ask how agents in a kind of veil of ignorance might agree to subject certain activities to collective-decision rules. Rather than considering how an 'individual' can be offered incentives to help the aggregate, they look at how the aggregate through a kind of market will generate the

[43] According to Mueller (1989) public choice took off as a separate field around 1948, with the seminal works of Bergson (1938), Samuelson (1947), and Arrow (1951).

decision rules for the aggregate. Buchanan and Tullock ask: 'When will a society composed of free and rational utility-maximizing individuals choose to undertake action collectively rather than privately?' (1962: 43).

What is of interest to my present inquiry is their discussion in chapter 5, which sets up their approach to how and why organizations may evolve from an individual calculus of self interest (this does not exclude altruism). It offers a gold-mine of meanings of the notion of externality which have clearly influenced later views of the concept. Externality is at the heart of their theory of collective choice.

An individual maximizes the utility derived from some activity when the 'net costs' of organizing this activity are minimized. There are two elements in the expected costs of human activity. 'First, there are costs that the individual expects to endure as a result of the actions of others over which he has no direct control. To the individual these costs are external to his own behaviour, and we shall call them *external costs*, using conventional and descriptive terminology. Secondly, there are costs which the individual expects to incur as a result of his own participation in an organized activity. We shall call these *decision making costs*' (1962: 45).

Together external costs and decision-making costs are called 'interdependence costs'. The object of the rational agent when considering institutional and constitutional change should be to minimize these costs. It is assumed that human and property rights have already been defined so that questions of forming institutions go beyond this initial stage. There are three forms of activity '(1) purely individualistic behaviour, (2) private, voluntary, but jointly organized, behaviour, (3) collective or governmental action' (1962: 51). For different activities one can associate a cost to the three different modes of carrying them out.

In choosing the colour of one's underwear there are (according to the authors) no external costs imposed on others, and while there are decision costs, they are small, and for the purpose of their exposition can be ignored. Such an activity would entail zero interdependence-cost when undertaken individually, and it would thus make sense that a constitution allows such activities to be private. The colour of one's automobile will likely have some impact on friends; they may find it revolting, their utility ever so slightly diminished. Yet while there are external costs, the decision cost required to deal with them may outweigh the 'external' costs. It would still be best to leave these activities to the private domain.

The activities that we normally associate with market transactions fall into the second category (private, but jointly organized). Collective decisions are confined to protecting the freedom of private contract. Market transactions occur through binary consent: they are not completely private, and external costs are not eliminated, since exchanges that take place affect other agents' opportunity sets. The business firm is a privately organized institution and it is 'the best single example of an institutional arrangement or device that has as its purpose the internalization of external effects' (1962: 53). In all these cases presumably the combined external costs and decision-making costs are less than they would be under a collective decision-making rule, i.e. government. There are also activities for which the interdependence costs will be quite similar under alternative modes of organization: for example, in education 'many individuals may prefer to accept the expected costs of private decision-making in this area rather than undergo the expected costs of collectivization, which represent yet another kind of externality' (1962: 54).

I will not carry on listing activities and the merits of alternative institutional arrangements. My purpose was to give a sense of Buchanan and Tullock's framework (and vocabulary), from which one can better understand their senses of externality.

The classical examples of external economies and diseconomies constitute only a small set of activities, and no one has discussed carefully the criteria for determining when an externality resulting from private behavior becomes sufficiently important to warrant a shift to the public sector. Few scholars in the field have called attention to the fact that much voluntary behavior is aimed specifically at removing external effects, notably the whole economic organization of activities in business enterprises. The limit to voluntary organization, and thus the pure *laissez-faire* model of social organization, are not defined by the range of significant externalities, but instead by the *relative costs of voluntary and collective decision-making*. If decision-making costs, as we have defined them, are absent, the pure *laissez-faire* model will be rationally chosen

for all activities. All externalities, negative and positive, will be eliminated as a result of purely voluntary arrangements that will be readily
negotiated among private people. Almost by definition, the presence of
an externality suggests that 'mutual gains from trade' can be secured
from internalization, provided only that the decision-making costs do
not arise to interfere with the reaching of voluntary agreements.

Although it has surely been widely recognized, to our knowledge no
scholar has called specific attention to the simple and obvious fact that
collective organization of activities in which decisions are made through
less-than-unanimity voting rules must also involve external costs for the
individual. (Buchanan and Tullock 1962: 62)

15.1.1. Three Distinct Meanings Extracted

Buchanan and Tullock use the term 'externality' in many different ways. By considering the context I have extracted three distinct meanings that they attribute to the notion.

1. Externality is equated to general interdependence: any
   potential impact that an agent's decision can have on
   another agent, is an externality.
2. Externality is equated to some notion of inefficiency, or
   potential gains from trade, since voluntary private behaviour is a way of eliminating externality.[44] If they are to be
   consistent they must mean that 'Pareto-relevant' externality
   is eliminated, since interdependence remains, but affected
   parties have consented to it, and many mutual gains to
   trade have been eliminated. Importantly, the formation of
   voluntary institutions is linked to the elimination of externalities, in the sense of inefficiency, or untapped mutual
   gains.
3. Externality is *actuated* influence or imposition of costs or
   benefits by any means (direct or indirect). This differs from
   general interdependence which may be present potentially.
   A decision rule of unanimity eliminates all externality. 'The
   only means whereby the individual can insure that the
   actions of others will never impose costs on him is through
   the strict application of the rule of unanimity for all decisions, public and private.' (1962: 72.) Of course, often such
   a rule carries a high decision-making cost. That prevents it
   from being an optimal rule. So while unanimity may imply

---

[44] Of course general interdependence cannot be eliminated.

losses in potential mutual gains, there will be no externality in the sense of coercion if it is a costly mechanism. It isn't potential interdependence that characterizes externality here, but simply actual coercion or exercise of influence.

Any collective-decision rules which depart from unanimity will imply the existence of externality since some group will have costs imposed on them. The existence of decision-making costs will almost inevitably imply that some external costs should remain in an optimal organization, in the sense of coercion.

While one can sometimes gather the particular meaning through the context, it is quite confusing to have 'external' in so many different guises. Externality becomes a very broad notion, when it refers to general interdependence, coercion, or some kind of failure (but not necessarily market failure since now we are in a context that is outside a specific institution or decision making mechanism like the market). Also 'consent' became strongly associated with the notion of externality, the latter being unconsented to activity.

15.2. Property Rights and Externality[45]

In the orthodox exchange model individuals seek to maximize their welfare given some initial endowment of goods. Optimizing behaviour takes place within a context of specific institutional rules—those that make up the competitive market process. Property rights are fully defined and enforced, and all action takes place through the consent of individuals exchanging mutually recognized rights. From early on in the debate on externality it was seen that externality was associated with some kind of deficiency of institutional rules, or lack of some rule. Meade's 'unpaid factors' seem to signal some deficiency in the ownership over certain goods. This naturally led to the question of why ownership rights had not been established in certain instances. It seemed that a better understanding of why and how property rights are established would offer insights as to why certain activities seemed to remain 'unowned'.

More economists started working on models of human

---

[45] See also Bush and Mayer (1974) and Umbeck (1981), for the relationship of property rights and externality.

interaction in contexts where institutions were in large part endogenously determined, rather than starting from a framework where institutions had been fully established and enforced. Rules that governed exchange were not already established but were the outcome of interaction. The objectives of these economists were often diverse, but they had in common the departure from the standard model of optimization within well defined institutions.

Demsetz (1967) was concerned with forming a theory of property rights that explained the function and formation of alternative property-right structures. Like Buchanan and Tullock he focused on the function of institutions. Unlike them he did not take as a starting-point a pre-constitutional state in which no institutions existed, but considered institutional change in a world where rules of interaction may exist but were also endogenously determined. There was no pre-constitutional mechanism of consensual agreement that determined what institutions should exist. Rather there was individual interaction in more-or-less organized societies that led to the establishment of institutions by a kind of 'invisible hand'. He considered institutional change in history, whether this was the transition from feudalism to capitalism, or from a hunting-gathering community to one based on animal husbandry. The motor behind institutional change is a discrepancy between the net benefits attainable through human interaction under some existing property-right regime and those possible under an alternative property-right system. In short institutional inefficiency provides the incentive for institutional change. As a crude illustration, the shift from a hunting-gathering society to one based on animal husbandry could be seen as resulting from the increased efficiency of the latter form of organization over the former as conditions change. Population growth may strain the natural stock of animals in a given area, increasing the cost of maintaining a given level of food. Know-how on animal breeding may improve. Increased population may make it easier to defend a given territory from poachers. Territorial boundaries are defended in order to secure animal husbandry. This form of communal property evolves as the costs and benefits associated with alternative modes of organizations change.

Prior to the evolution of communal property, one could say that hunters were imposing external costs on each other which they did not take into account, but the external effects were small and so it did not pay to take them into account. With increased population and the development of a lucrative fur trade, these external effects became significant and it became profitable to find institutional means of internalizing these effects. Communal property and husbanding meant that these external costs imposed on one another could be 'internalized'.

Externality is an ambiguous concept. For the purpose of this paper, the concept includes external costs, external benefits, and pecuniary as well as nonpecuniary externalities. No harmful or beneficial effect is external to the world. Some person or persons always suffer or enjoy these effects. What converts a harmful or beneficial effect into an externality is that the cost of bringing the effect to bear on the decisions of one or more of the interacting persons is too high to make it worthwhile, and this is what the term shall mean here. 'Internalizing' such effects refers to a process, usually a change in property rights, that enables these effects to bear (in greater degree) on all interacting persons.

A primary function of property rights is that of guiding incentives to achieve a greater internalization of externalities. Every cost and benefit associated with social interdependencies is a potential externality. (Demsetz 1967: 348)

Demsetz begins with the broadest view of externality—general interdependence or any and all effects of others' actions on an agent. Then he narrows it down, and externalities are those effects that are not worth taking into account. If I smile at you and that has a pleasurable impact on you, you would have more to gain if I smiled even more, but the effort or cost it would take me to induce you to smile more outweighs the gain. There is an organizational cost involved in influencing agents to act in certain ways. Institutions like property rights that limit and channel agents' activity are costly, and if we are going to assess the overall efficiency of a system these costs have to be part of the optimizing calculus. Some of the actions of agents in an economy which affect others may not have a substantial impact, or it may be that the cost of influencing these actors somehow outweighs the benefits of doing so.

Interestingly, neither of Demsetz's broad and narrow senses of externality are associated with inefficiency. In a simple exchange economy with fully defined property rights, Pareto-inefficiency is simply the presence of mutual gains through trade, given some initial endowments. In Demsetz's model inefficiency is simply the presence of mutual gains through institutional innovation, given some existing state of interdependence: the possibility of taking more 'external effects' (interdependent actions) into account. Externality as such has nothing to do with inefficiency. In a world of general interdependence all that matters is that whatever mutual gains are available, through making actors consider the effect their actions have on others, are attained.

Demsetz envisioned a kind of self-organizing *laissez-faire* system in which potential mutual gains among agents would provide the impetus for institutional change. If a factory was spilling smoke into the environment this did not necessarily mean inefficiency. If some institutional mechanism existed that could provide the parties harmed and benefited by this activity with gains from reduction in smoke and also pay for the cost of organizing such compensation, then the institution would be established and the system would be optimal. Demsetz was not saying that the system was transaction-costless, in which case it would be efficient tautologically, but that in the presence of transaction costs the agents making up the system, in perpetual pursuit of profits, would create those institutions that were least costly given the existing conditions, and which represented Pareto-gains.

Consider the cattle-rancher–farmer example. Cattle are straying on to the farmer's field and destroying crops. The farmer might be able to come to some agreement with the rancher and get compensation for the damage. If there were no transaction costs then an optimal level of farming and cattle-ranching would ensue. Suppose, however, there are costs of bargaining, forming, and enforcing a contract. If the costs exceed the potential mutual gains then no contract will be made and given the real transaction costs this will be an efficient outcome. The same could be said about a monopoly. If there are potential gains in a more competitive organization of production, and the costs of organizing activity in such a fashion are less than the benefits, then the change will occur. Presumably all institutional ways of squeezing any mutual gains from cooperation will be examined and if a way exists which allows both parties to gain, then it will be taken. At any given point in time the system will be optimal, given the existing know-how, transaction costs, etc.

Demsetz's context is very different from Buchanan and Tullock's although the meanings they both attach to externality seem to be similar. Buchanan and Tullock are considering a model in which agents are hypothetically discussing at a table what rules should guide their lives, without knowing in what position they may find themselves in the polity they are constructing. In this context there is some moral weight behind the assertion that selection of rules of voluntary decisions, collective decisions, or 'private' decisions to govern activity, will be efficient, although one may disagree with the ethical principle. In the case of Demsetz's analysis, agents find themselves immersed in the real world, and any decisions about 'internalizing' activity will be a function of the decision-making processes to which activity is already subject. It is hard to see how the evolving system will be efficient unless that can be said of the already existing institutions. It is not clear what the standard of efficiency is.

15.3. Externality as Coercion

Irrespective of how externalities have been characterized over the years, there has been a strong tendency to focus on areas for which mutual gains can be made. Whether or not pecuniary externalities should concern us would depend upon whether Pareto-improvements were possible. 'Pareto-relevant' externalities were those which held some promise of mutual gains from trade. The possibility of Pareto-improvements was closely linked to the importance of externality, sometimes determining what would be called an externality, and at other times carving out a subset of externalities worthy of concern. 'Internalization' was a process by which untapped mutual gains were appropriated.

Samuels (1972) strongly criticizes any such narrowing of focus:

With *coercion* defined as the impact of the behavior and choices of others upon the structure of one's opportunity set and relative costs of alternatives, *externalities* comprise the substance of coercion, namely, the injuries and benefits, the costs and gains, visited upon others through the exercise of choice by each economic actor and by the total number of economic actors. (1972: 52)

To exclude pecuniary and Pareto-irrelevant externalities is to exclude behavior only because the coercion is conditional; but coercion is both conditionally and unconditionally imposed. (1972: 58)

To talk about Pareto-better trades one has to assume that property rights are already established. To create new property rights on the basis of existing ones is simply to acknowledge the legitimacy of some existing structure of property rights which gives rise to the costs and benefits attached to activities. The essence of the argument is that a given legal structure, rules of contract, remuneration, initial property rights, forms of enforcement, etc., determine both the array of benefits and costs that agents attach to different activities, and the overall costs of transacting. To look for potential gains of trade on the basis of these costs and benefits, is simply to accept the entire institutional structure as legitimate, an apology for the status quo. For Samuels the job of the welfare economist is to evaluate the entire set of institutions on the prior decision of who is to count or what weight agents should be given in resource-allocation decisions.

Demsetz's argument is that agents will seek out ways of minimizing transaction costs, or 'internalize' untapped potential mutual gains. In a similar vein Posner (1986) suggests as a policy that institutions are selected according to the criterion of transaction-costs minimization. Specifically, a kind of Kaldor–Hicks compensation rule[46] should be used to bring about potential Pareto-improvements in institutions. Those institutions that maximized total benefits over costs given relative prices would be most efficient: 'internalize' most externalities. Samuels' criticism naturally extends to this proposition of efficient institutions. Schmid (1987) and Bromley (1989) offer such an extension:

The potential compensation test cannot be a guide to shifting rights without presuming who had rights before the shift . . . Efficiency calculations always depend on where you start, but they can never validate that starting place. Therefore, a benefit-cost analysis of alternative rights is always a partial analysis. Efficiency calculations always presume some set of rights and therefore cannot be a guide to rights, unless the prior rights are legitimated. (Schmid 1987: 248)

In essence when Samuels objects to the narrowing of externality to some idea of untapped mutual gains, he is objecting to the notion that Pareto-efficiency can be meaningfully applied to institutional evaluation.

---

[46] This wealth-maximization principle has undergone several refinements and is still a source of heated debate.

15.4. Externality Does Not Matter

If decision-making costs, as we have defined them, are absent, the pure *laissez-faire* model will be rationally chosen for all activities. All externalities, negative and positive, will be eliminated as a result of purely voluntary arrangements that will be readily negotiated among private people. (Buchanan and Tullock 1962: 62)

Thus if one assumes rationality, no transaction costs, and no legal impediments to bargaining, *all* misallocations of resources would be fully cured in the market by bargains. (Calabresi 1968: 67)

When looking at inefficiency or market failure through the visors of the 'institutional' perspective, all failure must simply be some impediment to making some mutually beneficial exchange. The economists cited above recognized the unlikelihood of a 'frictionless' world, but wanted to emphasize that the 'efficiency' of a system must be based on a measuring-rod of the resources expended in sustaining the system. If the market was optimal, it wasn't because it attained an ideal allocation of resources (which could only happen if transaction costs were absent), but because it attained some desirable allocation of resources while expending fewer resources than alternative institutional structures. Demsetz (1969) called the former approach the 'Nirvana' approach and the latter, 'attainable' efficiency.

Increasingly 'institutional' economists criticized the traditional economists' notion of optimality and market failure. If monopoly indicated a smaller output than what would exist under 'ideal' competitive conditions, this did not imply that there was failure. Failure elicited the notion that some real improvement could be achieved, possibly by government intervention. But if there were real transaction costs that meant that alternatives to monopoly organization would engender costs of organization that exceeded any expected benefits, then surely monopoly was the most efficient of feasible institutions.

This kind of reasoning is easily extended to all forms of market failure as traditionally understood. This divergence of private and social cost was a divergence in conjunction with an unattainable ideal. These potential mutual gains were fictitious. They did not represent or indicate 'real' failure. To focus on this kind of failure, this 'externality', was simply wrong. In this vein, Zerbe

(1976) argues that externality[47] is not a 'useful phenomenological category', while transaction cost is. Dahlman points out that 'externalities and market failure are not what is the matter with the world . . . our sad state of affairs is rather due to positive transaction costs and imperfect information' (1979: 161).[48] If there are activities which are not internalized by the agents taking the decisions, then this must imply the presence of transaction costs. The question is not whether there are 'externalities' but whether there are transaction costs that can be reduced.

Dahlman was making a wholesale rejection of traditional notions of market failure and 'externality' as market failure. In the general-equilibrium framework a comparison was being made between a Pareto-optimal point in a transaction-costless world and an equilibrium generated by a Walrasian auctioneer in a system with 'missing markets'. Hence 'externalities' were preventing the attainment of Pareto-optimality. A comparison is being made between a model without transaction costs and one with transactions costs. To look for ways of improving on the 'externalities'-infested economy in order to attain the Pareto-optimal point was misdirected since the Pareto-optimality of a transaction-costless world is a fiction. He was advocating a different notion of assessing institutions and the market: Demsetz's 'comparative-systems approach'. The focus would be to select institutions that reduced transaction costs. He reasserts and elaborates upon Coase's position.

To a large extent externality for the 'institutional' group has been a kind of a tool that, by virtue of focusing on the boundary of the well-defined institutional world of the neoclassical model with the beyond of 'institutionlessness', has helped uncover serious limitations of that model. By trying to understand how institutions 'internalize' activity, an introspection has been forced into the meaning and function of institutions as well as the notion of

---

[47] Note that Zerbe (1976) and Dahlman (1979) are referring to externality mainly in the senses given by Bator (1958), Arrow (1970), Heller and Starrett (1976). They do away with this sense of externality and do not comment on externality as Buchanan and Tullock (1962), or Demsetz (1967), view it.

[48] Dahlman (1979) deals largely with different notions of transaction costs, arguing that some of the notions used in general-equilibrium models are far too restrictive and miss the real import of transaction costs, and in that sense fail to treat institutions endogenously. He forms a definition of transaction costs; in effect that they are equivalent to information costs.

efficiency. What are firms, markets, property rights, institutions? What function do they serve? What are transaction costs? What is the meaning of efficiency? Is the Pareto-criterion of any value in a world of ubiquitous transaction costs?

16. CONCLUSION

Looking back a hundred years, if I were to follow the custom of dividing history into stages, I would suggest the following three: For the first, the forty years from 1890 when Marshall first used the term 'external economy' to about the time that Viner made his contribution in 1930, the issue centred on the clarification of the upward and downward-sloping supply curves. With this clarification seemingly complete, it looked as if external economies might recede into the margins of economic analysis. The next stage would cover about thirty years up to 1960 with Coase's seminal article. This was a time of accumulation of new interpretations of external economies largely in response to the many examples of phenomena that economists were associating with the notion of external economies or 'externalities'. Externality was seen as either a subset of market failure or coextensive with it. It was also seen as a cause of market failure. The third stage covers the last thirty years. The central features of this phase are (*a*) the rising interest in environmental matters forging a strong association of externalities with pollution and raising interest in the externality question; (*b*) the ascendance of an institutional dimension in economics, concurrent with the notion of transaction costs, which came under focus with the debate on externalities; (*c*) an increasing separateness of the contexts of debate over externalities; this of course reflects the general trend of specialization and compartmentalization of economic discourse.

Of these three trends, the second one (growing institutional awareness) has perhaps had the largest impact in the metamorphoses of the notion of externality. One might say that through the medium of externality, the recognition of institutional costs has been transforming the way economists treat or understand the causality and nature of market failure, and more generally institutional failure or institutional evaluation. The remaining lack of clarity in the notion of externality must in large part lie in the unsettled nature of the theory of market failure. Perhaps clarity will be attained when the institutional dimension of economics can be better comprehended.

There is one persistent problem reiterated throughout the history of the notion of externality, and that is the sense that no good characterization of externality exists. One of the few books devoted entirely to the theory of externalities entitled *The Theory of Externalities, Public Goods, and Club Goods*, by Cornes and Sandler, opens its chapter on externalities with the following statement: 'There is a strong temptation to avoid an explicit definition of an externality, since even this first step has been a fertile source of controversy' (1986: 29). I believe economists should resist this temptation to avoid explicit definition, since an understanding of the notion of externality seems to be tied intimately with the most central of issues, the appraisal of an economy and its institutions.

3

Phenomenological Characterization

1. INTRODUCTION

The growing awareness of pollution and its rise on the political agenda in the early 1960s offered an important focal point for the concept of externality which had been struggling to find a real-world counterpart that would do full justice to the attention economists had bestowed on it. Pollution and externality became nearly synonymous. This grounding of the term to something tangible or physical, heightened the sense that externality had a separate 'existence' of its own, that it was an identifiable phenomenon. It also intensified the feeling that it was a narrower category than general interdependence or coercion that warranted separate classification, although this has always been the prevailing sense in traditional economic models.

In the early 1970s two important books came out that dealt with externalities, focusing on environmental issues; James Meade's (1973) *The Theory of Economic Externalities* and Baumol and Oates's (1975) *Theory of Environmental Economics*. Both offer characterizations of externality that elicit the sense of there being some identifiable phenomena or events that can be classified without reference to institutions. Meade's distinction between events that are external and internal rests on two key notions, consent and appreciable effect. Events having 'appreciable' effects (benefits or costs) on agents who did not 'consent' to the decisions leading to the events in question, are deemed externalities. By varying the notions of 'consent' and 'appreciable', externality could span all human interaction or it could be drastically narrowed down (for instance Marshall's original sense).[1] Meade (1973: 15) says, '[in] fact the problem of deciding exactly where to draw the line between an internality and an externality

---

[1] Meade (1973: ch. 1) offers an interesting discussion on the nuances in the possible meanings of consent.

in economic analysis is not at all straightforward; and the definition which I have adopted casts the net very widely'.

Unlike Meade in this latter respect, Baumol and Oates are
keener to narrow the scope of externalities. Their characterization
seemingly carves out a smaller, more precise, subset of economic
interaction. This way it lends itself to appraising the problems of
forming a precise phenomenological characterization of externality. In this chapter I will focus on their characterization as representative of attempts to specify some well-defined phenomena as
externalities (narrower than general interdependence or coercion),
whose existence is independent of there being consequences in
terms of efficiency. Though I offer a detailed criticism of a single
characterization, my goal is to illustrate the inherent difficulty of
associating externality with a specific category of phenomena, as
well as to question the need for such a category.

Baumol and Oates's (1975) characterization of externalities,
quoted earlier, involved two conditions:

Condition 1. An externality is present whenever some individual's (say
A's) utility or production relationships include real (non-monetary) variables, whose values are chosen by others (persons, corporations, government) without particular attention to the effects on A's welfare. (1975:
17)

Condition 2. The decision maker, whose activity affects others' utility
levels or enters their production functions, does not receive (pay) in
compensation for this activity an amount equal in value to the resulting
(marginal) benefits or costs to others. (1975: 18)

Condition 1 is the test of whether an externality exists.
Condition 2 refers to whether an externality leads to inefficiency.
Rather than initially discussing how Baumol and Oates arrive at
this definition or what they really have in mind when using this
definition, I will examine first what someone may understand by
reading this definition on its own without further explanation.
The first purpose of this exercise is to use the definition as a
springboard to uncover some problems with this particular view
of externality, and by extension, with other similar phenomenological views. I will do this by looking independently at the problems posed by each of the clauses used to delimit the scope of
externality (real variables, monetary variables, 'chosen by others',
etc.). After, a contrast will be drawn between what the definition

allows one to perceive as externality and what Baumol and Oates meant, in order to highlight the underlying assumptions made. Finally, I will consider the merits of this characterization.

2. REAL VARIABLES

Heller and Starrett (1976) argue that this kind of definition is not very useful, 'at least until the institutional framework is given'. It would mean that in a two-person economy (e.g. barter economy) all exchanges would entail externalities. In a barter economy an individual's utility depends directly on the decision of another when the two are exchanging goods. In a definition of the kind offered by Baumol and Oates, externality would seem to include non-atomistic market interaction (in effect too few agents). In which case agents have some control over others' objective functions.

Delegation of decision-making would be seen as an externality on a strict reading of the definition. Individuals or firms may delegate certain areas of choice to others for a number of reasons (common interest, time-saving). In fact it could easily be stretched to entail any interdependence. Recall Buchanan and Stubblebine's characterization that uses almost identical wording and general interdependence can easily be implied.

3. MONETARY VARIABLES[2]

If individuals' utility were a function of income distribution, changes in relative prices would directly affect them. Price changes would alter the distribution of income and so the level of satisfaction or dissatisfaction derived by the individual.[3] Likewise altruism or envy would imply a sensitivity to relative price changes through its effects on incomes. What Scitovsky (1976) calls ranking would come under this category. Individuals attach importance to their income position relative to others in some reference group (neighbourhood, age, etc.). Again price changes will affect them directly.

[2] The use of this term is misleading since it refers to relative price changes.
[3] Ng (1973) has dealt with income distribution treated as a public good.

In the presence of transaction costs,[4] relative price changes become important in determining whether externalities are present. The private disposal of garbage on a neighbourhood street may be alleviated by a change in transaction costs. Changes in proximity or communication costs could make it easier to coordinate a market for garbage collection. An effect that may be established through relative price changes leads to the internalizing of an externality.[5] Or the opposite may happen: the earthquake in Sicily a few years ago, made enforcement costs rise, resulting in high rates of stealing and mugging.[6]

Suppose transaction costs for some good are high, and an alteration in the location of agents, brought about through the smooth functioning of the price mechanism, pushes the transaction costs down. What was previously an externality may no longer be. For example, say that the market leads an externality-generating firm to a less populated area (not because of the pollution but for private cost reasons), price changes alone have reduced externality, actually eliminated it. Similarly, changes in technology (brought about through the market) may make exclusion costs disappear for some good, again altering the externality space. These points become clearer when the concept is approached from a more analytical point of view in Chapter 4.

4. VARIABLES 'CHOSEN BY OTHERS'

Here we have the same factors as those in section 2 where the emphasis changes from 'real variables' to 'chosen by others'. Non-atomistic interdependence, increasing returns to scale, and delegation of decisions, all entail situations where choices are made by others.

In condition 1, it is stated that 'values are chosen by others',

[4] On some very broad definitions of transaction costs, externalities would not exist but for the presence of transaction costs. The issue of transaction costs will be discussed later.

[5] Heller and Starrett (1976) present a small model to illustrate these dynamic effects.

[6] Becker (1968) applies microeconomic analysis to the activity of crime and law-enforcement. No doubt crime involves the kind of 'direct interaction' implied in condition 1 of Baumol and Oates's definition, although it can't be said that crime is propagated 'without particular attention to others'. Condition 2 would rule it out as a cause of inefficiency if law-enforcement was 'optimally' applied.

are they chosen exclusively by others? Does A have no control over the effects on herself? How about A's ability to neutralize the effects by moving away from the externality-generator or by using other forms of deterrence? What precisely is the scope of control that an individual must wield over an activity for it not to be an externality?

5. VARIABLES NOT 'CHOSEN BY OTHERS'

The term 'chosen' seems inappropriate for a large category of externalities, where individuals' actions have an influence on variables without a conscious choice over the specific variable being made. In fact it conflicts with the clause 'without attention', since choice implies a conscious decision. A more consistent term may be 'influenced' by others.

6. WITH INTENT

An issue that often comes up in definitions, is whether an externality-generating act was intended or not.[7] In condition 1, the phrase 'without particular attention to the effects on A's welfare', indicates this concern with intent. Does this mean that if B acts on purpose to alter A's welfare, this would not be an externality? Or shall the degree of intent be an issue? Would the degree of awareness alter the picture? B may be aware of the effects his action has on A but the effect is unintentional. If a firm chooses a slightly cheaper production technique that has a higher social cost, and is aware of this, is such a choice without intent?

It seems better if the definition of externality did not make it dependent on whether the act was willed or not. First, it is very difficult, if not impossible, to determine whether some effect of an act was intended or not. Second, whether an act was done with intent or not, does not mean that the act has no direct effect on the receiver. The allocation consequences are still present. B may purposefully block A's view of the sea by building a high enough fence. In fact where compensation rules are not in effect,

---

[7] The inclusion of intent in the definition of externalities can be attributed to Mishan (1971).

B may generate an externality in order to enhance his bargaining position over A (more on this aspect later).

7. COMPENSATION

In condition 2 of the definition a new qualifying factor is brought into the account. Compensation is given a central role in determining what is considered a relevant externality. A is punched in the nose by B who receives an amount 'equal in value to the resulting (marginal) benefits or costs' on A. Accordingly, this is not a Pareto-relevant externality. There is an important qualitative difference between the compensation offered to agents through the smooth functioning of market transactions or private bargaining, and that offered either by coincidence (when externalities offset each other), or by some alternative mechanism (taxes, penalties). In the first case, the agents can decide whether to partake in a transaction or not. When in disequilibrium, there is an incentive to trade in order to reap some of the mutual gains from trade. In fact, with an auctioneer, agents know what they will get before they exchange goods. The act is taken in full awareness of the consequences, while, with externalities, compensation is offered after the effects of the action have been registered. Agents have no choice, the transaction is forced.

The question arises whether the externality-generating individual is able to compensate the receiver. Furthermore, unless compensation is simultaneous to the act, we move into a dynamic framework. The compensation after the act may be a different quantity, since 'time heals wounds'.[8] Should the compensation take into account the 'victim's' prior best response to the externality?[9]

Nozick (1974) points to some interesting issues concerning the inability of compensation to deal with fear. He says: 'A system that allowed assault to take place provided the victims were compensated afterwards would lead to apprehensive people, afraid of

---

[8] The issue of *ex post* and *ex ante* liability has far-reaching implications in a dynamic context. One perspective on the matter is offered by Buchanan and Faith (1981).

[9] Oates (1983) and Shibata and Winrich (1983) investigate what happens when victims take action to counter the externality.

assault, sudden attack, and harm' (1975: 66). And even if those attacked are compensated, 'who will compensate all the other apprehensive persons, who didn't happen to get assaulted, for their fear?' (ibid.). This further highlights the distinction between prohibition, and compensation after the act.[10] Market exchange entails a kind of prohibition (e.g. a prohibition to steal), and ensures that consent is prior to the act of exchange. In the case of externality there is no prior consent, compensation follows after the act.

Another way in which compensation may differ between market exchange and externality concerns the division of benefits resulting from trade. Two individuals in an Edgeworth box (competitive behaviour, convex preferences), trade from a point off the contract curve. The resulting gains from trade will be distributed in an arbitrary fashion between the two of them (depending on the utility functions). Arbitrary in terms of the distribution of utilities, but may be specifically determined by the market mechanism. In the case of an externality, if all that is required is that the offended be fully compensated, then the total net benefits are reaped by the generator. Full compensation means that the offender has to give enough to return the offended to her original indifference curve. Generally, if 'compensation after externality' $= a$, and 'market compensation' $= b$, then $a < b$ (a will be smaller than b). This implies that the individual with externality-inducing technology has an edge in the terms of trade. Bargaining over rights to offend may alleviate this problem, but that requires that *ex post* rights be defined (as opposed to *ex ante* or liability rights).

I have touched on only a few of the issues concerning the differences between property rights and liability rules. A lot has been written in the Law and Economics literature on these issues. The question being raised here, is whether what is called externality should depend on the kind of entitlement protecting an activity.

There is another problem with the compensation principle as stated in condition 2. It says that the 'decision maker, whose activity affects others' utility levels or enters their production

---

[10] An interesting discussion on the issues of prohibition and compensation can be found in Nozick (1974: ch. 4). Becker (1968) discusses the different implications of fines and punishment as applied to criminal activity.

functions, does not receive (pay) in compensation for this activity an amount *equal in value to the resulting (marginal) benefits or costs to others'* (Baumol and Oates 1975: 18, my italics). Fulfilment of this condition would require interpersonal comparisons. The decision-maker should not be receiving an amount equal to the benefit (or costs) the others *actually* receive, but equal to what they would be *willing to pay* to receive (or avoid) the benefits (or costs) arising from the decision-maker's action.

8. BAUMOL AND OATES'S JUSTIFICATION OF THEIR DEFINITION

Baumol and Oates formed a definition of externality in order to offer an alternative to the very broad definition given by Bator (1958) and Buchanan and Stubblebine (1962), even though definitions such as theirs (Baumol and Oates) abounded as they acknowledged. They did not want to include such phenomena as increasing returns, as this 'problem is ultimately quite different from that of the more conventional externalities that constitute the primary threat to the environment and to the quality of life more generally. It therefore seems preferable to hold to a narrower . . . interpretation of the term' (1975: 16). They also felt that these definitions focused too much on what externalities do rather than what they are. Is the reason for narrowing the definition to be closer to the 'conventional view'? Is it to focus on something that is very important, 'the environment and the quality of life'? Are these appropriate justifications?

Despite their intentions, Baumol and Oates's definition, in some respects, seems to be broader than Bator's. It allows non-atomistic market interaction to pass as externality (see the argument on real variables in section 2 above) while this would only be included in Bator's definition if it implied market failure. It is not clear whether this is intended by the authors. Furthermore, it could allow for economic interdependence generally. Clearly this is not what Baumol and Oates intend, and they say so explicitly. '(The) definition should not be misunderstood to be a simple equation of externalities with economic interdependence' (1975: 17). But the definition does not tell us that. At this point you may object and tell me to stop being pedantic and simply add a clause to the definition excluding general economic interdependence. Although this may deal with the problem at hand, there are more fundamental problems with the definition which are partly signalled by the need for such a clause.

What separates general economic interdependence from the kind that Baumol and Oates imply? Market interdependence from non-market interdependence? A utility function $U_a(x^a, y^a)$ from a utility function $U_a(x^a, y^a, x^b)$? What is the distinction that the authors are aiming at? What is implicit in a normal utility or production function is that the goods in the model (resources, commodities, inputs) are privately owned. Control over these goods has been fully assigned to agents in the economy. Control is nowhere disputed. It is not that decisions that others take do not affect you (just as their preferences affect you through prices), but that they cannot take certain actions without your consent. When John purchases an apple or a car, it is not that he does not affect his friend Willa, because he reduces the apples and cars available to Willa by one and alters their price (in a non-atomistic environment). However, in taking such action, John has to get the consent from some owner of these goods. These goods are privately owned by some agent. It is the assignment of property that is behind the distinction between the two utility functions. The general economic interdependence that Baumol and Oates want to exclude is this market kind (or even the private-bargaining kind) that is regulated by the institution of private-property rights. Only when property rights are not defined (or assigned) does one get the kind of utility functions that are used to represent externalities. What separates a utility function of the form $U_a(x^a, y^a)$ from a utility function of the form $U_a(x^a, y^a, x^b)$ is that in the normal utility function property rights are fully defined implicitly, while in the latter function, property rights over x are not fully defined. The full force of the point can be seen when considering a state of nature prior to the establishment of property rights.[11] In this state if one were to write a utility function of the agents over some good, say food, it would take the form used to represent an externality. Since no

[11] Some models where property is derived from a state of nature are offered by Bush and Mayer (1974) and Umbeck (1981). There is substantial literature on the role of property rights in economic models, see Furubotn and Pejovich (1972), Demsetz (1967), and more recently Eggertsson (1990).

one owns[12] the good, whoever acquires the food is directly affecting the other's utility. Externality is pervasive. Private-property
rights are critical in the separation between general economic
interdependency and market interdependency (many agents is the
other critical factor). Baumol and Oates should replace the first
condition with the following:

> Externalities are present wherever property rights are not
> fully defined.

or

> Externalities are synonymous with the non-existence of prop-
> erty rights.

This makes externality dependent on a specific institution (property rights). Is this what Baumol and Oates meant by externality?
The wording in condition 1 seems to purposefully avoid any reference to institutions. Other passages in their paper would seem
to confirm that they want a definition free of institutions. They
make a distinction between depletable and undepletable externalities. As examples of depletable externalities they cite the training
of unskilled labour and exhaustible common-property resources
(fishing). Undepletable externalities are public goods for which
'an increase in the consumption of the good by one individual
does not reduce its availability to others' (Baumol and Oates
1975: 19). The example they cite is 'the familiar case of the local
flower garden'. One could add television, defence, goodwill, etc.
They make this distinction in order to offer a parallel
with Buchanan and Stubblebine's 'Pareto-relevant' and 'Pareto-
irrelevant' externalities. Accordingly, 'where there are no legal or
institutional restrictions inhibiting the pricing process, a
depletable externality will usually be permitted to persist only if
the cost of collecting a price for it exceeds the potential gains'
(Baumol and Oates 1975: 20).[13] This is the traditional transaction-cost argument that optimal accounting of externalities will
take place unless transaction costs prevent it. If the transaction
costs are higher than the gains from eliminating the externality

---

[12] There is an important distinction between possession and ownership (see
Perrings 1987), but for our present purposes we need not delve into these sub-
tleties.
[13] As I noted earlier, Buchanan and Stubblebine (1962) did not offer this interpretation of Pareto-relevancy, although it may be seen as a natural extension.

then it is optimal to allow the externality to persist. Such externalities are Pareto-irrelevant. What is not clear is why this reasoning should apply only to depletable externalities. 'If the cost of collecting a price for (a depletable externality) exceeds the potential gains,' this can only be due to some institutional constraint or cost. But the same would apply to an undepletable externality. If technology of institutions allows, or transaction costs allow, undepletable externalities could be dealt with efficiently by the price mechanism. That they are not must be because the institutional costs (transaction costs) are too high.

The parallel between depletable–undepletable and Pareto-relevant–irrelevant does not seem right. Baumol and Oates 'suggest that it may be preferable to think of depletable externalities not as externalities at all, but as cases where institutional impediments make it impossible to impose the appropriate prices. For this reason one may want to include condition 2 as part of our definition' (1975: 23). I repeat, both externalities are 'cases where institutional impediments make it impossible to impose the appropriate prices', not just depletable externalities.

Why this confusion? Partly, it stems from the conflict between their desire to form a definition of externality without reference to institutions while at the same time implicitly referring to property rights in condition 1. It also stems from their attempt to offer an alternative definition to that of Buchanan and Stubblebine's where externalities are not defined by 'what they are but what they do' (Baumol and Oates 1975: 17). Baumol and Oates are looking for phenomena that can be labelled externality and not the consequences related to these phenomena. And this is supposed to be satisfied by condition 1: 'an externality is present if the activity satisfies condition 1' (1975: 18). Condition 2 is added to show the relationship between their definition and Buchanan and Stubblebine's. Accordingly condition 1 depicts the phenomena and condition 2 represents the set of such phenomena that have inefficiency as a consequence.[14] In Figure 3.1 a 'cleansed' version of Baumol and Oates's definition is represented.

There are two possibilities of what externalities are: first definition, externalities are those cases where property rights have not

[14] Depletable and undepletable externalities are not the basis of such a distinction.

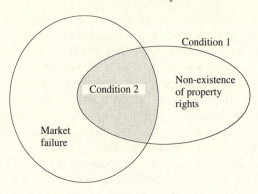

Fig 3.1.

been defined (revised condition 1), or, second definition, externalities are those cases where property rights have not been defined and inefficiency is present (revised condition 1 and condition 2 or shaded area in diagram). It is that subset of market failure that is related to the non-existence of property rights.

Does the revised definition offer an understanding of what externality is as opposed to what it does? Revised condition 1 seems to offer such an understanding. If one includes condition 2, externality is defined both by what it is (non-existence of property rights) and by what it does (inefficiency). The apparent clarity of this scheme, however, is based on there being a very crisp and clean distinction between the existence of private property and non-existence. Such precision is possible in an Arrow–Debreu world, but is questionable in a world of ubiquitous transaction costs where the notion of private property is diluted by the degree of protection or excludability offered by various mechanisms of enforcement. On close scrutiny it is apparent that the problem of identifying some subset of general interdependence by reference to the degree of control that an agent has over events, is translated into a problem of defining the institution of private property.

Even if private-property rights can be defined appropriately, is there any fundamental reason in adhering to the first definition? Is there any basic reason why one should focus on that activity over which property rights have not been defined, especially if these do not lead to inefficiency? If we are concerned about inefficiency why narrow it down to the inefficiency associated with the non-existence of property rights (second definition)? These problems need to be resolved. Could a resolution be found in a definition of externalities that makes no reference to institutions (what Baumol and Oates seemed to be seeking for)? Is such a definition possible?

9. CONCLUSION

In my introduction I distinguished the phenomenological, general-equilibrium, and institutional approaches to the concept of externality. I noted that these approaches do not entail distinct views of externality but that they provide heuristic devices to distinguish the main differences among the many characterizations in the literature. In fact, most characterizations tend to associate (at least implicitly) externality with some specific category of phenomena. In this chapter, I focused on a particular phenomenological characterization to bring out, *inter alia*, two general problems that confront any association of externality with a distinct set of phenomena: first, the difficulty of providing a clear distinction between external and internal activity that is not consequence-related; secondly, the difficulty of justifying or explaining the need for such a distinction, i.e. providing the motivation behind such a distinction.

4

General-Equilibrium Approach

1. INTRODUCTION

A different perspective on the nature of externality was provided by economists approaching the question from a more analytical vantage point; specifically attempting to identify its meaning and place within the general-equilibrium framework. Rather than trying to identify some event or some feature of an agent's control variables, the focus was on finding the boundaries between such concepts as market failure, public goods, non-convexities, and externality. The main motivation was to fully grasp the sources, or causes, of market failure within the rigorous Arrow–Debreu framework. Understanding the consequences of externality in terms of efficiency took primacy over establishing its existence as a phenomenon.

Despite the valuable insights that are gained from this approach, the notion of externality whether seen as equivalent to market failure, as Bator (1958) treats it, or as a subset of market failure, as Arrow (1970) and Heller and Starrett (1976) treat it, ultimately remains vague and imprecise. This imprecision may not be such a big problem on its own, but it reflects a growing imprecision in a series of key concepts like market, market failure, optimality, etc., along with the very methodology (General-Equilibrium Theory) from which these terms are interpreted.

In attempting to fully specify the causal mechanism underlying market failure and to establish externality's place therein, the authors gradually alter the very notion of market failure. The key element behind this transformation is the introduction of transaction costs within the general-equilibrium framework. Transaction costs are invoked to explain why property rights or markets are not established, but the full implications of introducing organizational costs are not worked out. Rather than starting with a model where transaction costs are fully endogenous and reinterpreting such notions as market failure, externality, and non-convexity, one gets the sense that the authors transplant these concepts as understood within a transaction-costless (Arrow–Debreu framework) model to a world of ubiquitous transaction costs. In other words, the authors are trying to explain phenomena in a world of transaction costs with conceptual tools tailored to a model without organizational costs.

In section 2, I discuss Bator's (1958) contribution to the notion of externality. According to him externality is equivalent to market failure, but externality should also be used to classify alternative causes of market failure. I argue that the distinctions he makes concerning alternative causes are unclear primarily because the ramifications of incorporating transaction costs in the model are not confronted. In particular the very notion of market failure needs revision once transaction costs are endogenous, and thus causes of market failure must be reinterpreted.

In sections 3 and 4, I discuss Arrow's (1970) and Heller and Starrett's (1976) contribution to the notion of externality. Both formulate new senses of market failure, 'relative-market failure' and 'private-economy failure', in response to endogenizing transaction costs. Both treat externality as a subset of causes of the non-existence of markets (or market failure), although they have different interpretations of the relationship of non-existence of markets with market failure. I argue that their revised notions of market failure are inadequate for models with endogenous transaction costs. Their causal explanation of failure as the non-existence of markets while appropriate for a transaction-costless model, tends to confuse when applied to a model with endogenous organizational costs.

While these attempts to characterize externality are rich in insights, and induce a revision of the Arrow–Debreu general-equilibrium framework, the authors discussed here only go part of the way in working out the implications of incorporating organizational costs in the model. The notions of externality and market failure remain vague. In section 5, I use the classic apple–honey externality example as a more concrete illustration of the gradual transformation of the notion of market failure, and in what ways this transformation is incomplete. In section 6, I make some additional points on why non-existence of markets is not a good way of viewing market failure or externality in models with transaction costs. And the introduction of transaction costs seems inevitable if one is to make sense of the notion of externality.

2. EXTERNALITIES AS MARKET FAILURE AND THE CHALLENGE TO THE TRADITIONAL VIEW OF MARKET FAILURE

In his seminal article 'The Anatomy of Market Failure', Bator (1958) sets out 'to explore and order those phenomena which cause even errorless profit- and preference-maximizing calculation in a stationary context of perfect (though limited) information and foresight to fail to sustain Pareto-efficient allocation' (1958: 352). He starts by setting 'out the necessary conditions for efficiency of decentralized price-profit calculations both in a 'laissez-faire' and in a 'socialist' setting of Lange–Lerner civil servants' (ibid.). Having set out four conditions for static efficiency, departure from which represent 'modes of failure', Bator proceeds to associate his work with the relevant literature. He argues that the 'literature is rich but confusing. It abounds in mutually reinforcing and overlapping descriptions and explanations of market failure: external economies, indivisibility, non-appropriability, direct interaction, public goods, atmosphere, etc. In a sense, our problem is simply to sort out the relations among these' (1958: 356).

With this task in mind Bator discusses the existing views on externality. He rules out pecuniary externalities as legitimate externalities since no Pareto-inefficiency is implied. For him, externality is equivalent to market failure; accordingly externality is to 'denote any situation where some Paretian costs and benefits remain external to decentralized cost revenue calculations in terms of prices' (1958: 362). He takes issue, however, with the prevailing view that market failure, or externality, should be seen as non-appropriability:

The doctrine of 'direct interaction' . . . consists in interdependencies that are external to the price system, hence unaccounted for by market calculations. (1958: 358)

But in a sense it only begs the fundamental question: what is it that gives rise to 'direct interaction,' to short circuit, as it were, the signalling system? (1958: 361)

Most modern writers have let matters rest with the Ellis–Fellner (1943) type explanation: 'the divorce of scarcity from effective ownership.' Does nonappropriability then explain all direct interaction? In a sense it does . . . Moreover, in one sense in which nonappropriability fits all cases of direct interaction, it explains none. If all it denotes is the failure of a price-market game properly to account for (to appropriate) all relevant costs and benefits, then it is simply a synonym for market failure (for generalized externality), and cannot be used to explain what causes any particular instance of such failure. I use it in a much more narrow sense, to mean the inability of a producer of a good or service physically to exclude users, or to control rationing of his produce among them. (1958: 361)

Bator's problem with the Ellis–Fellner type characterization,[1] is not that it treats all market failure as externality, since that is his own view. Instead, he is critical of viewing all market failure as non-appropriability.[2] He thought that by taking such a broad view of non-appropriability one loses insights into the causal mechanism of market failure. By narrowing the definition of appropriability he attempts to make room for other causes of market failure (increasing returns to scale, public goods), and he asks: 'If non-appropriability is, by itself, too flimsy a base for a doctrine of generalized (statical) externality, what broader foundation is there?' (1958: 363).

2.1. Externality as a Causal Explanation of Market Failure

Bator proceeds to offer a classification of causes of market failure in terms of three different kinds of externality called Ownership Externalities, Technical Externalities, and Public-Good Externalities. The discussion is of interest because it reveals an attempt to separate what may be viewed as 'institutional' explanations or causes of failure (Bator's non-appropriability), from technological, or other explanations of failure. I will argue that an institutional element permeates all his explanations of market failure, defeating his purpose. The problem stems from an arbitrary reference to transaction costs as a cause of failure in certain cases, with an equally arbitrary neglect of them in others.

---

[1] My own interpretation of Ellis and Fellner's characterization differs from Bator's; I don't think they took as broad a view of externality as Bator attributes to them.

[2] Note the problem with non-existence of property rights as a subset of market failure in Ch. 3, since if non-appropriability is seen as non-existence of private-property rights then market failure can be seen as non-existence of private-property rights; see Louis DeAlessi (1980).

More importantly the introduction of transaction costs casts a shadow on the very notion of market failure used by Bator.

As mentioned above, Bator argues that we can classify causes of failure into three polar types: (1) Ownership Externalities, (2) Technical Externalities, and (3) Public-Good Externalities. The first category, ownership externalities, entails failure caused by deficiency in institutional arrangements; in particular, it is not feasible to keep tab of certain values, it is too costly to enforce payments for certain activities, which as a result, escape accounting. The presence of transaction costs implies that efficient institutional arrangements are lacking, and are thus a cause of departure from an ideal allocation. According to Bator, only this type of externality is due to non-appropriability, i.e. this is the only 'institutional' cause of failure.

The second category, technical externalities (not to be confused with Viner's technological externalities), represents failure caused by technology that 'exhibits indivisibility or smooth increasing returns to scale in the relevant range of output' (1958: 365). Finally, the third category, public-good externalities, entails failure caused by 'outputs with important "public" qualities' (1958: 370). Bator argues that in fact the first category (ownership externalities) is insignificant since in most cases it 'is really a compound of Types (2) and (3)' (1958: 371). As one of the 'non-trivial' examples of ownership externalities, he discusses the failure associated with skill-formation of labour (suboptimal levels due to inability of employers to insure returns on investment, i.e. ownership of labour), which could (when coupled with the fact of non-durability and uncertainty) really be seen as emanating from the fact that the mode of organization of labour (non-slavery) is 'in the nature of a public good which enters people's preference functions' (ibid.).

Bator says that 'where bookkeeping feasibility appears to be the cause of the trouble, the question arises why bookkeeping is less feasible than where it is in fact being done' (ibid.). In other words, the institutional difficulty associated with effective control over skill (the valued good), may be ultimately caused by the fact that property rights for labour enter preferences as a public good. Bator emphasizes the public-nature aspect as being the cause of failure. But by allowing preferences for institutions in his model, Bator is actually increasing the importance of institutional explanation of failure. The difference between saying that private ownership of labour (slavery) is costly to enforce, and saying that it is hard to enforce because people have an aversion to slavery, is simply that there is an added dimension to institutional costs. It is no longer just a question of enforcement costs, one has to consider how different institutions affect agents' utility directly. Since institutions govern human interaction they are inherently public in nature, this is so irrespective of whether institutions enter agents' utility functions. If individuals place special value on institutions beyond their functional value, the importance of institutions is enhanced. In that sense, the way Bator has framed this example would seem to greatly increase the importance of institutional causes of failure[3] (non-appropriability) rather than shrink them.

On close inspection it would seem more natural to collapse public-good externalities on to ownership externalities. After all, the 'publicness' or 'privateness' of a good is dependent on institutional factors; presence of exclusion cost is fundamental in making such distinctions:[4]

Deeper reflection indicates that the distinction between private and public goods according to the notion of exhaustibility by a single individual is superficial. Indeed, when goods are defined in an appropriate manner, individual consumption always leads to exhaustion by private use. Instead of talking about national nuclear defences, we could consider the simultaneous protection of millions of units of space. If person i occupies space l, he consumes the good 'protection of space l' and prevents person j from benefiting from this good. Since it is impossible (or at least far too costly) to exclude only one particular space l from protection, the good will be called national nuclear defence and we can say that it is not exhausted in private use. (Laffont, 1988: 34)

Bator was not unaware of this fluidity of concepts, but then why argue that public-good externalities are more important than

---

[3] Introduction of institutions as 'objects of desire' is not the same as introduction of transaction costs into economic models, so it may be inappropriate to treat them both under one heading ('institutional causes'). The point I'm making here, however, is that Bator's attempt to contract the explanatory value of 'exclusion cost' by reference to 'publicness' has actually increased the relevance of exclusion cost.

[4] For an interesting discussion on the institutional nature of public goods and the kind of problems one gets into when not fully recognizing or incorporating the institutional context in defining public goods, see Cowen (1988).

ownership externalities? Are not the costs associated with institutions (exclusion costs) fundamental in understanding public goods? Throughout his analysis Bator tries to limit the role of institutional explanations of failure. After all, he started by pointing out that if institutions were defined broadly (non-appropriability), they could explain all failure, but that such explanations were vacuous. Despite his intentions, his reference to skill-formation of labour puts institutional factors in the forefront. Public-good externalities are best understood in an institutional context.

Bator also discusses how technical externalities (indivisibilities) may provide a better explanation of failure than ownership externalities. In certain examples he argues that technical externalities can be traced to public-good externalities. Given our previous discussion this would seem to enhance the institutional understanding of failure. In one example of a technical externality he considers falling average-cost curve, or a firm with increasing returns to scale. Bator argues that 'the institutional reorganization required to get correct decentralized calculation involves horizontal and vertical integration, and the monopoly or oligopoly problem looms large indeed' (1958: 376). It could be that vertical or horizontal integration does not lead to too few agents. This will also depend on the demand for the good in question (size of market), which in turn will depend on the distribution of income, which is a function of property rights (institutions). But even assuming too few agents, a perfectly discriminating monopolist could overcome efficiency losses associated with increasing returns. Bator points out that this would require complete knowledge of individual preferences. One could always argue that the institutional costs of acquiring such information is the cause of failure,[5] and increasing returns are what make such information necessary. Just as there are institutional costs associated with bringing a price to bear on a detrimental externality, such as soot emanating from a factory that soils neighbouring laundry, there is an institutional cost associated with getting a firm under increasing returns to 'price' the positive effects associated with production of some good. In some sense, the producer is unable to 'physically . . . exclude, or to control the rationing of his pro-

---

[5] Many do argue that transaction-costs cause all market failure, see Calabresi (1968), I shall discuss this view in Ch. 6, below.

duce among' (Bator 1958: 361) consumers. One may object that price discrimination is contrary to the notion of a market and in effect a market fails or does not exist if price discrimination is required.[6] In this sense, it might be legitimate to treat increasing returns to scale as a cause of market failure.

There is another sense in which increasing returns are not collapsible on to ownership externalities as are public-good externalities. While the concept of publicness hinges on that of exclusion costs, increasing returns to scale or non-convexities are concepts independent of exclusion costs (though they may affect exclusion costs, their meaning does not hinge on exclusion costs). Still, the presence of exclusion costs (and other transaction costs) indicates the need for a more sophisticated understanding of a causal explanation of market failure and the part that non-convexities will play in such explanations. The very recognition of ownership externalities (and public-good externalities) poses serious problems for causal explanations of failure. Though the presence of exclusion costs imply a departure from an ideal allocation by definition, at the same time they put into question the conventional notion of an ideal allocation and the corresponding notion of market failure as a departure from that ideal. An ideal allocation of resources (Pareto-optimal) does not abstract from production costs, why should it abstract from exclusion costs, or, more generally, transaction costs? Are not transaction costs real costs? If there are costs to 'a producer of a good . . . physically to exclude users', should these not be taken into account in discerning ideal allocations? Is market failure to be found in the fact that these costs exist or in the fact that they are not somehow taken into account? It seems almost paradoxical that Bator's externality which identifies failure as the inability to account for costs, should treat as failure the mere presence of costs and not the taking into account of these costs. The presence of exclusion costs may imply that property rights should not exist for certain goods, i.e. in an optimal allocation some activities should not have property rights defined over them.

To point to the presence of exclusion costs as a cause of market failure is a bit like pointing at the presence of production costs as the cause of market failure. Failure, as Bator's own

---

[6] This is the view that Arrow (1970) seems to take which I discuss in sect. 3, below.

intuitive notion of externality seems to insist, is the failure of the system to take into account certain costs. The introduction of exclusion costs into economic models throws the traditional concept of market failure and optimality off-balance and raises the spectre of a reinterpretation of market failure. In section 3 I discuss how Arrow (1970) begins to carry out this task.

2.2. A Note on Non-appropriability

Since the notion of non-appropriability often crops up in discussions of externality, sometimes in different guises, e.g. non-existence of private-property rights, I would like to make some clarifying statements about the concept before moving on. Ellis–Fellner give a very broad definition of non-appropriability: 'divorce of scarcity from effective ownership'. What precisely is meant by 'effective ownership'? In the previous chapter non-existence of private-property rights was seen as one source of market failure, but with a broad-enough use of the term one could treat all market failure as the inability to exclude. Yet treating inability to exclude as a cause of failure is again like treating the existence of transaction costs as a cause of failure rather than the inability to take transaction costs into account effectively. If it is very costly to exclude others from some activity, it may be best that the system does not invest resources in enforcing exclusion. This is essentially the Coasean reasoning that if the cost of organizing the internalization of pollution is greater than the gains, then the system is more efficient if it does not enforce exclusion. If transaction costs are to be included in the calculus of optimality, then there may be many cases where costs and benefits of activities should not be appropriated because the costs of appropriation are too high.[7]

[7] Non-appropriation in this case does not signify market failure unless costs and benefits calculated also account for the costs of organizing appropriation. One could reinterpret non-appropriability so that it takes transaction costs into account. It could be so broad that it includes any entitlement structure, i.e. public ownership, hierarchical rules, markets, in effect all institutions (institutions can also be more or less broadly defined). If broadly enough defined, non-appropriability could mean generalized system failure, and not just market failure. That is, any system could be said to fail because there are sources of gain that are not being 'effectively appropriated' by the existing institutions. But this is clearly not the meaning that Ellis and Fellner (1943) or Bator (1958) attach to non-appropriability.

2.3. Main Points on Bator

There are two main thrusts of Bator's work. First, externality is synonymous with market failure. Pareto-inefficiency is the hallmark of externality; this shows a consequentialist concern since the defining attribute is inefficiency, activity that is external to the control of the decentralized private ownership economy. Externality is a description of failure. Second, externalities are associated with a causal explanation of market failure. His attempt to treat non-appropriability, public goods, and non-convexities as separate causes of failure seems to be problematic. The main difficulty arises from the challenge posed to the traditional view of market failure once institutional costs are incorporated in the model. A reinterpretation of market failure will affect any causal analysis of market failure. In sections 3–5 I discuss how Arrow, and Heller and Starrett, take up this challenge and form two different notions of market failure: relative market failure and, what I call, private-economy failure respectively. Though these go some way in revealing the difficulties in reinterpreting such concepts as market failure when transaction costs are incorporated into a general-equilibrium framework, the notions of externality and market failure remain unclear.

3. FROM ABSOLUTE TO RELATIVE MARKET FAILURE

As Bator was trying to clarify the concept of externality we saw that the very notion of market failure was put to task. Bator never confronted this issue head on. Arrow (1970), on the other hand, who was also trying to distinguish between, and clarify, such concepts as market failure, public goods, externalities, non-convexities, sees the challenge posed by the incorporation of transaction costs, and initiates a change in the way that market failure should be perceived. He felt that in order to understand the notion of externality, which had always been closely clustered together with market failure and increasing returns to scale, one needed to better understand these latter terms. He does not offer an explicit definition of externalities but he says that they are a subset of market failure, while market failure can be seen as synonymous with the non-existence of markets.

To follow his argument it is important to understand how Arrow moves from what he calls 'absolute market failure' to 'relative market failure'. Again no explicit definition for absolute market failure is given but one can be derived from his analysis, and I will suggest a definition shortly. Essentially absolute market failure entails the traditional Arrow–Debreu notion of market failure, while relative market failure is an attempt to incorporate transaction costs into our understanding of market failure. I will argue that Arrow's characterization of market failure as non-existence of markets prevents him from making a clean break with absolute market failure and ultimately confounds his attempt to clarify the concept of externality and market failure, or 'relative market failure'.

3.1. Absolute Market Failure

Arrow points out that

key points in the definition [of perfectly competitive equilibrium] are the parametric role of the prices for each individual and the identity of prices for all individuals. Implicit are the assumptions that all prices can be known by all individuals and that the act of charging prices is not itself a consumer of resources (1970: 61).

He further argues that 'two hypotheses [made about perfectly competitive equilibrium] frequently not valid are (C), the convexity of household indifference maps and firm production sets, and (M), the universality of markets' (1970: 61). By universality of markets he means 'that the consumption bundle which determines the utility of an individual is the same as that which he purchases at given prices subject to his budget constraint and that the set of production bundles among which a firm chooses is independent of decisions made by other agents in the economy' (1970: 61). If Arrow's proviso that prices are parametric applies to this definition of universality, then universality boils down to two conditions: (1) private-property rights are assigned for all goods and services,[8] and (2) interaction among agents for all goods occurs via parametric prices, i.e. 'auctions' are set up for all goods and prices are treated parametrically.

---

[8] It is implicit that there is no cost in assigning and enforcing private-property rights.

Arrow's equation of market failure with non-existence of markets comes from this framework (absolute market failure). Given the strict definition of markets, any departure from parametric prices would be seen as non-existence of markets. Oligopoly, monopoly, or any situation where there are too few agents would be treated as non-existence of markets since prices would not be treated parametrically; failure of market and non-existence of markets in this case are the same thing.[9]

I will now try to zero in on absolute market failure. Arrow presents the welfare theorems in terms of the two hypotheses non-convexity and non-universality. Non-convexity could prevent markets from attaining an equilibrium, parametric prices don't work. Non-convexity could be seen as a cause of the market system failing either because a competitive equilibrium is not achieved given some initial allocation of property rights, or, certain Pareto-optimal allocations are not attainable through the market (Second Welfare Theorem). If convexity holds but there is a breach of market universality, a competitive equilibrium exists, but it is likely to be suboptimal (exceptions being coincidental or situations like non-paternalistic sentiment: see Winter (1969) and Archibald and Donaldson (1976)). One could say there is failure to achieve optimality due to non-existence of markets (whether because of lack of property rights or parametric prices). Failure by non-convexity and non-universality is treated as absolute because there is no reference to other modes of organization in describing this failure. We can view absolute market failure as *failure of hypothetically costless markets from attaining Pareto-optimal allocations attainable in an ideal world of no costs of organizing exchange.*

3.2. Relative Market Failure

Current writing has helped bring out the point that market failure is not absolute; it is better to consider a broader category, that of transaction costs, which in general impede and in particular cases completely block the formation of markets. (Arrow 1970: 60)

[9] Naturally, Arrow does not equate the market with private exchange as is sometimes done in the literature; see Hodgson (1989: ch. 8) for the many definitions of the market in economics. Arrow says: 'The price system, for all its virtues, is only one conceivable form of arranging trade, even in a system of private property. Bargaining can assume extremely general forms' (1970: 61), (parametric prices being a *sine qua non* of 'market' bargaining).

Market failure has been presented as absolute, but in fact the situation is more complex than this. A more general formulation is that of transaction costs, which are attached to any market and indeed to any mode of resource allocation. Market failure is the particular case where transaction costs are so high that the market is no longer worth while. (Arrow 1970: 68)

This is all that Arrow offers on the notion of relative market failure. Unlike Bator, transaction costs become central to the notion of market failure, but like Bator, it seems that the very presence of high transaction costs is associated with failure. Is it useful to describe failure of the market *system* as the case where some *particular* market is not worthwhile? If it was too costly to make it worthwhile forming a market for the nectar provided by the apple-growers and the pollination services offered by the apiaries, would we treat this as market failure?

Before attempting to answer these questions, let us see why absolute market failure is inadequate. The limitations of absolute market failure can be seen when one looks for an explanation of non-existence of markets. We can associate a specific 'real-world' meaning to non-convexity without altering the calculus of the general-equilibrium problem, but this is not so with non-existence of markets. Why are certain markets absent? The familiar answer to this question is that there are costs associated with either (1) property rights or (2) the price mechanism. One could leave it at that by saying simply that there are costs to markets which prevent one from attaining Pareto-optimality. This would correspond to absolute market failure. The transition point from absolute to relative market failure comes from recognizing that transaction costs are legitimate resource costs[10] (or affect agents' actions so that actual resources are affected) that have to be calculated in the general-equilibrium framework. Resources needed to organize economic activity, like the institution of private property, the firm, and the market, should be calculated in the overall evaluation of resource allocation. Failure because of non-existence of markets is not failure in a real sense unless we know something more about these costs. To treat it as failure is like setting an ideal allocation where there are no production costs

[10] Arrow (1970) points out that production costs depend only on technology and tastes while transaction costs are a function of the mode of resource allocation.

and then pointing at the existence of production costs as a cause of failure to attain an optimum (recall Bator's identification of transaction costs with failure).

Non-universality is a meaningful explanation of absolute market failure, i.e. in a general-equilibrium model in which transaction costs are not invoked, but once transaction costs are incorporated and one moves to a new sense of market failure it is no longer apparent that non-universality is a good way of explaining market failure. One would expect that a 'relative' notion of market failure would involve comparison of the market with alternative modes of organization. The market would be said to fail when an alternative mode of organization could allocate resources better (or with less organizational costs). It would not be the non-existence of a market *per se* that revealed market failure but the existence of an alternative mode of organization that could outdo the market. The problem is that Arrow never discusses a comparison set of modes of organization and we are left with non-existence as an explanation of failure. More importantly, to really understand the ramifications of endogenizing transaction costs into a general-equilibrium framework, and the implications for a notion of market failure, one has to rethink the entire theoretical model of an economy.[11]

3.3. Externalities as a Subset of Market Failure or Non-existence of Markets

Having stated some preliminary reservations on the usefulness of non-existence of markets as a causal explanation of relative market failure, let me return to Arrow's discussion on externalities. It is from the enriched concept of relative market failure that Arrow tries to establish an understanding of externalities. Transaction costs are central to such an understanding. Arrow says:

I contend that market failure is a more general category than externality; and both differ from increasing returns in a basic sense, since market failures in general and externalities in particular are relative to the mode of economic organization, while increasing returns are essentially a technological phenomenon (1970: 60).

---

[11] See Green (1982) for one such endeavour.

Arrow introduces a simple model of a pure exchange economy and shows how

by suitable and indeed not unnatural reinterpretation of the commodity space, externalities can be regarded as ordinary commodities, and all the formal theory of competitive equilibrium is valid, including its optimality. It is not the mere fact that one man's consumption enters into another man's utility that causes the failure of the market to achieve efficiency (1970: 65).

If there were a full set of markets there would be no externality.

Given this formulation, one might expect Arrow to simply define externalities as synonymous with the non-existence of markets; however, he treats externalities as if they have a separate existence of their own. In fact it would sound dissonant to say 'markets for externalities' if externalities were simply equivalent to non-existence of markets, since the very presence of markets would imply that they are ordinary commodities, not externalities. He treats externality as a subset of non-existence (or of market failure) and as somehow causing the non-existence, i.e. there are more fundamental factors associated with externality that cause non-existence. So Arrow seems to have in mind some other condition (separate from the non-existence of markets) that defines or characterizes externalities, but it is not at all clear what condition this could be. 'The problem of externalities is thus a special case of a more general phenomenon, the failure of markets to exist. Not all examples of market failure can fruitfully be described as externalities' (Arrow 1970: 67).[12]

Two examples of non-existence of markets that would not be fruitfully described as externalities are offered: 'markets for many forms of risk-bearing and for most future transactions do not exist and their absence is surely suggestive of inefficiency' (ibid.). But what makes these different from other instances of non-existence of markets? Arrow seems to suggest that the causes for the non-existence of markets may be a source of distinction, where non-existence of markets caused by '(1) inability to exclude' and '(2) lack of the necessary information to permit market transactions to be concluded' (68), might be the *sine qua non* of externalities. He argues that the failure of future markets cannot be explained in these terms. But on close inspection lack of future

---

[12] It is not clear what the basis of a 'fruitful' description of failure is.

markets can be the result of the two types of transaction costs stated (or the non-existence of complementary markets which itself is a function of the two transaction costs).[13] Surely one could make finer distinctions within the gambit of transaction costs, for example distinctions between different kinds, or degrees, of excludability, or kinds of information lacking, etc., so that instances of market failure or non-existence of markets could be distinguished according to the specific causes. But would there be any compelling reason to group certain of these causes under the heading of externalities? Until a justification is offered there does not seem to be a good reason to treat externalities as a subset of market failure as Arrow has defined the terms.

Another perplexing feature of treating market failure as non-existence of markets is revealed when considering increasing returns to scale. Increasing returns to scale, large relative to the market, could lead to failure to achieve optimality despite universality of markets. What of the equation of market failure with non-existence of markets? Recall, 'market failure is the particular case where transaction costs are so high that the existence of the market is no longer worth while' (Arrow 1970: 68). Here is an instance of market failure that is not equivalent to non-existence of markets. Even if the transaction costs associated with the market are zero, optimality cannot be achieved because there are no equilibrium prices.[14] One could say that if non-convexities are large relative to demand for the good in question, a market will fail to appear, since no firm would operate. Since no parametric price exists no market exists. The root of these conceptual difficulties, I think, lies in the fact that the notions of non-convexity and non-universality, to which Arrow refers, are anchored to the traditional view of absolute market failure, and must be reinter-

---

[13] For a good discussion on this point see Heller and Starrett (1976).

[14] Another semantic issue can be raised concerning the concept of transaction cost. Is transaction cost simply the cost of forming an institution, or is it the opportunity cost associated with the presence of some institution? In the literature the first seems to figure, but the latter seems to comply better with the 'correct' notion of costs. If one were to treat it as opportunity cost, then even a 'costless' market in the presence of increasing returns could very well be costly if it prevented another mode of allocation which was more efficient. Or more generally the cost of an institution would not be the actual resources needed to create and enforce an institution, but the resource loss when compared to the best alternative institution which may allocate more efficiently.

preted (or even discarded in the case of non-universality) when one considers a model with endogenous transaction costs.

3.3.1. Enter Heller and Starrett

Inspired by Arrow's imagery of externalities as non-existence of markets, Heller and Starrett (1976) carry on the search for a clear understanding of externalities. They argue 'that situations usually identified with "externality" have more fundamental explanations' (1976: 10). Four fundamental explanations for market failure associated with externality are cited. First, non-exclusiveness of commodities, alternatively property rights, cannot be easily defined, and this leads to market failure. Either the cost of creating and enforcing property rights is too high, or the nature of the good (interdependency) is such that it is not deemed desirable to exclude, e.g. parks, national defence. Second, non-convexities will lead to an inefficient allocation of resources, even if a market exists for the externality.[15] One can show that by extending the production space to include a detrimental external-ity, the 'new' production space is fundamentally non-convex (by fundamental, meaning that due to the negative sign of the exter-nality non-convexity is a mathematical certainty). Furthermore, there may be non-convexities in setting up a market. Third, non-competitive behaviour resulting from the kind of interdependency involved is a source of failure. Even if a market can be created, there may be too few agents. Arrow (1970) has argued that the lighthouse case could easily be viewed as a case of too few agents. Fourth, imperfect or incomplete information especially concerning future actions results in inefficient allocation of resources. Lack of a future market can be viewed in two ways. It could be non-convexities in the transaction cost of creating a future market (or complementary insurance market), or, it could be due to a kind of myopia in the agents, obstructing their ability to see the potential profits.

Given this reduction of externality 'to some more fundamental problem having to do with market failure . . . one might take the position that the concept of externality should be dropped alto-gether' (Heller and Starrett 1976: 20). However, echoing older characterizations, e.g. Bator (1958), they point out that 'we might

---

[15] More on this in Ch. 5, below.

still like to put the label "externality" on market failure due to interdependencies not properly taken into account by price-taking agents. One might be tempted to identify these situations with item 1 [non-exclusiveness] above.[16] However . . . the distinctions are not so clear-cut. The absence of a market for pollution may be attributable to either nonexclusiveness or to non convexities in the technology of setting up property rights' (Heller and Starrett, 1976: 20).

Like Arrow there is a desire to treat externality as a subset of market failure; in particular they point out that non-convexities in production technology and noncompetitive behaviour constitute their own type of market failure ('not something we would like to call "externality"' (1976: 16)), yet they indicate that clear distinctions are not easily made. For both Arrow, and Heller and Starrett, externalities are a subset of non-existence of markets, yet what identifies this subset is unclear. They both refer to some underlying causes of failure: certain underlying kinds of interdependency that seem to cause market failure (more specifically causes of non-existence of markets). There is no criterion, however, that links these causes of market failure together. A principle of distinguishing externalities among causes of non-existence is totally lacking. Heller and Starrett close on a rather disheartening note: 'it seems to us that the intuitive concept of externality must remain somewhat imprecise' (1976: 20).

While non-existence of markets seems to be intimately linked to externalities, in both Arrow's and Heller and Starrett's characterizations it actually describes a type of market failure which is a broader category than externality. Externality (in these characterizations) remains a poorly defined subset of market failure. A further source of vagueness in these views comes from the tension between externality as a description (activities for which no markets exist) and externality as a cause (underlying interdependencies or features that prevent markets from forming). This tension is unresolved, but I think that the authors, like Bator, are primarily concerned with finding a causal explanation of market failure, and therefore, like to see externalities as causal factors behind failure. In Chapter 7 I will discuss why I believe it is not

---

[16] Recall that Bator treated 'interdependencies not properly taken into account by price-taking agents' as equivalent to market failure, not just non-exclusiveness.

useful to treat externalities as a subset of market failure, nor for that matter as a cause of market failure.

Despite their attempt to identify a well-defined subset of market failure to label 'externality', this intuitive concept seems to seep into all descriptions of market failure. If it were just a question of having a poorly defined term which provided a different perspective or feel about things one could rest with Heller and Starrett's verdict of impreciseness. The problem is that this intuitive concept raises questions about a series of key concepts (market, market failure, optimality, etc.) and its imprecision reflects on these concepts along with the methodology (General-Equilibrium Theory) from which these terms are interpreted. Awareness of this problem has provided an important motivational force in attempts to define externality and it indicates that such attempts should not be abandoned unless one is content on living with a hole in the theory.

4. FROM RELATIVE MARKET FAILURE TO PRIVATE-ECONOMY FAILURE

Until now I have been treating Arrow's and Heller and Starrett's characterizations of externality and market failure as if they were fundamentally the same; however, Heller and Starrett introduce a twist in their concept of externality (and market failure) not present in Arrow. It is important to consider this difference because it raises some interesting issues about the concept of market failure, and it also helps reveal some further semantic problems with the concept of non-existence of markets. Although this difference is not emphasized by the authors it is apparent from a close reading of their characterization of externality, as well as from certain categories or failure they introduce (in particular, non-convexity in costs of forming property rights and markets). As quoted earlier, Heller and Starrett give the following as a definition of externality:

One can think of externalities as nearly synonymous with nonexistence of markets. We define an externality to be a situation in which the private economy lacks sufficient incentives to create a potential market in some good and the nonexistence of this market results in losses in Pareto efficiency. It is general enough to include both pecuniary and nonpecuniary externalities. (1976: 10)

Externality and the accompanying market failure can be seen as the failure of the 'private economy' to form a market when 'the non-existence of this market results in losses of Pareto efficiency'. So market failure (or at least one type of market failure) is not failure of the market system *per se*, but failure of a pre-market private economy. It is failure of some kind of pre-market equilibrium process not failure of a market system.[17]

It is easy to lose sight of the distinction: in Arrow's definition of relative market failure, the market fails where it is too costly for it to be worthwhile; in Heller and Starrett's case, the private economy fails because a market is not created where one should be created. For Heller and Starrett it would not be failure if a market did not exist because it was too costly; it would be however, if a market did not exist despite it being worthwhile. There may be non-convexities in creating property rights or markets, this would imply failure of the private economy to create the market but it would not be market failure in Arrow's sense, since the implementation of a market (by government subsidy for instance) could lead to efficiency. The differences can be seen as follows:

1. *Private-economy failure*: failure of a private economy to create markets where Pareto-optimality could be achieved through the formation of markets.

2. *Relative market failure*: non-existence of a market because of high transaction costs (issue of how markets evolve not in question).

(1) and (2) are not equivalent, and (1) may not entail (2). In fact the optimality of a pre-market process is much more demanding since one would have to go as far as envisaging a property-less world and expect institutions to evolve efficiently. This is more demanding than imposing some institutional structure and considering whether it is efficient. But Heller and Starrett are not simply considering the failure of a private economy to create optimal institutions, but failure of a private economy to create markets where Pareto-improvements could be attained by their existence. What if a market does not exist and

---

[17] Unless the market is defined as being this private economy. This might fair well with Becker's (1976) characterization of a market, where even marriage is treated as a market activity, but surely not with Arrow's more demanding definition.

the implementation of a market leads to Pareto-improvements, but other institutions could be created and run at even lower costs? If the private economy spontaneously forms private-property rights and markets where other institutions could do better, would this not also be private-economy failure?

Heller and Starrett don't give an explicit account of how a private economy might function, so I will spell out what seems to be implied. Private property has been defined for many activities. Many markets either already exist, or they spontaneously evolve as profit-seeking agents recognize gains in forming markets. In other words, the presence of property rights (and possibly many markets) are given exogenously. However, certain gaps are left open. There are some activities over which no property rights have been defined, and accordingly no markets exist, and there are activities over which private-property rights exist, but markets have not evolved. It is on these gaps that attention is focused. If markets evolve spontaneously in these activities, the externalities will be eliminated. The story is that transaction costs may prevent such a spontaneous event, either because market set-up costs are non-convex (in which case the government could subsidize the creation of a market), or because transaction costs are too high (in which case, the market shouldn't be formed anyway). Also, property rights may not have been defined and the cost of creating and enforcing may be too high or not.[18] In any case, wherever these gaps are a source of inefficiency, it is implied that the government should intervene to enforce some institution, either market or non-market institutions, whichever minimize transaction costs.

Heller and Starrett seem to presume that markets that evolve spontaneously will be efficient and so attention can be focused only on those activities for which markets have not evolved. However, there is no reason why the spontaneous creation of institutions will result in efficient institutions, or, more specifically, efficient markets.[19] The existence of a market cannot be

[18] Interestingly, Heller and Starrett do not mention non-convexity in set-up costs of property rights as they do with market set-up costs. This may be explained by the fact that they are not considering the creation of property endogenously.

[19] There is an expanding literature on the role and formation of institutions. Brennan and Buchanan (1985) offer an evolutionary theory of the private-ownership economy. Coase (1937) offers elements of an evolutionary explanation of the

taken as proof that other institutions could not have provided a better allocational mechanism (even if that only meant lower set-up costs).[20] It could be that markets evolve, given the existence of other markets, where other institutions would have been more efficient but do not evolve spontaneously because of non-convexity in their creation and enforcement. Once transaction costs are introduced in evaluating institutions it must be applied to all institutions. The markets that exist must also pass the test of minimizing transaction costs, otherwise they will not be efficient. While Heller and Starrett emphasize the need to compare alternative institutions in discerning which modes of organization minimize transaction costs,[21] they confine this evaluative process to those activities where markets have not evolved.

The insight that minimization of transaction costs is unduly confined is conveyed by Ledyard (1976) when he points out that had Heller and Starrett followed the kind of reasoning following from their own statement that one 'cannot ignore the costs of institutions in making social decision', one could say that the costs of institutions 'must be considered when choosing between a centrally planned economy and a market system. That is one should be interested in *net* optimality, the level of social satisfaction attained after institutional costs are netted out' (Ledyard 1976: 26). Ultimately even the maker of social decisions should be treated endogenously if one is searching for net optimality. Heller and Starrett treated several institutions exogenously—private-property rights, some markets, and the government—and therefore net optimality cannot be discerned. Once transaction costs have become a central criterion of efficiency it makes little sense to apply it selectively to areas of activity where markets have not formed to the neglect of activities over which markets and property rights are established.

formation of firms. For a good review and critical appraisal of the evolutionary arguments see Langlois (1986a: introd.), also see Schotter (1981). See Akerlof (1984) for an interesting analysis of the 'evolution' of stable and inefficient institutions.

[20] The whole question of evaluating alternative institutions is a complex one, but I assume for the sake of argument that there is a basis for making evaluative judgements.

[21] Minimizing transaction costs is seen as the basis of determining the most efficient institution, this complies with the prevailing view in the Law and Economics literature on assigning efficient property rights. In Ch. 9, below, I discuss the problems with this view.

5. ILLUSTRATION AND COMPARISON OF ABSOLUTE AND RELATIVE MARKET FAILURE

It is time to consider a more concrete example in order to illustrate the point that all institutions, including markets, need to be evaluated in their ability to efficiently organize economic activity (minimize costs of organization), but also to clarify many of the distinctions made in this chapter. To this end I use Meade's (1952) classic apple–honey problem discussed in Chapter 2, where two 'externalities' are involved. The apple-grower provides nectar to the bees which helps honey production in the neighbouring apiary, while the bees provide fertilization to the apple-grower. Calling the apples good-x and the honey good-y the problem can be formalized with the following simple model denoting the profit functions of two firms:

$$\pi_x = \max_x p_x x - l(x) + E(y)$$
$$\pi_y = \max_y p_y y - L(y) + e(x) \qquad (4.1)$$

p_x is price of apples, $l(x)$ the cost of producing apples (which is a function of the number of apples produced), and $E(y)$ represents the benefits ('externality') received from the apiary which (for simplicity of exposition) is a function of honey production. A similar interpretation follows for the profit function of the apiary. It is further assumed that both cost and externality functions are increasing and convex.

The private-ownership competitive equilibrium outputs x_c, y_c for the two-firm two-good model are given by the first-order conditions

$$p_x = l'(x_c)$$
$$p_y = L'(y_c). \qquad (4.2)$$

From society's point of view these outputs are too small since both firms, unable to receive payments for the benefits that they bestow on each other, take into account only the private benefits they receive from the sale of their conventional goods. The socially efficient levels of production can be seen by maximizing joint profits where interdependencies are fully accounted for:

$$\pi_{x+y} = \max_{x,y} p_x x + p_y y - l(x) - L(y) + e(x) + E(y). \qquad (4.3)$$

The first-order conditions give us the Pareto-efficient levels of output

$$p_x = l'(x) - e'(x)$$
$$p_y = L'(y) - E'(y). \tag{4.4}$$

Note that standard general-equilibrium theory would compare the competitive equilibrium output in (4.2) with the outcome attainable in a hypothetical world of zero transaction costs (4.4) and treat the discrepancy as evidence of market failure, or as Arrow puts it 'absolute market failure'. This failure would be seen to derive from the non-universality of markets, or 'missing markets' (see Ch. 1 sect. 14.4). In particular, two markets are missing, one for the fertilizing service of bees and one for the nectar production of apples. Had there been a full set of markets (as well as convexity of production functions), no Pareto-inefficiency would have occurred. With the appropriate commodi-fication of 'externalities', we have the following profit functions for the two firms:

$$\pi_x = \max_{x_{11}, y_{12}} p_x x_{11} + p_{21} x_{21} - l(x_{11}) + E(y_{12}) - p_{12} y_{12}$$
$$\pi_y = \max_{x_{21}, y_{22}} p_y y_{22} + p_{12} y_{12} - L(y_{22}) + e(x_{21}) - p_{21} x_{21} \tag{4.5}$$

where the subscript i in x_{ik} and y_{ik} tells us whose production function the input (output) is in, and the subscript k tells us who 'produces' the input (output). For instance, the apple-grower (x-firm) receives $p_{21} x_{21}$ from the apiary for providing for the nectar service, and pays $p_{12} y_{12}$ for the fertilizing service provided by the bees. Note furthermore that due to the specific technology (apples and fertilization are joint products) the following must hold in equilibrium:

$$x_{21} = x_{11}$$
$$y_{12} = y_{22}. \tag{4.6}$$

With (4.6) in mind the first-order conditions for the two firms are

$$p_x + p_{21} = l'(x_{11}) \qquad p_y + p_{12} = L'(y_{22})$$
$$p_{12} = E'(y_{12}) \qquad p_{21} = e'(x_{21}). \tag{4.7}$$

From (4.7), and using (4.6), it can be seen that the two-firms–four-goods competitive equilibrium will generate the following efficient equilibrium outputs:

$$p_x = l'(x_{11}) - e'(x_{11})$$
$$p_y = L'(y_{22}) - E'(y_{22}).$$

(4.8)

Thus absolute market failure is simply due to the lack of a universal set of markets. Taking a prescriptive vantage point one may be tempted to say that market failure could be eliminated by forming a full set of markets. Alternative remedies have been suggested, such as the merging of the two companies where joint profits would be maximized, or the imposition of a set of Pigouvian taxes. The following subsidies in the two-firm–two-good model would do the trick:

$$s_x = e'(x)$$
$$s_y = E'(y)$$

(4.9)

In a zero-transaction-cost world there is no way to distinguish the relative merit of these alternative remedies. Furthermore, there is no way of explaining why the two markets (nectar and fertilization services) have failed to form. The recognition that transaction costs have to be incorporated in the model provided the impetus for a changing characterization of market failure. As a heuristic device I will suggest, in oversimplified terms, a way in which transaction costs could enter into the decision problem of a government as well as that of the agents, which in our case are the two firms. For a government, the problem is to maximize the difference between the joint profits of the apple and honey firms and the organizational cost[22] incurred in the process. The joint profits as well as the transaction costs incurred by the government, would depend on the kinds of institutions or rules set up. The government's decision problem could be expressed as

$$\max_{g} J(g) - T_G(g)$$

(4.10)

where $J(g)$ represents the two firms' joint profits as a function of government action g, and $T_G(g)$ represents transaction costs that are particular to the government (thus the subscript G) and which are also a function of government action. I will not make any assumptions about functional form since my only concern here is with the conceptual issues raised by incorporating transaction costs, not in deriving results. Note that there is now a basis for distinguishing among different 'remedies' for the 'externalities' on the basis of the net benefits associated with different institutions instigated by the government.

[22] Costs of gathering information, creating, monitoring, and enforcing rules.

The decision problem for the apple-producing firm (a symmetrical argument would apply for the honey-producing firm) might take the following (mathematically inelegant) form:

$$\max_{x,\, a_1,\, a_2} \pi_x = p_x x - l(x) + E_x(y(a_1)) + e_x(x(a_2)) - T_x(a_1, a_2). \quad (4.11)$$

Each firm may have certain actions, a_1 and a_2, that it can take that could affect the level of the other firm's ('external') activity and the potential profits from its own 'external' activity. In the case of the apple-grower the amount of 'external' activity received is shown with the function $E_x(y(a_1))$ (the subscript x indicating that this is a different function from $E(y)$), reflecting the apple-grower's potential influence on the fertilizing 'externality'. For instance, the apple-grower may enter negotiations with the apiary, lobby for a subsidy, promote a merger, etc., all of which are costly activities. The apple-grower will undertake such activity as long as the marginal benefit outweighs the marginal cost. The function $T_x(a_1, a_2)$ represents the transaction costs associated with different levels and kinds of organizational activities. The term $e_x(x(a_2))$ is meant to indicate potential profits that the apple-grower could get from 'selling' the benefits it bestows on the apiary; these depend on actions a_2 which the apple firm can take. The apple-grower could, for a colourful example, make a claim on the air over the apple grove demanding 'access fees' from infringing bees. More realistically (but still colourful), it could threaten the apiary with a fine meshed net obstructing the little intruders unless a fee was paid. Again, such actions would be contemplated to the extent that their net expected gains were positive.

The question of interest here is How does the inclusion of transaction costs affect the characterization of market failure? Arrow's 'relative market failure' could be seen as the absence of markets due to high transaction costs in forming markets, whether these are transaction costs faced by the government in (4.10), or transaction costs faced by the two firms (4.11). The inadequacy of such a description of market failure is apparent since the non-existence of markets may be warranted by Pareto-efficiency. This is clearly so if transaction costs of forming markets outweigh the benefits of forming them in the government's decision problem.

Heller and Starret's 'private-economy failure' could be

interpreted as the case where market-forming is not a profit-maxi-mizing action for the farmers (4.11), but none the less is a wel-fare-maximizing action for the government (4.10). That is, given the nature of transaction costs that the farmers face, markets for nectar and fertilizing services do not 'spontaneously' evolve.[23] But if the government were to impose markets, Pareto-gains could be attained. The problem with such a notion of market failure can be illustrated by an alternative scenario. It could be that transaction costs are such that, given time, the spontaneous functioning of the private economy leads to the creation of mar-kets for the 'externalities' and this leads to Pareto-improvements. Now assume that further Pareto-improvements could be achieved (by a further reduction of transaction costs) if the apple–honey production was organized by a very different set of institutions than the market (e.g. a hierarchical structure or some cooperative enterprise, or simply a single owner of both activities), but the transaction costs for setting up this mode of organization are such that these institutions do not evolve spontaneously from the actions of the farmers (e.g. transaction-cost technology may be non-convex). The private economy may not create the most effi-cient institutions. Once transaction costs have been introduced into the model there is no reason why the most efficient institu-tions will evolve as a result of transactions among profit-seeking agents. Part of the problem is that no account is offered as to what a private economy is, or what the mechanism is by which institutions evolve. There seems to be an implicit identification of existence of market institutions with optimality of institutions.[24] If one is to assume that the institutions that evolve 'sponta-neously' are optimal one has to make rather restrictive assump-tions about the mechanism by which institutions are created.[25]

The literature on the creation of institutions is still very lim-ited. Umbeck (1981)[26] has offered a model illustrating the emer-

[23] It could be that the farmers do not have the kind of information available to the government, or that the initiating farmer bears too high a cost to make it worthwhile. There are many possibilities on the nature of the transaction-technol-ogy functions.

[24] Demsetz (1967) effectively takes the position that existence of an institution is equivalent to its being optimal, I will discuss problems with this view in Ch. 8, below.

[25] Esp. given the inherent public-good nature of institutions.

[26] I discuss Umbeck's model at greater length in Ch. 8, below. A similar model is offered by Bush and Mayer (1974).

gence of property rights from a property-less world, and though he shows how an optimal set of property rights may emerge, rather restrictive assumptions are made concerning the costs of forming property rights. Unless restrictive assumptions are made about the costs of creating and enforcing private-property rights, those that emerge spontaneously could very well be inefficient as well as the resulting markets that are created. Once more, the existence of private-property rights or markets is not sufficient proof of their optimality.[27] Unless one has good reason to believe that the spontaneous formation of institutions will (1) produce optimal institutions, and (2) that these will be markets, and (3) only where markets have not been formed will there be inefficiency, Heller and Starrett's private market failure, with the accompanying notion of externality, seems problematic.

6. SOME MORE PROBLEMS WITH NON-EXISTENCE OF MARKETS AS A CHARACTERIZATION OF MARKET FAILURE

Given the widespread use in the literature of non-existence of markets as a characterization of externality and market failure, I would like to point out some general points about treating market failure as the non-existence of markets (in a framework of endogenous transaction costs).

A central problem is that one can always treat a failure of an institution in taking into account certain consequences as resulting from the lack of some private-property right and/or market. But what this really gauges is absolute market failure, which is inadequate for understanding failure in models with transaction costs. In an imperfect world of organizational costs the question is not whether actions or consequences of actions (actual and potential) are taken into account but whether, given the cost of taking consequences of action into account, the most consequences and/or most important consequences are taken into account. Imperfections in the market system can be interpreted as non-existence of markets, but imperfect markets are created where perfect ones cannot thrive, and given transaction costs

---

[27] These issues are taken up extensively in Ch. 8, below.

these may or may not be optimal. In a world of ubiquitous organizational costs one is judging the efficiency of imperfect markets not the existence or not of perfect markets.

Akerlof (1984) has presented several models where markets are inefficient due to lack of information. In one model he shows how a market for skill can lead to an inefficient allocation of labour. Because skill cannot be detected directly (transaction costs prohibitive), a proxy is formed for skill to determine where the workers will be allocated in the production process, and what their remuneration will be. The model shows how the use of a proxy can lead to an inefficient allocation of labour. Appropriate taxation can lead to a Pareto-optimal allocation of labour. In this case one might say that because of the inability to form private-property rights for skill, and by extension a true market for skill, there was market failure. However, one could construct other examples where proxies or 'indicators' for skill (or other economic 'goods') lead to the most efficient allocation of resources possible given transaction costs.[28] The non-existence of private-property rights over the ultimate good in question, (and by extension the non-existence of a market for that good), would no longer indicate market failure. Some markets for 'proxies' or pseudo-markets, may be the best institutions given transaction costs.[29]

If the problem is stated in a counterfactual way so that one asks if the system would have been optimal had there been a market for the 'externality', one is tempted to say that the non-existence of such a market is what prevents the system from being optimal. But this is a return to the absolute market failure which abstracts from transaction costs. Once transaction costs are incorporated in the model there is failure not because some market is missing (since that may be prescribed by the transac-

---

[28] Akerlof (1984) was interested in showing how lack of information could cause failure when it leads to use of proxies, and thus warrant government intervention. However, there would be no difficulty constructing models where certain proxies provided the best allocation devices given transaction costs.

[29] In a world of ubiquitous transaction costs one could argue that many property rights are simply proxies for ultimate objects of desire, e.g. there is no way to define a property right for my desire for greater mobility (ultimate good); instead I express my demand for this desire by purchasing imperfect proxies for this good like a car, bicycle, etc. The fact that a market for the ultimate good 'mobility' cannot be formed does not warrant saying there is failure due to the non-existence of this market.

tion costs associated with such a market), but because there may be an alternative institutional structure that could do better. Furthermore, one cannot focus on the efficiency of an institution that governs interaction over some particular activity, in abstraction from the surrounding institutional environment. The existence or non-existence of a specific institution cannot tell us whether resource allocation is efficient unless we know more about the general institutional environment. It is only in reference to absolute market failure that non-existence stands alone as a cause of failure.

As an illustration of the nature of the problem consider the following example. The formation of skill is a familiar externality problem in the literature. Firms tend to under-invest in skill, fearing that labourers will leave the firm before the firm can cover the investment costs. Japan has been cited by many authors (e.g. Morishima 1982; Dore 1987) as exemplary in the way its economy deals with this inefficiency. A system of loyalty ensures that workers will stay with one firm for most of their lifetimes, virtually alleviating any reservations with skill-formation of labour. Though loyalty is the distinctive institution singled out in explaining this efficiency, loyalty as an institution may not be viable or not have the aforementioned effects if it were not supported by other institutions in the system, e.g. dual-market structure of Japanese economy, educational system, etc. If one could transplant the Japanese ethos to workers in a western society one should not necessarily expect the successful results evinced in Japan. The success of an institution is found, in large part, in the way it interacts with other institutions and values, and alternative modes of behaviour.[30]

Treating market failure as non-existence of specific markets over specific activities fails to capture the interdependent nature of institutions. While an inefficiency may seem to reside in a single activity, an appropriate institutional solution to this inefficiency may require new modes of organization that cover more activities than the one under scrutiny. As with the apple–honey example failure of the system may not be understood by simply focusing on the activity over which a market does not exist (there

---

[30] In Ch. 10, below, I argue that in order to give content to the notion of 'efficient' or 'optimal' institution, one has to introduce behavioural models which make room for greater behavioural diversity.

are three activities; apple production, honey production, 'external' activity). While that might lead to a partial-equilibrium solution (optimal institution for external activity given existing institutions for apple and honey production), a general-equilibrium approach would assess the 'joint' activity of apple–honey-externality production. The optimal institutions resulting from such an approach may entail a different 'optimal' institution for the 'external' activity.

Another tension is present in the non-existence approach: on the one hand, market failure means failure of the market system; on the other hand, it is failure of a specific market. There is a tension between the market viewed as a system and the market viewed as an institution over a specific activity. The non-existence approach is unable to discriminate between these two. If for some activity a market does not exist, does this imply failure of the market system? Would the presence of vertically integrated firms imply systemic failure? Non-existence of markets is too absolute a concept to afford an institutionally rich understanding of market failure. The market system is not a simple sum of markets, it is made up of legal structures, hierarchic firms, administrative bodies of government, etc. Introduction of transaction costs entails an introduction of institutional complexity and a fundamental reinterpretation of market failure. This reinterpretation is not well served by the inflexible concept of non-existence of markets.

The following is a brief summary of the problems associated with viewing market failure, or a subset of market failure, as the non-existence of markets:

1. It presumes that the existence of a market is sufficient to establish its efficiency, i.e. existing market equals optimal institution. Once transaction costs have been incorporated fully into a model of the economy, the modes of organization of economic activity become users of resources, and one has to consider whether a certain constellation of institutions actually economize on resources. One cannot focus on a single activity to discern what is the optimal mode of organization for that activity in isolation, since the costs of setting up an allocation mechanism over any activity is inextricably linked to the general institutional environment. If several activities are organized by markets this will have

repercussions on the cost of institutions in other activities. The simple presence of an institution, market or non-market, is no evidence that it uses resource efficiently in the organization of economic activity.

2. It is indirect and perhaps misleading in avoiding explicit mention of a comparison set of institutions. Once transaction costs have been introduced, the failure of a market is deduced by comparison to alternative institutions and not by whether a market exists or not.

3. It treats all imperfect markets as non-existent markets, and this includes markets for proxies. In a world of transaction costs many markets will be 'imperfect', or many private-property rights may be 'imperfect', yet one could not deduce inefficiency from this alone. This is part of the more general problem that non-existence seems to refer to an absolute failure, in that any imperfect institution may be treated as the absence of a perfect market, but in doing so one forgets that these imperfect markets may be optimal institutions, i.e. there is no failure, and the market (albeit imperfect) still provides a good allocational mode.

4. Distinction between specific market and market system blurred.

5. Finally, a lot of the conceptual problems present in Arrow's notion of relative market failure and Heller and Starrett's notion of private-economy failure, seem to emanate from the transference of non-existence as a cause of failure in a transaction-costless world, to a model with endogenous transaction costs.

7. CONCLUSION

There is no question that non-existence of markets (or property rights) is a good metaphor in conveying the highly contingent nature of the thin line separating commodities from 'externalities' in a general-equilibrium model. The concept of universality of markets and its complement, non-existence of markets, are appropriate within the confines of the mathematical model of general-equilibrium; used out of that context they tend to confuse. The movement from absolute market failure to one that incorporates transaction costs should be accompanied with an abandonment of non-existence as a characterization of failure. Non-existence is an absolute concept inappropriate for an understanding of failure of imperfect markets relative to alternative imperfect modes of organization.

While Arrow moved away from absolute market failure by putting transaction costs at the centre stage, Heller and Starrett move even closer to the 'institutional' school of thought[31] by taking what seemed to be a 'process' view of the economy. Transaction cost has come to pre-eminence on the backs of 'institutional' (more recently 'new institutional') economists, who represent a very different methodological school than the one Arrow has been a founder of. By introducing transaction costs into a general-equilibrium setting Arrow makes an important step outside the Arrow–Debreu programme closer to an institutional perspective. No wonder O'Driscoll (1986: 156) says that 'the literature on process and institutional analysis would find congenial much of the recent work on transaction costs and externalities'. However, he also notes the 'pitfalls of the marriage of externality analysis and neoclassical economic theory', when he quotes from Dahlman (1979: 153): 'if it exists, it must be optimal, and if it does not exist it is because it is too costly, so that is optimal too'. This poignantly captures the quagmire that the 'non-existence' view of market failure is in. Arrow's identification of non-existence of markets with relative market failure does not confront the fact that non-existence of markets may be optimal, and should not necessarily be described as market failure, or that markets may exist and be suboptimal (since they may not minimize transaction costs). Heller and Starrett's characterization of externality and failure recognizes that non-existence may not entail failure of the market, but other pitfalls ensue having to do with the efficiency of the pre-market system. The source of the problem is not the introduction of transaction costs, but the concept of non-existence of markets which is too closely tailored to the requirements of the Arrow–Debreu model and the associated absolute market failure.

Despite some of the problems with Arrow's, and Heller and Starrett's, characterization of externality, an important lesson is

---

[31] This does not represent a homogenous group, see Langlois (1986a) for a representative sample of 'new' institutional economists.

learnt. The search for an understanding of externality forces a departure from the Arrow–Debreu model as we know it. Externality is not just a condition the absence of which implies the optimality of markets in a general-equilibrium model; it is a signpost demanding a revamping of the general-equilibrium model. An understanding of institutions and their economic function becomes a central objective. 'The identification of transaction costs in different contexts and under different systems of resource allocation should be a major item on the research agenda of the theory of public goods and indeed of the theory of resource allocation in general' (Arrow 1970: 60). It is necessary to construct institutionally rich models which will bring new interpretations of fundamental concepts like market failure, markets, market system, optimality, etc. Institutional economists, though not a homogeneous group, by virtue of making institutions a central part of their analysis, may provide important insights in understanding the implications of including institutional costs in models of the economy, and therefore seeing in what ways such concepts as optimality, externality, and market failure, have to be reinterpreted.

5

Non-Convexity and Entitlements

1. INTRODUCTION

In the previous chapter the notion of non-convexity came up under three different guises: first, as a cause of 'absolute market failure', which is the traditional view of non-convexity in general-equilibrium models; secondly, Heller and Starrett (1976) talked about 'fundamental' non-convexities arising from forming markets for detrimental 'externalities'; and thirdly, non-convexities in the formation of property rights or markets. In this chapter I will take a closer look at the notion of non-convexity and its relationship with externality. I shall be dealing with the first two kinds of non-convexity which are present in models without endogenous transaction costs, i.e. this chapter is about non-convexity in 'frictionless' models. It is from these models that the notion of externality as missing markets has derived.

Section 2 will restate the causes of failure in the Arrow–Debreu framework. Sections 3, 4, and 5 will look at the relationship between non-convexity and detrimental interaction under alternative 'entitlement' regimes: Pigouvian taxes, Lindahl markets, ownership of previously 'free' scarce resources. The emphasis will be on the institutional nature of non-convexities and failure; in particular that non-convexity and failure are determined by how the economic units (agent, property right, market, firm) are defined. Section 6 will discuss the relationship between non-convexity and beneficial interaction. Section 7 will look at the relationship between non-convexities and locational interaction, pointing to the pervasive nature of 'externalities' (missing markets) arising from locational interaction. Finally, in section 8, I will consider the implications of the discussion on non-convexity on the notion of externality as 'missing' markets. I will point out, once again, how the very notion of externality forces a move away from the Arrow–Debreu framework, thus leading to a reinterpretation of central concepts like market failure and externality.

2. MISSING MARKETS AND NON-CONVEXITY OF PRODUCTION SETS IN FRICTIONLESS MODELS

There are generally two kinds of failure in general-equilibrium private-ownership economies: (1) competitive equilibria that are not Pareto-optimal and which are often described as resulting from missing markets, (2) non-existence of competitive equilibrium due to non-convexity in consumption and production possibility sets. In general, if markets can be established for all 'goods' (all things that influence welfare), then description of market failure can be reduced to non-convexities. Non-convexity represents one class of situations where private profitability may diverge from social profitability in private ownership economies. Non-convexity poses no problem for the validity of the First Theorem of welfare economics.[1] If all competitive markets equilibrate despite non-convexity, then the equilibrium will be Pareto-optimal. The Second Theorem requires convexity. Not all Pareto-optimal states can be sustained by the decentralized price system. If increasing returns to scale in some activity is large relative to the market for any distribution of income, then no competitive equilibrium is possible. Conversely non-convex economies may equilibrate for certain distributions of income, depending on the nature of the non-convexities.

Detrimental spillovers among agents have come to be closely associated with non-convexity. Strong detrimental activity gives rise to non-convexity in production sets that confound standard Pigouvian tax solutions to externalities. Formation of Lindahl markets for detrimental spillovers result in 'fundamental' non-convexities preventing competitive equilibria. If intermediate property rights are well specified, Lindahl markets for 'externalities' can lead to competitive equilibria, but these may not be Pareto-optimal.[2] The next three sections of this chapter will take a closer look at the relationship between detrimental spillovers, non-convexity, missing markets, and inefficiency.

---

[1] Though it affects its reach and domain.

[2] See Starrett (1972) and Baumol and Bradford (1972). Interestingly, if Lindahl markets are seen as competitive markets, this point compromises the validity of the First Theorem of welfare economics.

3. DETRIMENTAL INTERACTION AND PIGOUVIAN TAXES

Consider a very simple example of two firms with detrimental spillover in their activities. Firms 1 and 2 produce goods y_1 and y_2 respectively, which they sell in a competitive market. The production of y_1 imposes a cost on firm 2 that shows up in its cost function $e(y_2, y_1)$. Suppose the technology is such that y_1 units of output cannot be produced without generating y_1 units of pollution that harm firm 2. With p_1 and p_2 being the prices of output, the profits of the two firms are given by

$$\pi_1 = \max_{y_1} p_1 y_1 - c(y_1) \tag{5.1}$$

and

$$\pi_2 = \max_{y_2} p_2 y_2 - e(y_2, y_1). \tag{5.2}$$

Both cost functions are assumed increasing and convex.

The equilibrium outputs (and level of pollution y_1) are given by

$$p_1 = \frac{\partial c(y_1)}{\partial y_1} \tag{5.3}$$

and

$$p_2 = \frac{\partial e(y_2, y_1)}{\partial y_2}. \tag{5.4}$$

The output of y_1 is too large from society's vantage point since it does not take into account the detrimental impact on firm 2. The efficient level of output and pollution would have to maximize the joint profits of the two firms

$$\pi_{1+2} = \max_{y_1, y_2} p_1 y_1 + p_2 y_2 - c(y_1) - e(y_2, y_1), \tag{5.5}$$

with first-order conditions

$$p_1 = \frac{\partial c(y_1)}{\partial y_1} + \frac{\partial e(y_2, y_1)}{\partial y_1} \tag{5.6}$$

and

$$p_2 = \frac{\partial e(y_2, y_1)}{\partial y_2}. \tag{5.7}$$

One of the standard policy instruments to align the competitive-equilibrium output with the socially efficient output level is the Pigouvian tax. In this case, firm 1 could be taxed by an amount t per unit of output, so that the first-order condition profit-maximization becomes

$$p = \frac{\partial c(y_1)}{\partial y_1} + t. \tag{5.8}$$

If we set $t = \dfrac{\partial e(y_2, y_1)}{\partial y_1}$, and the cost functions are convex as assumed, this tax will induce the firm to produce the desired level of output.

3.1. Non-convexity in the Social-Production-Possibility Set when the Detrimental Interaction is Strong

Baumol and Bradford (1972) have shown that if the detrimental spillover between two firms is strong enough, the combined production set of the two activities will be non-convex.[3] As an illustration they consider an electricity plant that emits smoke which soils laundry of a laundry service. It is assumed that there is no market for smoke and the laundry service takes the spillover as a given; it is not a control variable. The labour requirements of the two firms are:

$$l_1 = \frac{y_1^2}{2} \text{ and } l_2 = \frac{y_2^2}{2} + \alpha y_2 y_1 \tag{5.9}$$

where l_1 and y_1 are the input and output levels of the electricity firm, and l_2 and y_2 are the input and output levels of the laundry firm. The parameter α represents the strength of the detrimental effect suffered by the laundry service as a result of smoke emitted by the electricity plant. For simplicity it is assumed that a unit increase in electricity evokes a unit increase in smoke. As α is positive, an increase in electricity (and thus smoke) implies that the production of a given level of laundry service will require a higher

---

[3] While the individual cost functions may be convex in the inputs which the firms can control, if one includes 'pollution' as an input in the production process then the convexity of the cost functions is lost (at least when the detrimental interaction is strong).

input. By substitution one can get the production-possibility curve for the marketed goods

$$\frac{y_1^2}{2} + \alpha y_1 y_2 + \frac{y_2^2}{2} = l_1 + l_2 = L, \qquad (5.10)$$

L being an exogenous labour supply. By differentiation the relationship between the marginal rate of transformation and the pattern of output can be expressed as

$$\frac{dy_2}{dy_1} = -\frac{y_1 + \alpha y_2}{y_2 + \alpha y_1}. \qquad (5.11)$$

If α is greater than 1, the production-possibility set becomes non-convex.

Even as the production-possibility set of two activities is non-convex, the individual-production sets are convex in their respective control variables (production of y_2 treated as a function of l_2 alone), so the competitive market equilibrates. The equilibrium will be inefficient, but with appropriate Pigouvian taxes the decentralized market could be relied on. The problem that strong detrimental activity poses in this context is that due to the non-convexity of the social-production-possibility set, even if the authorities know the entire set of feasible output vectors, equilibrium prices no longer tell us whether the current output is Pareto-optimal, or what the direction of improvement should be. There are multiple Pigouvian tax-compensated equilibria. A Pigouvian tax-adjustment mechanism that relies on information of marginal damages may move the economy to a suboptimal equilibrium.

3.2. Illustrating the Problem for Pigouvian Taxes when the Social Production Set is Non-convex

The problem for Pigouvian tax-mechanisms, when the social production set is non-convex, can be illustrated with the help of a few more equations and some figures.[4] Let the production possibilities for our electricity and laundry firms be represented by the following general functional forms:

---

[4] The exposition in this sect. and in sect. 4, below, follows quite closely that of Dasgupta and Heal's (1979).

$$y_1 \le h(l_1) \tag{5.12}$$

where $h(0) = 0$, $h'(l_1) \ge 0$ and $h''(l_1) \le 0$,
and

$$y_2 = \frac{f(l_2)}{1 + v(y_1)} \tag{5.13}$$

where $f(0) = 0$, $f'(l_2) \ge 0$ and $f''(l_2) \le 0$ $v(0) = 0$ and $v'(y_1) > 0$.

The production function of the electricity firm (5.12) is straightforward. The production function of the laundry firm (5.13) incorporates the detrimental impact of the electricity firm's output, though the particular functional form of the detrimental impact is left unspecified. The government wants to induce the electricity firm to produce an output (and pollution) level that will maximize the joint profits of these two firms. It is helpful to look at the maximum attainable profits of both firms at different levels of pollution (or electricity output), i.e. the two firms choose the profit-maximizing input levels for different levels of pollution (for the electricity firm this means simply to pick the profit-maximizing labour-input level):

$$\pi_1(y_1) = \max_{l_1}[p_1 y_1(l_1) - w_1 l_1] \tag{5.14}$$

and

$$\pi_2(y_1) = \max_{l_2}[p_2 y_2(l_2, y_1) - w_2 l_2]. \tag{5.15}$$

The functional form of the two profit functions can take any number of shapes. For illustrative purposes, I will assume the profit functions, along with the resulting marginal-profit functions $d\pi_1/dy_1$ and $d\pi_2/dy_1$, take the reasonable shapes depicted in Fig. 5.1a and b. The interpretation of these specific functions is straightforward. For the electricity firm the first units of output (and unavoidably pollution) bring in the greatest profits. Additional increments of output raise smaller amounts of profit. For the laundry firm that is receiving the pollution, the impact of the first units of pollution on its profits is small. But as pollution accumulates, it seriously damages productivity. At some point however, after the serious damage has been done, additional units of pollution will no longer have an impact on the spillee.

Fig. 5.2a is a vertical summation of the two profit functions giving us the joint profits of the two activities associated with

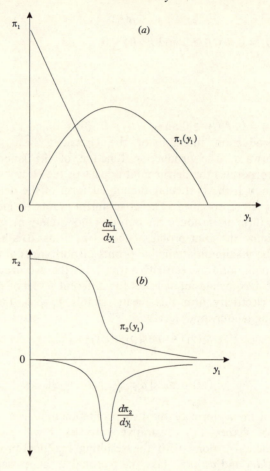

F<small>IG</small> 5.1.

different levels of pollution. Noting that the marginal-profit functions can be interpreted as the marginal-benefit and -cost functions associated with different levels of pollution, and taking the
absolute value of the marginal-cost function and superimposing
the two curves, we have the marginal benefits and costs of alternative levels of pollution in Fig. 5.2*b*. Under certain assumptions
about the marginal benefits and costs of pollution, such as a substantial degree of detrimental impact (which would stretch the

marginal-cost curve upwards), or a relatively low profitability of the polluters' activity (shifting the marginal benefit down or the marginal-cost curve up), we could easily get the kind of cost curves depicted in Fig. 5.2*a* and *b*. Given these functions, point E^* is an equilibrium point associated with the joint-profit-maximizing level of output y_1^*. Output level y_1^0, is associated with a local maximum of joint profits. If the authorities adjust Pigouvian taxes according to marginal damages done by the

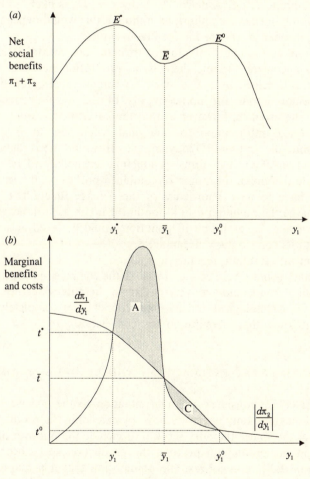

FIG 5.2.

polluting firm, then depending on the initial level of pollution (beyond $\bar{y}_1$), the economy could easily end up at a suboptimal competitive equilibrium with a pollution level y_1^0. While marginal benefits and costs may be equal with respect to pollution, there are higher net benefits associated with a substantially lower level of pollution where marginal benefits and costs are high. Pigouvian taxation based on marginal damages may lead to a tax-supported competitive equilibrium that is not Pareto-optimal. In this case there are three Pigouvian tax-compensated competitive equilibria, E^*, $\bar{E}$, and E^0. The latter one, E^0, is likely to be a dynamically unstable equilibrium, although this would depend on the adjustment procedure for the Pigouvian tax.

As long as the two firms do not treat the detrimental interaction as a control variable there is no production outcome that cannot be attained by a Pigouvian tax-compensated competitive equilibrium despite the non-convexity of the social-production space. The problem, however, is that the government cannot rely on marginal information (or marginal willingness to pay) to determine the optimal Pigouvian tax. It would need detailed information of the two firms' production technology to be able to locate the global maximum of combined profits. At the least it would have to have knowledge of the damage function $\pi_2(y_2)$, and charge the polluting firm a non-linear tax in accordance with this schedule, i.e. each unit of pollution would be taxed at a rate equal to its contribution of damages.

Pigouvian taxation remains a solution when the detrimental externality is not severe enough to make the combined-production-possibility frontier non-convex, but again the authorities need to know the technological and economic possibilities completely, in order to know that there are no non-convexities.

4. DETRIMENTAL INTERACTION AND LINDAHL MARKETS

Starrett (1972) considers a similar situation to the one we have been discussing, only he shows how, by extending the production space of the spillee (laundry service) to include the spillover as an input in the production process, the production space becomes 'fundamentally' non-convex; the point being that if a market is created in the spillover and it becomes a control variable in the individual production processes, the production space becomes non-convex irrespective of the severity of the detrimental externality. As the intensity of the detrimental effect increases (even if the overall effect is minimal) either there will come a point where increases will no longer have an effect on the spillee, or a point where it will no longer be profitable for the spillee to remain in business. Either way, the change in the marginal effect from negative to zero implies a non-convexity in the expanded production space (see Figs. 5.3*b* and 5.4*b*).

If a market for the detrimental interaction existed, the two firms (laundry and electricity) would be maximizing the following profit functions:

$$\pi_1 = \max_{y_{11}} p_1 y_{11} - c(y_{11}) - r y_{12} \qquad (5.16)$$

and

$$\pi_2 = \max_{y_2, \, y_{12}} p_2 y_2 - e(y_2, y_{12}) + r y_{12}, \qquad (5.17)$$

where r is the competitive (Lindahl) price of units of pollution (treated as a separate commodity from output of the electricity firm) and noting that in this example $y_{11} = y_{12} = y_1$ by assumption. The first-order conditions can be written as

$$p_1 = \frac{\partial c(y_{11})}{\partial y_{11}} + r \qquad (5.18)$$

and

$$p_2 = \frac{\partial e(y_2, y_{12})}{\partial y_2} \text{ and } r = \frac{\partial e(y_2, y_{12})}{\partial y_{12}}. \qquad (5.19)$$

These first-order conditions should lead to maximization of joint profits. The problem, however, is that given the non-convexity of the production set, the competitive Lindahl market will not equilibrate. At a positive price for smoke the laundry service will not want to purchase any smoke, while the power station will be trying to sell. At a zero price the laundry service will still not demand any smoke, while the power station will pollute indiscriminately. Finally, with a negative price the laundry service will find it profitable to shut down and try to sell an indefinite number of pollution certificates to the power station. This problem is illustrated in Fig. 5.3*a* and *b*. Fig. 5.3*b* shows a functional form of profit-maximizing levels of laundry output

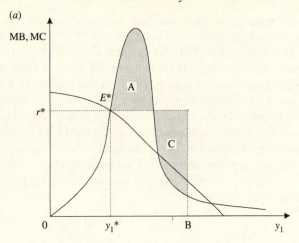

(*a*)

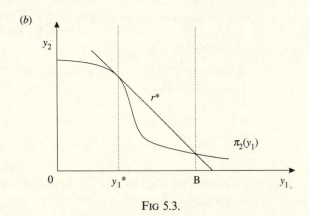

(*b*)

Fig 5.3.

(y_2), associated with different levels of pollution, as well as the Lindahl price (r^*) that would maximize joint profits. At that price the laundry firm could get more profits by selling more units of pollution than that indicated by quantity B. In fact at such a price (or any positive price) it would rather shut down and sell an infinite number of pollution certificates than the quantity that the electricity firm is willing to buy, and so there is no equilibrium.

4.1. Specifying Intermediate Rights

The lack of an equilibrium may be seen to result from the fact that no upper bound has been placed on the number of pollution certificates that the laundry firm is able to sell (or that pollution rights are not well specified). Looking at Fig. 5.3*b* again, it is apparent that if the total number of pollution certificates that the laundry firm was allowed to sell was just under quantity B, then the Lindahl price r^* would indeed support the Pareto-optimal allocation of resources because the laundry service could maximize profits by selling y_1^* units of pollution. Fig. 5.3*a* shows the same impact of putting a lid on total allowable pollution certificates. The two shaded areas in the diagram are equivalent in value, suggesting that the laundry service will be indifferent between selling y_1^* units of pollution and selling B units of pollution. The greater losses from allowing more pollution would be offset by the higher certificate revenues. If the total number of pollution certificates are greater than B there will be no competitive equilibrium.[5] Any benchmark under B would sustain a Pareto-optimal outcome.

The problem is How does the government select the total allowable pollution, i.e. determine the number of certificates? It is clear from Fig. 5.3*a* and *b* that the informational requirements to find this threshold benchmark would be great. One possibility would be to select a benchmark such that the production-possibility curve in Fig. 5.3*b* becomes convex. This would correspond with the peak of the marginal-cost curve in Fig. 5.3*a* (marginal costs and benefits become conventional). Again this would require more information than simply the level of marginal costs. More importantly it could impose an equilibrium that may not be optimal.

Under a different set of competitive prices for the laundry services and electricity (and/or different production functions), making the production function of laundry with respect to pollution convex could impose a suboptimal equilibrium. In Fig. 5.4*a* and *b*, it can be seen that E^* would be the equilibrium, but it would be suboptimal. Given the particular marginal benefits and costs associated with the two activities, joint-profit maximization

---

[5] Note that E is no longer an equilibrium as it was with Pigouvian taxes, it would only be an equilibrium if the benchmark happened to coincide with it.

would entail a lower level of provision of laundry services, E^0. Depending on the cost functions, it could be optimal for the laundry service to shut down. The difficulty is that by selecting a benchmark level that ensures convexity the authorities may be enforcing a competitive equilibrium that is not optimal.

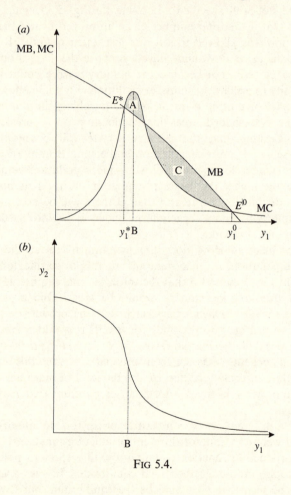

FIG 5.4.

4.2. Alternative Rights

Rights do not have to be described as a pollutee's rights to clean air, they could also be framed as the polluter's rights to pollute.

Authorities could endow the polluter with a level of permissible pollution, requiring the pollutee to purchase from the polluter the right to cleaner air. The firms would be maximizing the following profit functions

$$\pi_1 = \max_{y_{11}} p_1 y_{11} - c(y_{11}) - r(\bar{y}_{12} - y_{12}) \qquad (5.20)$$

and

$$\pi_2 = \max_{y_2, y_{12}} p_2 y_2 - e(y_2, y_{12}) + r(\bar{y}_{12} - y_{12}). \qquad (5.21)$$

This does not alter the outcomes discussed so far. The total number of certificates will determine whether there is an equilibrium or not. Changing the total number of pollution certificates that can be exchanged, or altering the initial distribution of certificates effectively alters the distribution of the combined profits of the two activities.

One is inclined to think of these Lindahl markets with benchmarks as simulating a Coasean zero-transaction-cost world where changes in benchmark represents changes in property rights, effectively redistributing the combined profits associated with efficient levels of production. The problem, however, with Lindahl markets is that the two industries or firms are not actually negotiating where they would bring to the table the full weight of their potential rents. Instead they face parametric prices which equate demand and supply of pollution certificates, and depending on how the benchmark is set the pollution market may settle at a local equilibrium. The benchmark determines not only distribution of profits but total profits as well. A Pareto-suboptimal equilibrium is possible with competitive Lindahl markets. The difficulty of finding an appropriate benchmark for the spillee's right to compensation, i.e. one that will maximize net benefits, is analogous to that of finding a global maximum of net benefits with Pigouvian taxes. The authorities require global information.

4.3. Reciprocal Spillovers

Detrimental externalities associated with the 'tragedy of the commons' like fishing from an open-access sea, or grazing on open-access land, differ from the previous example discussed so far, in that the spillovers are symmetrical in nature, meaning that these reciprocal spillovers have the same underlying technological basis. The detrimental effect is a function of the scale of a single productive activity, rather than a function of two (or more) different activities. In the case of detrimental spillovers created by fishing from a common fishing ground, every time a new vessel is brought into the fishing ground the fishing output of others is diminished. As was discussed in Chapter 2, this results in over-fishing since no one takes into account the reduction in others' profits from the more intensive use of the commonly used resource. Assuming for simplicity that vessels represent an aggregate of all inputs into fishing except the input sea, one could hypothetically establish Lindahl markets for vessels so that v_{ij} would represent the good: 'vessel used by i that enters into j's production function'. The formation of Lindahl markets, or markets in 'named' vessels, would lead to fundamental non-convexity in the extended production space of the individual firms. Unlike the case of Lindahl markets in pollution where there were different kinds of activities involved and where some range of the extended production space of the individual firms were convex, here the entire range of the extended production space of the individual firms will be non-convex even though the social production of fish (the input sea assumed constant) will be convex throughout. That is, Pigouvian taxes could be used to locate a global maximum in this case, whereas no benchmark in vessel-permits could generate a convex extended production space for the individual firm.

5. DETRIMENTAL INTERACTION AND ENTITLEMENTS

So far we have seen two ways of dealing with detrimental spillovers, Pigouvian taxes and Lindahl prices, each plagued in different ways with the problem of non-convexities.[6] Essentially

[6] Varian (1989) has suggested a rather ingenious compensation mechanism that would overcome the difficulty that Pigouvian taxes and Lindahl markets have in achieving a Pareto-optimal allocation of resources when there is non-convexity due to detrimental interaction. If the firm that generates the detrimental impact has good information about the costs she imposes on other firms, there is a neat scheme to ensure that resources are allocated efficiently. The firm that generates the detrimental activity is asked to announce the rate at which the receiving firm will be compensated per unit of output it produces (polluting activity). The 'victim' firm is asked to announce a charge that will be imposed on the polluting firm. In addition, both firms are charged a penalty that increases with the discrep-

the decentralized private-ownership economy is unable to rely on marginal information transmitted by parametric prices. Initially the inefficiency associated with detrimental interaction may have been described as arising from the lack of a market, but Starrett's example revealed that even with a 'fully' defined set of markets inefficient equilibria can exist.

There is another way, however, of viewing detrimental spillovers. Rather than extending the market space, or 'ownership' over activities, one could extend the property-right space to the channels of interaction. In the case of the laundry service and power station, the spillover occurs through the channel of air. Clean air is an input into the laundry service's production function. The problems arise because it is treated as a free good, when clearly it is very scarce. If the resource 'air' was owned by individuals, then sure enough a competitive equilibrium would result, as long as the new production space (that incorporates air as an input) of the individual firms turned out to be convex. The air would be distributed so that it was put to its most productive use. The laundry service and power station would bid for the use of air, and 'air'-owners would look to maximize rents. Only Pareto-optimal allocation would maximize rents. Air-owners would provide the global perspective missing with Pigouvian and Lindahl markets. Naturally it is difficult to envisage property rights to air, or 'plots' of air, largely due to the physical nature of this input which gives it attributes of a public good. But the difficulty of forming private-property rights over air is related to the costs of forming institutions, which do not enter into frictionless general-equilibrium models. What is important to note is that by changing the way property rights are defined, one is changing the definition of inputs that enter into production functions and

ancy between the compensation and charge rate, and is zero when the two announced rates are the same. After the rates and penalties have been established, the two firms determine their respective output levels. The structure of penalties is such, that each firm is induced to announce respectively, a charge and compensation rate that is equivalent to the social cost of the detrimental activity at the margin. This outcome is a 'subgame perfect equilibrium' based on each firm's rational conjecture of the other firm's rational conjecture. Specifically, the polluting firm has an incentive to match the announcement of the victim firm, since whatever charge the victim firm announces it will have to pay, it can only minimize its burden by minimizing the discrepancy between charge and compensation. The only point at which the victim firm would like to avoid any discrepancy between the compensation rate and the charge rate, is when the compensation rate is just equal to the cost of the detrimental activity at the margin.

thus altering the shape of production functions. A production function that is convex on one definition of inputs may be non-convex on another. Non-convexity (and thus failure due to non-convexity) is closely related to how property rights are defined.

The tragedy of the commons associated with fishing (or any activity) could also be turned into a conventional model by redefining the open-access resource as divisible private property. Fishermen would purchase well-defined rights to patches of sea. This in fact is a much more natural extension of property rights in the private-ownership general-equilibrium model than Lindahl markets. Lindahl markets set up exchange among individuals and firms in 'activities' rather than in resources or goods. In the case of 'named' vessels, firms are exchanging the right to use different levels of inputs. In the case of pollution, firms are exchanging rights over levels of detrimental activities.

Private ownership of some 'free' good (space, air, sea, etc.) would turn models of detrimental 'externalities' into conventional ones.[7] One can treat congestion as the imposition of costs by one activity on to another and consider the formation of markets for these interactions, or one can view the interaction as resulting from some good not being privately owned. Forming property rights for the detrimental effects that agents or firms impose on others in a congested inner-city area would be highly complicated, and would require a lot of information to result in a Pareto-optimal allocation of resources. Private ownership of the channels of interaction, space, roads, etc., may appropriately price use of scarce resources, although it might be extremely difficult, or impossible, in the real world to define and enforce such private rights. Furthermore, the incorporation of these newly defined inputs into production functions may lead to new non-convexities.

With Pigouvian taxes, rights are defined over the value of goods being produced; Lindahl markets establish rights over specific activity levels; and private ownership of previously 'free' resources establishes rights over resources. With appropriate information these alternative ways of defining rights lead to the

---

[7] It seems unlikely that all detrimental interaction can be usefully described as use of some open-access scarce resource even in a world of costless enforcement such as the one we are considering. To think of one ex., locational interaction does not seem to offer itself to such an interpretation.

same resource allocation. They are different ways of channelling agents' activity through manipulation of the constraints that agents face. In models with no transaction costs, there is little basis for preferring one method of defining property rights from another. It might seem natural to prefer a property-right structure that would avoid multiple equilibria. This itself, however, would require knowledge of the underlying production functions and the shape that they take under different property-right regimes.

Looking at detrimental interaction in terms of alternative property-right structures, emphasizes the institutional nature of what is labelled 'externality'. One could take any input into a production process and strip it of any private-ownership rights, effectively modelling it as an open-access scarce resource, a resource that should command a positive price but does not. If labour were treated as a free-access resource (although it is difficult to visualize this), then as firms used up labour in their production processes, they would be imposing a detrimental effect on other firms requiring this scarce resource. It might be objected that with pollution the detrimental interaction is strong or somehow direct, but surely one could construct an example where the detrimental impact of pollution is nearly imperceptible, and accumulates by very small increments. In the case of fishing, the effect of the first entrants into a common fishing area may be hardly perceptible. The using-up of clean air, or sea, is analytically analogous to the using up of free scarce labour.

If one were to draw the production function of a firm which required clean air as an input, and air could be purchased in plots (air of different qualities could be defined as different goods), the function might look something like that shown in Fig. 5.5*a* (the particular shape would depend on how this new input affected the production function). The point is that it would take a conventional form much as if one were to draw any other input, say labour, on the horizontal axis. In Fig. 5.5*b* the origin corresponds to zero output of goods and free access to clean air. Moving away from the origin indicates increases in pollution which can be treated as decreases in clean air. The 'fundamental' non-convexity arises precisely because of treating the activity of polluting as an input rather than the resource clean air. If the firm were confronted with air-owners it would not be

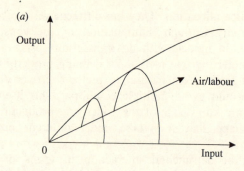

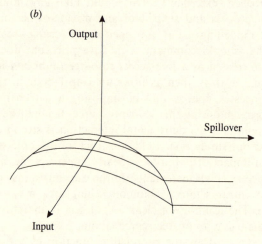

FIG 5.5.

able to begin production without purchasing some rights to (clean) air from them, and the production function would look like that of any other production function without detrimental interaction.

Pushing the analogy, if one were to form Lindahl markets for the detrimental interaction associated with firms' use of 'free' labour, the extended production space would be non-convex. The analogy with 'named' vessels would require that firms had to pay for the right to use other inputs in combination with the resource labour. No doubt this wrenches intuition but serves the purpose of emphasizing that the differences involved in the nature of interaction associated with use of labour and pollution cannot be the distinguishing feature separating 'externality' from 'internality'. In a transaction-costless world, property rights can be defined in numerous ways, nothing inherent in the nature of the activity can determine what kind of property right (if any) can be used. In this sense there is nothing inherent about production and consumption activities which warrants a distinction between external and internal activity.

6. BENEFICIAL INTERACTION AND NON-CONVEXITY

The focus has been on the relationship between detrimental spillovers and non-convexity, but what of beneficial spillovers which have been conspicuous for their absence in the non-convexity literature? The extension of a production set to include some beneficial spillover may also lead to non-convexity. Chipman (1970) shows how a perfectly competitive equilibrium may result with firms operating under increasing, constant, or decreasing returns to scale. The idea behind his model is that the scale of industry has an impact on the cost of production that each firm faces, yet each firm contributes so little to this scale effect that they do not take it into account. It can be likened to Adam Smith's pin-factory illustration. As a firm expands, new divisions of labour are possible, specialities develop, which then feed into a pool of labour which other firms can tap into. Each firm contributes to the process imperceptibly, and thus the firms regard the improvement in the quality and variety of the labour force as an exogenous variable. It is this dysfunction between the production function that each firm perceives and the underlying actual-production function, that allows an industry to function under increasing costs under perfectly competitive conditions. Each firm 'mistakenly' perceives a constant return to scale-production function because the beneficial interaction due to scale goes unnoticed.

Chipman argues that this can be seen as a kind of rehabilitation of Marshall's external economies of scale. Pigouvian taxes and bounties can be used to move the economy to a Pareto-optimal competitive equilibrium by taxing the decreasing-cost industries and subsidizing the increasing-cost industries, albeit there may be some balancing-budget problems. This result is similar to Baumol and Bradford's point that since the firms' individual production sets are convex in their control variables, Pigouvian taxes will do the trick. While in Baumol and Bradford's model the detrimental interaction was among dissimilar activities, and Chipman considers beneficial interaction among firms producing the same good, there is no reason why this could not apply to scale economies among firms with different productive activities.

One way to interpret this problem of beneficial spillover is that property rights for skilled labour are poorly defined. If one could form well-defined property rights over the attributes of labour, then the spillover model would turn into a more conventional model without spillovers, where firms would be able to reap all the benefits of training through the 'exchange' of workers of different skills. The interesting point here is that what was perceived as a convex technology by firms when property rights for labour were 'poorly' defined, may turn into non-convex technology (increasing returns to scale) when property rights for workers' attributes are well defined. It could be that in the extended-market model increasing returns to scale relative to the market would make production privately unprofitable (see Fig. 5.6). As another illustration, one could imagine that the apple–honey interaction is such that when pollination is included as a purchasable input in apple production, apple technology becomes an increasing returns to scale technology. Once again, it seems that alternative definitions of property rights, by altering the input space, will alter the production functions so that convexity becomes an attribute partially determined by the definition of institutions.[8]

7. INDIVISIBILITIES AND LOCATIONAL INTERACTION

Baumol and Bradford (1972) show that in the case of detrimental interaction, the introduction of space in the model, in which spatial separation can be seen as a palliative to the detrimental effect, will lead to non-convexities. The ability of a firm to control pollution as an input by moving further away from the pol-

[8] Note furthermore that property rights can also determine the definition of goods (outputs) and not just inputs.

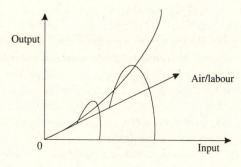

FIG 5.6.

luting firm, where location is not only important for its palliative effect but also gauges other inputs, such as transportation costs, communication costs, nearness to resources, etc., is likely to lead to multiple equilibria. It seems this has less to do with the presence of a detrimental effect like pollution, and more with the peculiar impact that locational questions have in the presence of indivisibilities. Quoting from Koopmans (1957: 154):

Preliminary exploration of models in the location of indivisible plants throws serious doubt on the possibility of sustaining an efficient locational distribution of economic activities through the price system. The decisive difficulty is that transportation of intermediate commodities from one plant to another makes the relative advantage of a given location for a given plant dependent on the locations of other plants. This dependence of one man's decision criterion on other men's decisions appears to leave no room for efficient price-guided allocation.

In the case of pollution with separation of activities as a palliative, private ownership of 'air' rights would no longer provide a way out of the multiple equilibria that the price system confronts. With pollution one can somehow identify a separate input (air) that comes into the production function of a firm, or is an output of some firm (different qualities of air). A price will be associated with specific quantities of the resource in question. Control over the potential detrimental effect seems well defined. The relational quality of locational interaction makes it much more complex to deal with through a price system. Control over proximity is poorly defined. Could there be Lindahl markets for 'nearness', a market for the 'externality' of locational choices? It strains the imagination to think of proximity as a commodity. I can only conjecture that locational interaction introduces a kind of indivisibility that pervades the entire economy even when all goods are locationally defined. If transportation costs are important and are an input in all production processes, then the production of any good (which is also specified locationally) is in fact a joint output in the production of all goods. If production of all goods took place within one firm then these interactions would be dealt with as long as there were no organizational costs.

No matter how entitlements are defined, spatial interaction seems to conflict in a fundamental way with decentralization of decision-making. Spatial interaction is rarely labelled 'externality' yet it differs from other interdependencies only in complexity. The ability to treat interdependencies effectively through parametric prices becomes increasingly difficult.

8. CONCLUSION: MISSING MARKETS, NON-CONVEXITIES, AND EXTERNALITY

One of the postulates made in the Arrow–Debreu model is that producers' production sets are 'independent of the choices of other decision-makers' (Koopmans 1957: 44). Another way of looking at this is that institutions (property rights, markets) and agents (firms) are defined so that all inputs in production sets are acquired exclusively through market transactions. In the case of the laundry and electricity firms, if we allow the physical interaction to go unmarketed, then the production set of each activity can be said to be 'dependent' on the other producer's decisions. By simply 'commodifying' the interaction, the production sets are said to be 'independent'. All effects of other agents' decisions are now transmitted through parametric prices. Alternatively, by redefining the unit of production to produce clean laundry and electricity jointly, interaction is 'internalized'. It seems therefore that 'independence' of production sets is synonymous with a complete set of markets for the relevant inputs. The independence of production sets is determined by how markets, commodities, and agents are defined; it does not have a separate status.[9]

[9] Quoting from Bator (1958: 361), 'The question of whether technological external economies involve shifts of each other's production functions, or mutu-

In general-equilibrium models of private-ownership economies without organizational costs, there are two ways of describing failure: non-existence of markets and non-convexity. In these models missing markets may be called externality; they are synonymous. There is no other meaningful characterization of externality. What markets do not exist, and therefore where externality is present, are partly determined at the outset by how the agents, commodities, and markets are defined. With few exceptions these missing markets imply failure of the competitive equilibrium in Arrow's sense of 'absolute' market failure.

By redefining the entitlement space so that there are no missing markets, failure can become an exclusive prerogative of non-convexity, either because no competitive equilibrium will exist, or because the competitive equilibrium may be Pareto-suboptimal if the complete set of markets include Lindahl markets with well-specified property rights. The nature and extent of non-convexity will itself be determined by the way institutions are defined. Different entitlement structures (whether these include Pigouvian taxes, Lindahl markets, private-property rights for previously 'free' scarce resources, or any other entitlement rules that can be imagined) will lead to differences in the shape and extent of non-convexity in the production space. Though there is a sense in which non-convexity may be a feature of underlying physical reality, in the space of economic activity, non-convexity will depend largely on the way institutions are defined.

In transaction-costless general-equilibrium models, missing markets (or 'externalities') and non-convexities, and the accompanying 'absolute' market failure will all depend on how institutions have been defined at the outset. A problem with the theoretical insights gained from these models is that they cannot be easily transferred to the real world, since the existence or not of markets, and the extent and kind of non-convexities present,

ally induced movements along such functions, is purely definitional. If one chooses to define each producer's function as to give axes only to inputs and outputs that are purchased and sold, or at least "controlled," and the effects of everything else impinging on production (e.g., of humidity, apple blossoms, etc.) are built into the curvature of the function, then it follows that externalities will consist in shifts of some functions in response to movements along others. On the other hand, if, as in our apple–honey case, it seems useful to think of the production function for H as having an A-axis, then clearly, induced movement along the function is a signal of externality.' The point is that the degree of independence of production sets is based on where market interaction is defined.

no longer bear the simple relation to optimality that they have in axiomatic transaction-costless model. One can set up models to comply with the way agents, markets, and commodities are defined in the real world and then consider the kind of problems that arise. In fact this is usually the motivation behind models with missing markets. The problem for the general-equilibrium theorist, however, in drawing implications from models with non-existent markets, is that the 'absolute' market failure that they represent in the models may tell us little about whether the institutions have failed in view of the costs of organizing institutions. Observations from the real world indicate that in many circumstances the formation of markets or the enforcing of property rights is too costly. Whatever intuitions one can draw from missing-market models will be limited unless one is able to incorporate more fully those factors that determine the size and function of the economic units; the agent, the firm, property rights, and markets. Whether to rely on Pigouvian taxes, form Lindahl markets, or redefine resource ownership cannot be surmised from models that do not incorporate organizational costs. The appropriateness of the alternative entitlement structures will depend, *inter alia*, on the informational requirements of the associated institutional structure, e.g. the information required for a Pigouvian tax may be less costly to acquire than the information to determine Lindahl benchmarks.

Laffont (1988: 7) has captured the need to incorporate organizational costs into general-equilibrium models in order to allow for useful interpretation of the role of externalities, or missing markets:

Starting with an economic system, that is, given a set of economic agents and existing markets, externalities may or may not come into play. *The existence, and eventually justification, of these external effects may be understood only after an explanation of the size of economic units and a determination of the number of markets is given* [*my italics*]. Unfortunately, the conventional wisdom about these two problems is quite limited. The impossibility of excluding users of a public good, technological nonconvexities and fixed entry costs on markets, transaction costs, the availability of information, and the cost of transmitting and acquiring information appear to be fundamental determinants of the size of economic units and of the number of markets. There is no general-equilibrium analysis that, starting from an elementary definition of agents and their objectives, yields endogenously the definition of an observed economic system (in the sense mentioned above).

Laffont's quote essentially raises the problem of 'absolute' market failure discussed in the previous chapter. We are not able to say whether missing markets are a problem, or by extension, whether the given shape of production functions are a problem, unless we understand something about the organizational costs which determine the institutional structure of the economy. It would be nice if a model could be formed where the institutional structure of the economy could be determined endogenously, as Laffont envisages. It would propitiate a more useful understanding of the efficiency effects of missing markets and non-convexity in the real world, where institutional costs are pervasive. However, in the process, the very notions of market failure and externality would be transformed.

In a model that incorporates transaction costs endogenously, the relevant area of economic interaction would not be limited to action taking place once the units (agents, property rights, markets, etc.) have been defined, but would extend to the very process by which these units are being shaped. The focus will shift to economic interaction among agents in forming institutions and not just the activity of agents once institutions are already defined. While one might like to label as external effects those interactions that take place outside markets once markets have been formed, what of the interaction of agents in the process of forming markets? Is that not action outside markets? Is it not essential in determining the efficiency of the system? It would seem to be a more important kind of interaction in that it determines the efficiency of the existing institutions.[10] Many questions can be raised about useful distinctions. Will it be useful to separate interaction prior to the defining of the system with that occurring after the system is defined? Will not the system and its economic units be perpetually in a process of being redefined? An understanding of externality seems to require an understanding of how the economic units are determined, but in so doing the notion of externality itself may change beyond recognition.

[10] It is the kind of process Heller and Starrett (1976) were dealing with in discussing private-economy failure. We saw there the problems of transferring the notion of non-existence of markets to describe pre-market failure.

The discussion in this chapter reveals that what is labelled a missing market (or externality for some), or non-convexity, in the Arrow–Debreu world, is largely a matter of how institutions are defined. Where externality is present and what effects it has, depends on where one wants to draw the boundary lines of economic units; how one specifies property rights, firms, agents, markets, all determine where a market will be 'missing' and where non-convexity will be present, as well as the efficiency repercussions of these factors *vis-à-vis* the transaction-costless benchmark. The minute one is interested in evaluating the implications of a 'missing' market or a 'missing' property right or the size and function of economic units, or even the importance of some non-convexity, one has to consider the factors that determine the size and function of the units, and that takes us out of the Arrow–Debreu framework. Once outside the Arrow–Debreu framework the concepts of market failure and externality require reinterpretation.

6
Relevant Causality

1. INTRODUCTION

A recurring theme in the literature on externalities is that of uncovering the causes of market failure. Although this is a central concern in the general-equilibrium approach, it is also an issue with the phenomenological characterizations when absence of property rights or consent are viewed with an eye to their effects. Is the non-existence of property rights a cause of market failure? Is the non-existence of markets a cause of market failure? It has been argued that the ultimate cause of market failure cannot be any institution, but the cost associated with institutions, that is the presence of transaction costs. Both Bator (1958) and Arrow (1969) treated the presence of high transaction costs as a cause of market failure. I argued that the simple presence of high transaction costs impeding the formation of property rights or markets was not sufficient for failure. It could be that no property rights should be assigned or enforced in the case in question, and this would be optimal. Lack of market or high transaction costs would not necessarily imply failure. On the other hand, if market institutions were present when other non-market institutions could allocate resources better, or at less organizational cost, then this would be market failure.[1] The market would fail relative to other organizational modes.

While it may be misleading to simply point to high transaction costs as a cause of failure, there is still a basis for treating organizational costs as an important element in a causal explanation of failure. However, it has been argued that transaction costs are the sole cause of market failure. In this chapter, two related issues will be discussed. First, I will present and contest the view that transaction costs are the sole cause of market failure.

---

[1] It is not clear how institutions are to be evaluated but it is assumed that evaluation is possible, and that therefore some comparative notion of market failure would ensue.

Second, I will raise a more general methodological point about discerning causes of market failure in economic analysis.

2. TRANSACTION COSTS AS THE SOLE CAUSE OF MARKET FAILURE

With the advent of transaction-cost analysis it has been argued by some that externality is no longer a relevant or fruitful category. 'For if we could eliminate transaction costs, externality would be of no consequence' (Dahlman 1979: 161). 'Transaction costs are an appropriate and useful phenomenological category. Externalities are not' (Zerbe 1976: 32). Their basic argument is that all market failure is caused by transaction costs, that externalities, which have been viewed as a cause of market failure (by many), or as synonymous with market failure (Bator 1958), are simply instances of transaction costs and therefore deserve no special status.

Calabresi says,

If one assumes rationality, no transaction costs, and no legal impediments to bargaining, all misallocations of resource would be fully cured in the market by bargains. Far from being surprising, this statement is tautological, at least if one accepts any of the various classic definitions of misallocation (1968: 68).

Given property rights are fully specified, bargains will eliminate any inefficiencies in the system. Even increasing returns to scale will no longer present a problem, as long as the consumers are able to compensate the producer for losses incurred. A monopoly would fully discriminate. Likewise inefficiency due to externality (in the traditional sense) is no longer a problem since any Pareto-optimal improvements will be costlessly bargained away. In order for this reasoning to be correct it requires a very broad definition of transaction costs. So broad that transaction cost itself may no longer be a 'useful phenomenological category.'

Dahlman (1979: 148) argues that '[1] search and information costs, [2] bargaining and decision costs, [3] policing and enforcement costs', provide 'the first approximation to a workable concept of transaction costs . . . Yet this functional taxonomy of different transaction costs is unnecessarily elaborate: fundamentally, the three classes reduce to a single one—for they all have in common that they represent resource losses due to lack of information'. Transaction costs have been transcended for the ultimate origin of market failure: information. Information comes as close to a panacea for market failure as one can get. If there was just complete information there would be no economic problems to contend with. The cause of all evil can be derived from missing information. But is it true that all three classes of Dahlman's transaction costs represent resource losses due to lack of information? There would seem to be no problem with the first two classes, but the third class, policing and enforcement costs, seems less likely to be reducible to information costs.

Dahlman (1979: 148) says that

policing and enforcement costs are incurred because there is lack of knowledge as to whether one (or both) of the parties involved in the agreement will violate his part of the bargain: if there were adequate foreknowledge on his part, these costs could be avoided by contractual stipulations or by declining to trade with agents who would be known to avoid fulfilling their obligations. Therefore, it is really necessary to talk only about one type of transaction cost: resource losses incurred due to imperfect information.

It seems, however, that there are costs which could naturally be placed under the heading of enforcement costs that Dahlman seems to exclude and that cannot be reduced to information costs. One could categorize them as follows: (1) Costs of enforcing entitlements (defining, distributing, and protecting property rights). These are costs of setting up the process of exchange rather than costs that agents face in the process of exchange. (2) Costs of determining or enforcing gains from trade. These are the costs of getting people to agree on the share of benefits arising from an exchange. One could call these secondary entitlements, since they are posterior to property rights. Dahlman's bargaining and decision costs focus more on the costs that agents incur in finding and communicating mutual-gain opportunities, rather than the cost of actually reaching an agreement once all parties are fully informed of such opportunities.[2]

---

[2] One might prefer to call these costs of reaching agreement, bargaining costs. I opt for the more general usage of enforcement costs as it does not exclude the sense in which agreement may in certain cases be partly enforced by the structure of exchange within which the agents interact. Also, the actual reaching of an agreement is a kind of enforcement in itself.

2.1. Costs of Enforcing Property Rights (Primary Entitlements)

Dahlman excludes the first category of enforcement cost (cost of enforcing entitlements) by definition. He assumes that property rights are fully defined (and thus enforced) from the start. But this is inconsistent with an analysis of externalities. If you are going to discuss externalities you cannot start by defining them away. If property rights were indeed fully defined,[3] then property rights for air would exist, and therefore the externality associated with pollution would never arise. It must be that certain property rights are not fully defined. If there are any undefined property rights in the system, it would have to be because of the presence of enforcement costs. It remains to be seen whether these enforcement costs will be eliminated by full information.

Consider a hypothetical state where no property rights exist but information abounds. The story of the rat race comes in handy. 'In the rat race the chances of getting the cheese increase with the speed of the rat, although no additional cheese is produced' (Akerlof 1984: 27). The problem arises because of lack of information. If the rats knew how fast they could reach the cheese, how quickly they could eat, how much shoving and pushing they would have to do to safe keep their heatedly contested gnawing position, they would know beforehand the outcome of the race. In this case they could save themselves the trouble of fighting over the cheese, by appointing to each what they all know they could have achieved had they fought (property rights). There is still a chance that some rats may break the agreement in the hope that they will run off with more than had been allotted to them. If enough rats break the agreement they will end up where they started.

Rats, known for their prescience, would have avoided this problem by agreeing to punish any rat breaking the rules. The punishment would have to be tough enough to deter the rats from perpetrating the crime. Having read Becker (1968), they may allow some crimes, only as long as the cost of apprehension and conviction did not outweigh the gains from prevention. Some of the intellectual rats may wonder whether punishment

---

[3] The statement 'fully defined property rights' is ambiguous as it depends on one's definition of property rights: another poorly defined term in the literature.

should be simply a compensation rule, or should be based on a principle of retribution.[4]

According to this story, in a world where property rights had not been defined to start with, full information did lead to an efficient allocation of resources (formation of property rights). It also entailed a specific distribution of resources that was based on might. For the present purposes the only concern is with the efficiency result. Although information did the trick here, it is not clear that it would pass the test at a deeper level of analysis. In Chapter 8 I show, in a similar model of anarchy where agents have full information, that inefficiency can easily ensue. It is premature to say that where property rights are not defined, full information will suffice to extricate enforcement costs (the actual loss or resources incurred in order to form and protect property rights).

2.2. Costs of Enforcing Agreement (Secondary Entitlements)

Consider now the second category of costs, the costs of reaching an agreement that Dahlman left out of the picture. Let us assume that property rights are fully defined so one is left only with these secondary entitlements to deal with. Does information do away with the cost of reaching an agreement? Cooter (1982) has shown that complete information is not enough to ensure efficient allocation of resources, even when property rights are fully defined. Any exchange entails mutual benefits. In the market when agents are many and thus behave competitively, the gains from trade are determined by the price mechanism. However, when the agents are few, and they perceive the control they can exert, there is no reason why they should agree on how to split the gains from trade. Full information does not solve this problem. Each individual has an incentive to hold out for a larger share of the gains. If individuals were to come to any agreement the outcome would be efficient, but there is no reason why they will agree. Their respective 'hold-out' levels may be incompatible, and the exchange may never occur even though it entails mutual benefits, thus perpetuating an inefficient allocation.[5] As an alternative to

---

[4] These rats have been reading Baird and Rosenbaum (1988).

[5] Note that even if agents know each other's bargaining strategies, this does not imply that they will agree, unless one assumes a deterministic model where

the Coase Theorem, Cooter has posited the Hobbes Theorem. Accordingly, an authority is required to enforce the gains from trade, so that individuals are cut short of incessant squabbling. He argues that the real world will lie somewhere in between these polar theorems; agents will sometimes agree, and sometimes will have to be forced to agree.

The real difference in the two theorems would seem to lie in the extent of authority required. The Coase Theorem brings in authority through the back door by requiring fully defined property rights. If these property rights have been defined by consent, this consent is of a different kind from that encountered in market exchanges. For property rights to be formed by consent, an implicit or explicit agreement is required by all parties concurrently, whereas exchange agreements require binary agreements, i.e. only the two parties in exchange. So even if property rights are formed by consent, a measure of authority is implied. In the case of the Coase Theorem authority is limited to enforcing property rights, while in the Hobbes Theorem, authority is extended to the gains from trade. Either way, authority is required for any economic system to function, and full information is not enough to ensure efficiency. Information is not a panacea.

If property rights are to be formed by consensus, the costs of enforcing agreement will apply to the costs of enforcing property rights. Complete information may imply that no force need actually materialize since agents will already know the outcome of a dispute (as in the rat-race story); however, in the same way that incompatible 'hold-out' levels lead to inefficient allocations in the bargaining problem, likewise, incompatible 'threat' levels will lead to inefficient stalemates (no agreement).

It is clear that full information is not enough for an economy to be efficient. Does this imply that the elimination of transaction costs is not sufficient to eliminate market failure? It depends on how broad a notion of transaction costs one has. Dahlman's notion is too narrow. Only by extending the concept to include the two enforcement costs discussed (enforcing primary and sec-

complete information entails foreknowledge of outcome of bargaining and agents simply accept the outcome which they know will occur by 'necessity'. I deal with a similar kind of problem in Ch. 10, below.

ondary entitlements),[6] will it be true that zero transaction cost implies efficient economy. But note, it implies efficient economy, not just efficient *market* economy. In fact a zero-transaction-cost world would be a world without institutions. Institutions (in this idealized world) exist in order to facilitate transactions, in order to reduce transaction costs. Without transaction costs institutions and rules will have no economic function.

As long as the benchmark for efficiency is what can be attained in a world where there is no cost of organizing the economy (in the broadest sense of organizational costs), one can point at the presence of some organizational cost (not just information), and argue that that is what prevents the attainment of efficiency. And then it cannot be argued that organizational costs are the cause of market failure, but the cause of institutional failure generally. However, if organizational costs are going to be incorporated in the notion of efficiency, so that the benchmark of an efficient allocation of resources is one that somehow economizes (minimizes) on organizational costs given some social-welfare goal, then organizational costs cannot be treated as a cause of failure. Rather, one has to look for reasons whether and why organizational costs were not minimized. Departures from such a benchmark could not be said to be caused in general by the absence of property rights or markets or high transaction costs.

3. USEFUL SPECIFICATION OF CAUSATION

The treatment of information as a cause of market failure brings out another more general issue. When does one distinguish something as a cause of market failure or institutional failure? What makes lack of information a 'cause' of market failure? What makes absence of property rights or of markets a cause of failure? What is a good way of specifying relevant causes of market failure?

An illustration will show why the absence of organizational costs (or information costs) is not a useful way of describing

---

[6] Arrow (1970: 60) has stated that 'transaction costs are costs of running the economic system': as a definition this is broad enough to include any costs of authority required to run an economic system.

causality of failure. Imagine there existed an elixir that could solve all problems of life and create full and healthy lives. One could not say that lack of this elixir was the cause of all ailments. Microbes, weak constitutions, viruses, etc., must partake in any causal explanation of the ailment. In their presence lack of this elixir would culminate in disease, but this does not mean the missing elixir is the cause. Information has much the same function for the economy as this hypothetical elixir has for the body. Abundance of information could rid the economy from many ailments, but this does not mean that lack of information is a cause of inefficiency. Some pertinent passages from Hart and Honoré (1985) will illuminate the issue:[7]

In most cases where a fire has broken out the lawyer, the historian, and the plain man would refuse to say that the cause of fire was the presence of oxygen, though no fire would have occurred without it: they would reserve the title of cause for something of the order of a short-circuit, the dropping of a lighted cigarette, or lightning. Yet there are contexts where it would be natural to say that the presence of the oxygen was the cause of the fire. We have only to consider a factory where delicate manufacturing processes are carried on, requiring the exclusion of oxygen, to make it perfectly sensible to identify as the cause of a fire the presence of oxygen introduced by some one's mistake. The general laws which we may need to demonstrate causal connection in these two cases of fire will not tell us that in one case oxygen can be sensibly cited as the cause of fire and in the other not. Yet in making this distinction it is plain that our choice, though responsive to the varying context of the particular occasions, is not arbitrary or haphazard. The question is, 'What sort of principles guide our thoughts?' (1985: 11)

What is the basis for contrasting mere conditions from a cause?

In the case of a building destroyed by fire 'mere conditions' will be factors such as the oxygen in the air, the presence of combustible material, or the dryness of the building. In a railway accident they will be such factors as the normal speed and load and weight of the train and the routine stopping or acceleration. These factors are, of course, just those which are present alike both in the case where such accidents occur and in the normal cases where they do not; and it is this consideration that

---

[7] The literature on causation, or what constitutes a cause, is vast. My discussion here is meant merely to exemplify some issues that need to be confronted when considering causes of market failure.

leads us to reject them as the cause of the accident, even though it is true that without them the accident would not have occurred. (1985: 34)

normal conditions (and hence in causal inquiries mere conditions) are those conditions which are present as part of the usual state or mode of operation of the thing under inquiry: some of such usual conditions will also be familiar, pervasive features of the environment . . . What is abnormal in this way 'makes the difference' between the accident and things going on as usual. (1985: 35)

So oxygen and dryness of the building are the normal conditions, while lighting the match makes the difference. Naming lack of information as the cause of market failure, in some cases, is a bit like pointing at the presence of oxygen as the cause of fire. Surely if oxygen were not present the fire would not have occurred. In many cases if there were full information there would be no market failure. In keeping with the spirit of Hart and Honoré we should single out lack of information as a cause of market failure if this represented the 'abnormal' element in our account of the event. In order to discern departures from 'normal' amounts of information, one needs to define what one considers the normal amount of information in the environment. Doubtless it would not be full information. Increasing returns to scale should remain a legitimate cause of market failure even though full information would allow the producer to perfectly discriminate with prices and so eliminate inefficiency. It is also important to note that what may be a cause of inefficiency of the market may not be for other institutions.

In summary, I have argued that organizational costs cannot be seen as an ultimate cause of all market failure. While one could say that there would be no market failure (or failure of any institution), if organizational costs (in the broadest sense of the term) were not present, this would not provide a useful understanding of causality of failure. The discussion by Hart and Honoré illustrates why and suggests the need to form an idea of 'normal' levels of organizational costs in order to arrive at a relevant concept of causality of market failure.

7

Underlying Motivations

Definition, define thyself. Dictionary entries are a far cry from what philosophers and mathematicians call definition. Dictionaries are for facilitating our negotiations in the language, and for that purpose it proves efficacious to resort only here and there to definition in the philosophers' and mathematicians' sense. Definition in the philosophers' and mathematicians' sense remains an important matter, however, deserving of a name. Such will be my sense of the word . . . (Quine 1987: 43)

1. INTRODUCTION

In this chapter I will try to illustrate the sources of the many meanings of externality in the literature. In section 2, I discuss two generic senses of externality which make no reference to specific institutions. These derive from two different connotations of the words external–internal, which seem to be present in most characterizations in the literature. Section 3 tries to bring out more clearly these two generic senses of externality, showing how they can be easily confused, and why there is good reason not to associate externality with a specific system, e.g. private-ownership economy. In sections 4 and 5, I discuss some of the difficulties, or problems, that existing characterizations of externality confront when they try to form a narrower view of externality than general interdependence or general institutional failure (or market failure). In section 6, I discuss two central motivations underlying the many characterizations of externality that are lost, or not well served, because of the inability to separate and treat independently the two generic senses of externality. I discuss two consistent approaches to the concept of externality based on the development of the two separate motivations. One approach, the consequentialist (sect. 6.1) sees externalities in terms of consequences, specifically as institutional inefficiency, which is a broader category than market failure. In the appendix to this chapter I offer a lengthy illustration of the difference between market failure and institutional inefficiency. The other approach, called the intrinsic-feature approach (sect. 6.2), emphasizes some intrinsic characteristic such as the absence of property rights or markets, in identifying externality.

The purpose of this chapter will be to throw some light on the question of what externality is by recognizing a class of concepts involved in this apparently homogeneous notion. It will help us bring out some of the motivations behind the many characterizations, to understand the basis of the distinctions and to evaluate their importance. It will show how central issues concerning institutional choices and behavioural assumptions have not been confronted. The object is not so much to look for the 'right' or 'best' definition of externality, but to relate the analysis of externality to the issues of institutional and behavioural choices for resource allocation.

2. TWO GENERIC SENSES: INTERDEPENDENCE AND INEFFICIENCY

The externality–internality distinction seems to have two generic senses which the many characterizations of externality draw on. These senses emanate from a different use of the roots 'external–internal'. One sense, which I will call the 'interdependence sense', comes from treating 'external' as activity that has effects outside some unit of account, whereby unit of account may be an agent, a household, a firm, an organization, or any aggregate of these so that the entire economic system could also be a unit of account. In contrast, in the other sense, which I will call the 'inefficiency sense', 'external' denotes action that was not properly 'accounted for' by some unit of account, or that the action taking place within some unit of account was somehow inefficient.

The first sense of 'external' (interdependence sense) also has the sense that those affected do not have complete control over the activity in question, so it's often associated with some kind of coercion. If the individual is the unit of account, all interdependence among individuals is 'external', since interdependence implies that an action by one individual will have effects on another. There is no attempt here to distinguish between separate consequences of some action. If the action by one individual has even a slight effect on another person, then this action will be deemed 'external'. The only 'internal' activity would be action that an individual takes that has no effect whatsoever on other individuals (this would entail a small subset of overall activity). As long as external refers to the individual, the externality is simply general interdependence.[1] Furthermore, there is no reference to institutions and thus any kind of institutional interdependence would be included in this sense since it would still entail influence by others over an agent's activities. Market interdependence, barter exchange, interaction within an organization according to the rules of that hierarchy, etc., would all entail external influence among agents. Importantly, this sense of 'externality' makes no reference to consequences of actions in terms of efficiency, it simply refers to interdependence; an 'external' effect is simply influence working outside some unit of account. If one were to look at activity from the vantage point of the system, so that the entire economic system were the unit of account, then all interdependence would be 'internal' to the system, i.e. all interaction would have effects within the system and there would be no external activity.

As long as one refers either to the individual from which all action ultimately originates, or the entire system within which all action takes place, 'external' and 'internal' are unambiguous. However, when referring to some intermediate unit of action like the firm, external and internal become somewhat ambiguous. For instance, activity by the firm that affects individuals within the firm may be thought of as 'internal' activity, but since labour is a potential resource for other firms, much of this activity would have some effects outside the firm and thus should be treated as 'external'. This is simply a reflection of the fact that interdepen-

---

[1] Buchanan and Tullock (1962) make a distinction between general interdependence and coercion, sometimes treating 'externality' as coercion. Coercion is viewed very broadly, it entails any influence one can exert on others, even market interaction would be some kind of coercion since decisions are taken by binary consent rather than unanimously. The distinction between general interdependence and coercion is based on the notion of unanimity, any decision not taken unanimously would entail coercion. This is one way of narrowing the scope of 'external' activity. Of course, unanimity could also be seen as a coercive process. It may diminish powers to control others or it may greatly enhance those powers.

dence is pervasive in a system, and there are very few actions that can be taken by some unit of account that will not have some effect on other units of account.

The second sense of externality comes from viewing 'external' (inefficiency sense) as action that is inefficient with respect to some objective; that somehow was not properly 'accounted for' by the unit of account.[2] For instance, an agent being rational will always 'internalize' activity with respect to her own welfare, i.e. will appropriately weight consequences of her actions given her environment. A firm will be 'internalizing' if it attains its objective of profit-maximizing. The market system will have 'internalized' activity if it attains some objective set for it, e.g. Pareto-optimality. Note that while agents may be 'internalizing' with respect to their separate objectives, their actions may be 'external' or inefficient with respect to some other global objective, in which case the institutions through which agents are interacting have not been able to 'internalize' their activity. Activity is external when institutions have not been able to 'perceive' or weigh certain consequences of actions appropriately.[3] In this sense externality is simply some kind of institutional inefficiency. It refers to the consequences of actions in terms of efficiency. As it does not refer to a specific institution it can be a broader notion than market failure; it can refer to the failure of any institution. To say that activity has been 'internalized' in this sense simply implies that the institution(s) in question has efficiently coordinated activity with respect to some objective.

These two generic senses of externality tend to gravitate towards each other. When one says that activity is internal to some unit of account it seems to imply that activity is fully 'controlled'. But while all interdependence is internal (interdependence sense) to the system, this does not imply that the system is able to 'internalize' (inefficiency sense) this activity with respect to some overall social-welfare objective. Both senses of 'external'

---

[2] While the inefficiency usually associated with externality is that of Pareto-suboptimality, I think it useful not to constrain this generic sense to a specific notion of inefficiency.

[3] This language gives the impression that institutions are like agents capable of conscious control over action. When we say that an action was 'internalized' by an institution or by the formation of property rights, it elicits a sense that institutions are able to consciously control actions. One could say that 'internalization' by an institution is a kind of 'institutional rationality'.

seem to be associated with some kind of lack of control. Interdependence implies that agents no longer have full control over outcomes. Inefficiency implies that activity was not optimally 'controlled'. But these are different senses of control. The discussion in the next section will try to bring out more clearly the two generic senses and suggest how they can easily be confused.

3. UNIT OF ACTION: DISTINGUISHING BETWEEN THE TWO GENERIC SENSES OF EXTERNALITY

In a simple Prisoners' Dilemma if one were to take the vantage point of one of the prisoners, one would advise the prisoner to follow the dominant strategy that is likely to lead the two prisoners to the low-level trap. From the vantage point of each agent this is the rational thing to do. What is an efficient act from one perspective is inefficient from a more distant perspective. It is with the ability to view the combined action of the agents, that one perceives of an alternative route. If only the unit of action was the combined action of the agents there would be no problem; if these agents were somehow unified there would be no Prisoners' Dilemma. The separation of decision-makers seems to be at the heart of the inefficiency. But this is misleading, since while it gives rise to the possibility of inefficiency, it is not the cause of inefficiency.

Alec Nove (1983) points out that under capitalism, the profit of each separately owned unit can contradict the profitability (interest) of the whole. He asks whether one can transcend this fragmentation if the means of production are commonly owned and answers in the negative.

Externalities arise not because of separation of ownership, but because of separation of decision-making units. Even in a university, room-allocation of timetable changes by one faculty office can have deleterious effects on students in other faculties, effects which are external to the faculty office in question. What is taken into account depends on the area of responsibility of the decision-maker. This is partly due to the interest (the decision-maker will be judged by how well he or she carries out his/her prescribed responsibilities), and partly due to information flows (effects external to the office concerned may simply not be known to the decision maker). (Nove 1983: 69)

In this view externality is not an inherent feature of a private-ownership economy, and non-existence of private-property rights is not the key element inducing externalities but the separation of decision-making units. No reference to a specific institution is made. This allows Nove to consider the presence of externalities in centralized economies, otherwise they would be precluded by definition wherever ownership was common. However, separation of decision-making could not be a sufficient test of externality in the sense of inefficiency, since that would identify externality with any interdependence.[4] Both generic senses of externality are present here: (1) general interdependence, as separation of decision-makers implies that there are effects 'external' (interdependence sense) to the agent, and (2) inefficiency, or effects 'external' (inefficiency sense) to the organization, arising from a dysfunction between decision-makers and areas of responsibility. Decision-makers have been allotted areas of responsibility in ways that do not make them 'appropriately' sensitive to the consequences of their actions.[5] Action is said to be 'internalized' (inefficiency sense) when the institutions ensure that they are coordinated with the organization's overall welfare objective.

Consequences of action may be unaccounted for when the unit of decision-making, or action, is different from the sphere of action being evaluated. In the case of a Prisoners' Dilemma, the sphere of action is the combined action of the agents, while the unit of action, or decision-making, is a subset of the sphere of action. As it were, the outcomes of the game are a function of the combined action of the agents while the source of decision is separate. It is this dysfunction that gives rise to the possibility of inefficiency, but importantly, it should not be seen as the cause of inefficiency.[6] Institutions provide a way of overcoming this dysfunction. By coordinating decisions of separate agents in certain ways, institutions can provide ways of 'internalizing' (efficiency sense) consequences of actions. The institution fulfils the

---

[4] The ease with which the two senses of externality can be conflated is apparent here; general interdependence gives rise to the possibility of inefficiency but is not a cause. To say that externalities are due to the separation of decision-making units makes it ambiguous as to which sense is implied.

[5] An area of responsibility can be envisioned as a set of constraints or incentives on action.

[6] In the same way that interdependence gives rise to the possibility of inefficiency.

task of a decision-maker at the level of the unit of action, it plays the role of a 'collective mind'. By reshaping the boundaries of agents' actions, by altering in effect the subjective outcomes that agents associate with their individual actions, the several consequences of agents' interaction are accounted for by the institution.[7]

An important point in contrasting the two generic senses of 'external' is made apparent in Nove's quote. The fact that activity takes place within an organization does not mean that all consequences of agents' action will be taken into account.[8] This will depend on whether the organization is able to shape agents' pay-off structures (altering the domain of responsibility) with incentive mechanisms at the organization's disposal, in order to align the separate decisions with the collective objective. The virtue of the market when it works is that it coordinates agents' decisions so that those consequences of individual action relevant for the sphere of action are 'internalized' (efficiency sense).[9] What consequences of action are taken into account and how they are weighted will depend on the particulars of the institutional structure, which should depend on the objective that is set for the collective outcome.

It is a misconception to always treat groupings of agents as the replacement of multiple decision-makers by a single decision-maker. While there may be occasions where it is convenient for analysis to make such assumptions, it is important to realize that such decision units are composite structures made up of several decision units.

The formation of decision units arises out of physiological necessity (as in the family), out of economic and social convenience (the kinship

[7] Unanimity might be thought to eliminate the dysfunction between the sphere of action and the unit of decision-making, since the unit of decision-making seems to be equivalent to the sphere of action. However, this is misleading, since if there are costs to decision-making (especially high under a rule of unanimity), then the consequences of organizing activity through unanimous decisions must also be taken into account, i.e. not all consequences of actions (including organizational consequences) are being taken into account appropriately.

[8] Here one sees the ease with which one confuses the two senses of internal. The fact that there is interdependence internal to the organization does not imply that it is 'internalized' in the sense of efficiency. It depends on whether the organization can ensure an appropriate incentive structure for those working within it.

[9] Another ambiguity with the word 'internalize' is that it sometimes refers to the agents taking the action, and sometimes to the institutions that make the agent act efficiently.

group), out of economic advantage (the firm), or out of the need for protection (the militia). Institutions, as the working rules of going concerns, define these decision units *vis-à-vis* other decision units, and they give structure and regularity to the internal workings of such units. (Bromley 1989: 52)

Neglect of the composite nature of many decision units has led economists to view centralized economies as avoiding externalities, in that the units of decision (centralized state) are identical with the unit of action (overall social interaction), the implication being that all decisions are internal to the organization. Here we can see how the two senses of externality are superimposed: while action is internal to the centralized state in the sense of interdependence occurring within the state, this does not imply that interaction will be efficient. The fact that final decisions are taken at the centre disguises the fact that these are based on myriads of decisions at lower levels of the hierarchy, and that for each agent in the hierarchy to be making the appropriate decisions requires that the organizational incentives are such that the 'important' consequences are taken into account and weighted 'appropriately'. Whether the collective decision-making of some hierarchic structure can 'internalize' (efficiency sense) the actions of its constituent agents will depend on the mechanism by which decisions are taken. The paradigm of a firm replacing the market in order to reduce transaction costs, and thereby 'internalizing' those costs, bias us towards treating increased hierarchy as increased efficiency ('internalization'); however, a market's existence (replacement of a firm) must also be rationalized on transaction-cost-reducing grounds. The 'decentralization' associated with the market has a counterpart in hierarchies, in that decisions by the agents within them are taken separately. The effectiveness of market and hierarchic organizations, or any institution, will depend on the nature of the interaction of agents and the costs of forming institutions.

'Internalizing' in the sense of efficiency can be thought of as a process of weighting the consequences of action according to some welfare function. In a Prisoners' Dilemma each agent will 'internalize' (take efficient account of) the consequences of her actions as they affect her welfare, the others' actions will not be treated as control variables. Rationality insures that each agent 'internalizes' (efficiency sense) all the actions she controls with respect to her own welfare, i.e. with respect to her own welfare she puts the appropriate weights on the consequences of her actions. As one abstracts and considers the welfare of both agents (or either agent), and considers the combined consequences of the agents' actions (i.e. treats the actions of both agents as control variables), one can see that what is efficient for both to do, is not efficient for each to do separately. Imagine a disinterested observer, or enforcer, who could alter the pay-off structures that the individual agents perceive by forming constraints on action (penalizing or subsidizing actions), and thus make them reap the cooperative gains. If the enforcer can do this then she will have 'internalized' (efficiency sense) the actions of the agents[10] with respect to some social-welfare objective. We might say that there is 'externality' (inefficiency sense) when the institutions or constraints that the agents face do not coordinate their actions so that some social-welfare objective is attained (the enforcer was unable to force proper accounting of their actions).[11]

3.1. Dividing the Individual into Sub-units: Externality within the Individual

Till now I have assumed that individuals can 'internalize' (efficiency sense) activity with respect to their own objective, i.e. they are rational. An interesting discussion by Elster (1989) on weakness of will shows how both senses of externality may pertain to the individual. He says: 'In a group of individuals, each can impose negative externalities on everyone else. In a succession of "selves", earlier selves cannot be hurt by the later ones' (1989: 23). Earlier selves, however, can harm later selves. By treating the

[10] It will look as if the agents are sensitive to the effects of their actions on others but they are no more sensitive than before, they simply face new constraints; looking from their eyes they are always internalizing with respect to their individual objectives.

[11] Further removed, one could treat the enforcer as an actor within an even larger unit of account, where new consequences arise 'external' (interdependence sense) to the enforcer. In this case, the question becomes how to form constraints on the enforcer's activity in order to attain some welfare objective in this larger unit of account. A real conceptual difficulty arises when one treats all enforcers endogenously, since there is no way to 'internalize' the 'internalizer' (efficiency sense). I deal with this issue at length in Ch. 10, below.

agent as a multiple-self, (in this case the separate selves are determined by a separation in time),[12] one can treat the agent much like a social system. Negative or positive externalities (interdependence sense) refer to negative and positive effects that the earlier self can have on the latter. This interdependence raises the possibility of inefficiency.

Whatever its shape, there must be some temporal profile of smoking and not smoking that maximizes lifetime utility, keeping other things constant. Assuming I know what that profile is, will I choose it? If I am subject to weakness of will, I will not. Instead, I will yield to temptation on each occasion, thereby making myself worse off at (almost) all times than I would have been had I abstained or chosen the optimal profile. (Elster 1989: 23)

Each present self is maximizing welfare with respect to that self's welfare function, i.e. she 'internalizes' (efficiency sense) activity. However, with respect to the composite self, interdependence is not being 'internalized' (efficiency sense). Weakness of will refers to the lack of control of some central enforcer over the composite self. If the composite self was 'rational' it could overcome this weakness of will and ensure that the proper constraints are set on the successive 'present' selves.[13]

4. EXTERNALITY AS A KIND OF INTERDEPENDENCE

The preceding section was meant to emphasize the difference between the two senses of externality (as well as the ease of confusing the two) and to show how certain aspects of economic activity (or general social activity) can be described in terms of these two distinct senses. The question I will turn to now is whether these two generic senses can have some useful function as classificatory principles in economics, i.e. to investigate whether there are some grounds for using the word 'externality' to describe some special category of economic activity, or some

---

[12] There are many ways to treat the agent as a multiple set of selves, e.g. H. Margolis (1982) considers a separation between a 'self-interest' self and a 'group-interest' self, (he does this in order to solve the voters paradox). For many other ways see Elster (1986).

[13] Schelling (1984: ch. 3) discusses this composite self as a manager of the several selves.

causal mechanism of failure. It is clear that the two generic
senses of externality are very different and though one may draw
connections between the two, it is important that one remains
aware of their separateness. In this section I will consider
whether externality in the sense of interdependence can have a
useful function, while in section 5 I will consider externality in
the sense of inefficiency.

In the first generic sense of externality, activity that is 'external' to an agent simply implies interdependence. This is not a
particularly interesting category: after all, why call interdependence externality and not just leave it as interdependence? In
many characterizations of externality, while 'external' essentially
meant interdependence, externality was seen as a certain kind of
interdependence, not so broad that it encompassed all forms of
interdependence. The distinction between technological and pecuniary externalities, for instance, was in part a subdivision
between kinds of interdependence. While this subdivision was
often interpreted as being between efficient and inefficient interdependence, in many characterizations externality was seen to
have a separate existence, irrespective of whether it led to efficiency or not. Accordingly, externality was seen as a special kind
of interdependence that could be identified independently of an
evaluation of consequences. There seemed to be an implicit belief
that behind the distinction between market and non-market interdependence there was a more solid 'real' basis distinguishing
interdependence labelled 'externality' and other kinds of interdependence. This is apparent both in Baumol and Oates's (1975)
characterization, which tries to establish externality independently
of inefficiency and institutions, and in Arrow's (1970), and Heller
and Starrett's (1976), which treat externality as one kind of
underlying cause of the non-existence of markets. While many
characterizations of externality seem to imply some underlying
category of interdependence, it remains unclear how such a category could be formed, or what its value would be.

4.1. *Kinds of Interdependence without Reference to Institutions*

One seemingly obvious way to discriminate between kinds of
interdependence among agents would be according to the kind of
institutions that mediate interaction. An alternative, which I will

consider first, is to see if there is a useful way to distinguish between different kinds of underlying interdependence without reference to institutions? There has often been a sense that externality could be associated with some kind of underlying physical interdependence among agents that exists independently of institutions. Could we set up some kind of taxonomy of different types of physical interdependence, some of which we might call 'externalities'? Notions like 'non-rivalry' in consumption, or 'non-excludability' of goods, seem to provide a way of distinguishing goods (and potential interdependencies among agents desiring these goods) by invoking physical attributes of goods. But though there are surely some physical attributes that contribute to goods being non-rivalrous or non-excludable, non-rivalry and non-excludability are largely determined by institutions,[14] so they would not be suitable as categories of purely physical interdependence.

In general one could try to separate the physical world which sets rigid constraints on human activity, from the institutional world which represents human constraints on human activity. Interdependence among individuals is determined both by the underlying state of nature and the institutions that mediate human interaction. The fact that I like food and you like food and there is a given amount of food in the world, and we have certain powers to act on our desires, implies a potential interdependence that is in the state of nature (it is a given). The nature of interdependence, or how we actually interact, will also depend on the institutions (or lack of institutions) that mediate our interaction. If we are able to identify the underlying physical interdependencies among agents, we may acquire a better understanding of how well institutions are likely to deal with these interdependencies. For instance, knowledge of the physical and biological nature of fisheries will be crucial in understanding how alternative institutional mechanisms will cope with the allocation of fishing activity.

---

[14] See my discussion in Ch. 4, sect. 2.1, above. The publicness or privateness of a good will depend on the way that property rights have been defined, in a transaction-costless world one can always redefine property rights for a non-rivalrous good so that it becomes rivalrous. In a world where organizational costs matter, the publicness of a good will be determined both by the physical attributes of the good, and the nature of the organizational costs of defining property rights over the good.

Although it is useful to recognize the underlying forms of interdependency, it is far from clear that some category of physical interdependence should be singled out as 'externality'; it is hard to envisage the classificatory principle. Non-convexity in production and utility functions,[15] detrimental interaction, beneficial interaction,[16] lack of information, too few agents, are all terms that could be used to describe certain underlying aspects of interdependence (prior to institutions), but there does not seem to be any justification for treating any of these descriptions of interdependence as a separate category called 'externality'. Recall that in terms of physical interaction, the consumption of an orange by one individual deprives another individual of consuming that orange, and is thus detrimental interaction in the same way that smoking a cigar would deprive some individual of 'clean' air. One tack might be to see which underlying physical attributes make it difficult to define private-property rights over goods. The problem is that there are likely to be many such attributes, all of which may affect the degree of difficulty in forming private-property rights, and there would be no rationale for picking some 'level of difficulty' in forming private-property rights to distinguish them. Finally, one might try to distinguish among different kinds of underlying interdependence by the strength of interdependence, or the degree of influence exerted by one individual over another,[17] but again the problem of demarcation would arise.

There is an attribute of individual preferences that could warrant the epithet 'external' without reference to institutions or consequences, and that is non-selfish sentiment. One might want to call altruism an 'external' preference since it entails sentiment about other agents, while preference for some good that one seeks for one's own benefit (but others also may desire) may not be labelled 'external'. This would dissociate the meaning of exter-

[15] Recall (Ch. 5, above) that non-convexity may depend on how institutions define goods and thus may be viewed as partly determined by institutions.

[16] The terms 'beneficial interaction' and 'detrimental interaction' would be used in this context to signify some description of potential physical interdependence among agents where the actions that one agent undertakes have beneficial and detrimental effects on another agent respectively, e.g. singing may have beneficial effects, while drinking water may deprive the other individual of some good.

[17] This would correspond to Meade's (1952) attempt to characterize externalities by the degree to which the influence that one's actions had on another represented 'appreciable effects'.

nality from consequences of actions, institutions, or from the fact of interdependence. Not that 'external' preferences would not have consequences, but that their being labelled 'external' would not be linked to the fact of there being consequences or interdependence. One would not call preferences 'external' because others have influence on you, since that would reinstate the fact of interdependence as a basis of classification. Preferences would be 'external' for the simple fact that they refer to others' preferences, without reference to their decisions having an impact. It seems, however, that the scope of such a characterization would be very limited. One might want to call such preferences 'external' but not 'externality' which seems to bring in some aspects of interdependence or consequences.

Besides this very narrow use of the word 'external', it seems to me that trying to narrow the notion of externality to a subset of general interdependence without reference to consequences or institutions proves to be a questionable task. And even if one did form such a category of underlying interdependence, there remains the question of what motivation would there be for such a category.

4.2 Kinds of Interdependence as Classified by Institutions

One way of narrowing 'externality' to a subset of general interdependence could be by classifying different kinds of interdependence according to different kinds of institutions. For instance, 'externality' might be interdependence where private-property rights have not been defined, or interdependence where markets have not been defined. At first glance this seems to be a simple way of classifying different forms of interdependence, but actually, once transaction costs are brought into the models, or one looks at the real world, these notions become highly blurred.

Trying to establish a definition of private-property rights, or institutions in general, is a task rife with problems.[18] If the basis

---

[18] Definitions of private-property rights, or property rights more generally, vary a lot. A small sample will make this apparent: 'The most general definition of an individual's sets of property is simply his opportunity set. Given this definition property rights are always defined' (Bush and Mayer 1974). Another definition has it that ownership rights are 'the expectation a person has that his decision about the uses of certain resources will be effective' (Alchian and Allen 1969: 158) 'Property is also the legal ability to impose costs on others' (Bromley

of such a definition is the degree of control that a private-property right offers an agent over certain activities, one is back to the problem of determining how much control warrants calling a property right 'private'. What degree of excludability must there be? The same kind of difficulties would arise if one treated externality as the non-existence of markets. As we saw with Arrow's strict definition of markets every 'imperfect' market would entail externality, and it is unlikely that in a world of transaction costs there would be any perfect market. The problem with both ideal types of 'private-property rights' and 'markets' is that most activity in the real world does not conform to these ideal types: accordingly almost all activity would be externality. Of course all non-capitalist societies would be externality-infested, but even market economies have a rich variety of institutions and entitlements that would not conform to these ideal types;[19] not to mention that all forms of activity organized through some kind of hierarchic structure would be seen as externality.

James Coleman (1990: 20–1) offers a general classification of interdependence of actions. Accordingly interdependence can be subdivided into six categories, (1) externality, (2) bilateral exchange, (3) markets, (4) collective decisions, (5) formal organizations, (6) norm-guided action. He doesn't actually define externality but alludes to some examples like the 'tragedy of the commons' to offer a sense of this kind of interaction. In fact, one can deduce from his subdivisions that externality is simply 'unorganized' interdependence, or non-institutional interdependence. This has some intuitive merit in that it does not become as broad a category as non-existence of property rights or markets, yet there is still the difficulty of identifying what is unorganized activity. Are imperfect markets a mix of markets and unorganized activity? Do Akerlof's (1984) markets for proxies represent market interdependence or externality interdependence?

In the externality literature most associations of externality with the non-existence of some institution reflect a concern about

1989: 206) 'Institutions are really nothing but specific collections of attenuated property rights' (Dahlman 1980: 213).

[19] A look at Schmid (1987: 189–93), who offers a long list of the kinds of rules and entitlements present in private-ownership economies, will convince one of the extent of oversimplification that terms like 'private property' entail.

the resultant consequences of the lack of an institution. It is clear that once transaction costs are incorporated in models there is no one-to-one correspondence between the presence of some institution and efficiency. Non-existence of property rights, markets, or institutions in general, cannot be said to lead to inefficiency unless one knows something more about the organizational costs and the welfare objective. It would seem, then, that distinguishing kinds of interdependence by the kind of institution that mediates interaction, in order to infer inefficiency, would not be a good basis for making such distinctions.

5. EXTERNALITY AS INEFFICIENCY

The second generic sense of 'external' (inefficiency sense) I discussed, treated externality as action that was not properly 'accounted for' by some unit of account. This is the generic sense that Bator (1958) is alluding to when treating externality as equivalent to market failure; it is activity 'external' to 'price-taking agents', activity outside the purview of the market system. But if externality is simply another word for market failure, or institutional failure, why come up with another word for market failure; the notion of externality becomes redundant. Bator tried to justify the separate need for a category of externality by breaking it down into separate causes of market failure, trying to distinguish institutional from non-institutional causes of market failure, but this proved to be problematic.

Arrow (1970), and Heller and Starrett (1976), are in the tradition of Bator, yet they do not equate externality with market failure; as a result it is not clear what 'external' refers to. While Bator treats increasing returns to scale in production as a cause of externality—in the sense that market institutions cannot quite 'control', 'internalize' or bring within its accounting the actions involved in this kind of interdependency—Arrow, and Heller and Starrett, do not consider increasing returns to scale as externality or a cause of externality. Inefficiency is not what makes actions 'external' to the system. Why abandon Bator's use of external? What new sense could take its place? Bator identified externality with Pareto-inefficiency, but his causal explanation of inefficiency seemed incomplete. The market was not taking certain actions or consequences into account, often because property rights did not exist. But why did property rights not exist for some goods? The reply would be 'transaction costs', but then the diagnosis of market failure is premature since if transaction costs are legitimate costs, and if property rights are not formed for that reason, it may have been optimal that the market was not taking certain consequences of actions into account. While increasing returns to scale were a familiar source of market failure, failure associated with non-existence of property rights, and for that matter markets, was more perplexing since it required further explanation (i.e. why the market did not exist), and an understanding of non-existence seemed to require a reinterpretation of market failure.

Arrow associated externality with non-existence of markets and in particular a subset of non-existence of markets. For Arrow externality was related to inefficiency, but wasn't coextensive with it. It seems that Arrow viewed externality as a causal factor of inefficiency, a phenomenon like increasing returns to scale that caused market failure but had a separate existence of its own (a special kind of underlying interdependence). Though Arrow's work was very perceptive and paved the way for important reinterpretations of key concepts as well as indicating a need for a methodological revamping, the concept of externality remained illusive; in fact, it lost a certain semantic clarity that Bator's characterization had. By making externality a subset of inefficiency and losing the sense in which 'external' was equated with actions that had escaped the account of the market system, Arrow had to find another criterion to identify externality. Could non-existence of markets be the criterion? But Arrow treated non-existence of markets as a broader category than externalities, i.e. externalities were certain instances of non-existence but not all, so some other criterion is needed. Arrow does not provide another criterion nor do Heller and Starrett who take a somewhat similar approach, and we are left with the impression that there is some underlying phenomenon called externality which we cannot fully comprehend. As discussed above, even if we could identify specific underlying phenomena or interdependencies it does not seem likely that 'externality' would be an appropriate epithet.

Bator's identification of externality with inefficiency has a semantic appeal, but as we saw, the absolute market failure that he discussed did not tackle the inefficiency that seemed to be implied by externality. The fact that institutions were costly and that the concept of market failure should somehow include that fact, was the important breakthrough inherent in the 'modern' view. The problem with Bator's absolute failure was that it simply equated the existence of transaction costs with failure, optimality being an ideal state where institutions are costless. Though institutions mattered, they were not made part of the calculus of optimality. If institutions are costly, maybe the given institutions are not the best? Shouldn't the cost of institutions be a variable that is included in the optimization calculus, and if so, shouldn't the concept of market failure be adjusted appropriately? It was this kind of reasoning that led Arrow to the concept of relative market failure and Heller and Starrett to private-economy failure. This process entailed a fundamental methodological departure from the Arrow–Debreu general-equilibrium model, requiring a reinterpretation of central concepts. The new views on market failure carried important insights, but were incomplete and vague. Their reliance on the concept of non-existence of markets served as an anchor preventing them from completing the break with absolute market failure. Non-existence of markets belies the comparative nature of failure; failure of the market relative to other modes of organization.

Institutional failure and market failure remain to be better defined. However, defining externality as institutional failure, or activities and consequences of activities that are outside the system's purview, seems to make it redundant. Why not call inefficiency (however defined) by its name? Finally, attempts to treat externality as a subset of market failure, or as a particular cause of failure do not seem to hold any promise.

6. UNDERLYING MOTIVATIONS: TREATING INEFFICIENCY AND INTERDEPENDENCY SEPARATELY

Most traditional characterizations of externality make reference to both generic senses of externality. On the one hand, in the generic sense of interdependence, 'external' would refer to some kind of lack of control by the agent, or coercion (external influence), or simply activity taking place outside some institution ('external to the market', or 'lack of property rights'). On the other hand, it was often used at the same time to denote inefficiency; an inability of some institution to 'take into account' action in accordance with Pareto-optimality. As my earlier discussion showed (section 3), however, there is no necessary connection between the two generic senses. A lot of the difficulties in characterizations of externality seem to derive from an intermingling of these two senses. Attempts, for instance, to forge intimate connections between activity not taking place within a market (or the non-existence of markets) and inefficiency tended to confuse. The confusion on the relationship between the 'existence' of externality and the 'consequences' of externality is another instance of confusing two separate generic senses.[20]

More importantly, this intermingling of the two generic senses of externality obscured some underlying motivations behind the two senses. In the case of the general-equilibrium approach, where the emphasis was on inefficiency, the connection with the first sense (interdependence sense) in the form of non-existence of markets (activity outside markets), seemed to stunt the development of a different understanding of market failure that Arrow (1970), and Heller and Starrett (1976) were driving at. On the other hand, there is another motivation that may derive from the first generic sense (kinds of interdependence), and that seems to underlie many characterizations, that is encumbered by a concern for consequences. Coercion, or lack of control over certain activities, is often seen as a problem in itself irrespective of overall economic inefficiency. Separation of kinds of activity by whether activity takes place through certain institutions, or by certain processes, without reference to consequences in terms of Pareto-optimality, may be justified on libertarian grounds. One could say that the two generic senses of externality are invoked by different motivations: first, a consequentialist concern that sees institutions primarily as instruments in advancing some welfare objective, and draws on the generic sense of externality as inefficiency; secondly, a non-consequentialist concern that values institutions, or forms of interdependence, on other grounds than

---

[20] With the two generic senses, the first (interdependence) leads to a sense of the existence of some phenomena, while the second is institutional inefficiency, and does not derive from the first.

efficiency, and draws on the generic sense of externality as inter-dependence, or kinds of interdependence.

In the remainder of this chapter I will try to pursue these two underlying motivations that seem to figure in most characteriza-tions of externality, but get obscured by not being dealt with explicitly. Under the heading of 'The Consequentialist Approach' I will develop the concern with inefficiency that underlies many of the attempts to understand externality, and which can be associated with the generic sense of externality as inefficiency. Under a separate heading entitled 'The Intrinsic-Characteristic Approach', I will develop the concern with the nature of interde-pendence, irrespective of whether there is inefficiency. I use this heading since the motivation being described seems to emphasize some intrinsic characteristic such as absence of property rights or markets, in distinguishing between different kinds of interdepen-dence. Naturally, this later approach can be associated with the generic sense of externality as interdependence.

6.1. The Consequentialist Approach

It is tempting to conclude after close inspection that all market failures are equivalent to external effects (inefficiency sense). In all instances of market failure certain activities are not accounted for or captured by the existing institutions. Any activity that is not harnessed to promote efficiency implies the existence of some unaccounted-for effects (effects not captured by the system). The rules or entitlements in the system are deficient. They are unable to fully capture all the relevant consequences of action. To a greater or lesser extent they guide our action into socially less productive activity. Rather than promoting our mutually benefi-cial interests, our conflicts surface instead, or we miss opportuni-ties to promote our mutual interests. I will argue that from one view, the concept of externality (in the sense of inefficiency) leads us to a notion of institutional failure that is broader than the notion of market failure.

Ledyard's (1976) idea of net optimality prompts the following thought-experiment.[21] Rather than seeking the minimum conditions required for the decentralized market system to be

---

[21] See Nelson (1981: 98) for a similar notion of net optimality.

Pareto-optimal, consider an alternative programme. Imagine a programme that could be run on a computer where one could specify (1) a behavioural model of the individual such that individuals maximize their own utility functions as in the general-equilibrium models, and where concern for others was not ruled out; (2) production functions representing the state of technology (which may or may not be fully convex); and (3) institutions and the cost functions associated with institutions (one could say institution functions representing the state of technology of creating and enforcing institutions). For the purposes of this discussion, institutions may be seen as any rules or regularities of economic interaction. This would include such things as entitlement structures (different kinds of property rights, entitlement to the product of one's labour, rules of exchange, etc.) and governance structures (firm hierarchies, governments, etc.). The computer would be asked to organize the economy in such a way as to maximize some social-welfare function. It would be selecting those institutions that best promoted social-welfare. It cannot be predicted what institutions will be provided or what the scope of the market would be. It may be that a centrally planned economy would be more efficient than a market economy, or some mix of market and planning institutions would be optimal. Whatever the system, it would achieve a kind of '*net* optimality, the level of social satisfaction attained after institutional costs are netted out' (Ledyard 1976: 26).

Depending on the social-welfare function being maximized one would get different results. If the social-welfare function was to include some criteria of justice or liberalism, it is likely that another set of institutions would be optimal. The 'optimal' institutions would vary according to the social-welfare criteria being used. One could further expand the set of possible institutions by making aspects of the behavioural model of agents vary. The computer could then come up with optimal behavioural norms or institutions as well. For now, however, assume the behavioural model is given and welfare is maximized in the space of utilities. Consider another problem for the computer. Assume there is a well-defined set of market institutions.[22] No doubt exchangeable

---

[22] This is no small assumption. Many institutions that make up a market system, or are present in a market system, may be present in non-market systems as well, so it's not clear how to define a set of market institutions. For the purposes

private property would be a cornerstone in this set, as well as certain institutions that result from contractual agreement. The computer could then be asked to maximize social-welfare subject to the constraint that only market institutions are used. One would be able to compare the social-welfare outcome achieved by this optimal market system, to the net optimality achieved when the computer is free to choose any institutions that maximize social-welfare. The difference in welfare attained by the 'optimal system' and the 'market system' would be a measure of market failure.

The market fails when market institutions fail to achieve net optimality;[23] for example, when private-property rights in a given context fail to support an optimal allocation, the market has failed. Consider a classical cause of market failure. In the presence of increasing returns to scale, a system of private-property rights and competitive exchange fails to allocate resources efficiently. There may exist other institutions that allocate resources in a more optimal fashion in the presence of increasing returns. In this case increasing returns to scale is a cause of market institutions failing. It may not cause other institutions to fail. Alternatively, assume for a moment that another (non-market) system of institutions does fail to allocate resources optimally in the presence of increasing returns to scale. This institutional deficiency could not be called market failure, yet it would correspond with externality in the inefficiency sense, since somehow actions were not being harnessed in the promotion of efficiency by the institutions. Note that the generic sense of externality as inefficiency focuses on the deficiency of the institutions, whatever these institutions are.

The consequentialist approach to externality leads us to a notion of institutional inefficiency, which is a far broader notion than market failure. Institutions are no longer treated as fixed, they are variable, and the criterion of efficiency can now be used to judge and compare institutions. Furthermore, the consequentialist approach leads to a reconceptualization of market failure where the market system is seen to fail relative to other institutions that can do a better job, rather than relative to an ideal

of the present thought experiment it will be assumed that such a set of market institutions is well defined.

[23] Again it is assumed that a well-defined set of market institutions exists.

world of zero transaction costs. This concept of market failure is
very different from Bator's market failure, yet not so different
from Heller and Starrett's. The latter emphasized the importance
of institutional costs and the relevance of externalities on institutional choice. However, they did not take their own logic far
enough; had they done so, they may have arrived at something
like the consequentialist view of externalities, i.e. that externality
is simply institutional failure. In the appendix to this chapter I
offer an illustration of institutional ineffiency, and I compare it
to the notion of market failure.

6.2. The Intrinsic-Characteristic Approach

The consequentialist approach developed a motivation that
underlied the generic sense of externality as inefficiency. I will
now suggest another motivation that seems to explain the other
generic sense of externality as interdependence, or some kind of
interdependence. In section 4 of this chapter, I described the difficulty in making clear distinctions between different kinds of
interdependence, and suggested that there does not seem to be
any good rationale for calling one particular kind of interdependence 'externality'. Despite these difficulties there would appear
to be an important motivation behind attempts to distinguish
between kinds of interdependence. In many characterizations of
externality some intrinsic feature is seen as a defining characteristic, specifically the absence of property rights, that of markets, or
action that has not been consented to by an affected party. A
possible motivation for such an approach may be that some feature or institution is seen as having some intrinsic value. In the
consequentialist view, consistent with a utilitarian approach, a
consequentialist view of institutions has been followed. This
means institutions have no intrinsic value of their own. The value
of an institution is a function of the consequences it has. In the
consequentialist context, 'external' simply referred to institutional
inefficiency, whatever the institution; no special status was attributed to the kind of institution. There is, however, another
approach to institutions. Rather than viewing them as instruments
wielded by governing authorities in pursuit of efficiency and distributional goals, institutions, and entitlements, may be treated as
exogenous to the policymaker. The protection of entitlements may

be seen as an end in itself, and for that matter, may act as a constraint in the promotion of other social objectives. This view emanates from the classical liberal framework where rights are seen as securing a realm of autonomy for the individual not to be compromised for other social ends.

An intrinsic-characteristic perspective may attribute intrinsic value to institutions, entitlements, and processes. Nozick (1974: p. ix) argues that 'Individuals have rights, and there are things no person or group may do to them without violating their rights.' Institutions in this view are not evaluated according to their consequences. Some rights should be upheld irrespective of whether they advance social-welfare or not. Within this perspective, 'external' might refer to those activities over which rules or entitlements have not been specified or are violated. In this view inefficiency will not necessarily imply 'external' activity. The inefficient allocation that may result from 'too few' agents would not signal an 'externality' as long as property rights have been defined, and property rights are deemed to have intrinsic value. It is not 'deficient rule' or inefficiency due to lack of rule, but 'lack of rule' as such that underlies this understanding of 'external'.[24] The intrinsic-characteristic view judges actions through the prism of legitimate entitlements and processes. In this perspective 'externality' is simply activity taking place outside some legitimate institution or process. If private-property rights are seen as the intrinsic feature, then common property would entail 'externality' irrespective of whether it is accompanied with rules of behaviour leading to optimal allocation. Likewise, the absence of markets may not mean that there is inefficiency in the system, yet an intrinsic-characteristic approach may treat it as 'external' activity. Market interaction may be seen as a legitimate process in contrast to other forms of interaction.

6.2.1. On Violation

In the consequentialist approach, violation of rules or rights does not imply institutional inefficiency. It depends on whether the

---

[24] In some sense this comes closer to the more narrow characterizations of externality (Baumol and Oates's first condition). A barter economy would be externality-infested according to the consequentialist view, while in an intrinsic perspective as long as property rights are defined and not violated no externality is present.

violation has somehow been 'foreseen' by the system. If the rule has been set so that an optimal number of violations occur, then no inefficiency is implied. Becker's optimal-enforcement rule is meant to prohibit those whose gains from violation are less than the loss inflicted by the violating action. Actual violators will be those whose gains outweigh the losses. In a sense the system deems that these violations should take place. If this is part of the efficient functioning of the system, violation will not entail inefficiency. Somehow the very word 'violation' is not appropriate in this view. It usually carries moral connotations. 'You should not commit a crime,' does not seem consistent with a consequentialist approach. 'You should only commit this crime if it pays off,' is more appropriate. Legal rules assign a price on actions aligning incentives to promote efficiency.

On the intrinsic-characteristic view, violation is singled out as illegitimate activity that is 'external' to some proper process. The rules should not be violated. 'You should not commit a crime.' A rule is more than a price on action.

6.2.2. The Value of Consent

A fundamental institution which has been at the centre of liberal economic thought is the institution of consent. The differences in the two motivations underlying externality can be illustrated further with respect to the value of consent. On the one hand, consent is meant to protect the individual from the society or from other individuals in society (Mill's sense). It defines a private domain over which the individual alone has absolute control. On the other hand, the function of consent has been viewed as a vehicle or ultimate guarantee of optimal decision-making in a decentralized fashion. In this view, if consent is required of any individual affected directly (private-domain-affected) by some decision or action, consent will be afforded only if the individual is somehow compensated for any loss, or has to gain by the action. In this latter respect, private domain should be defined in such a way as to enhance efficiency. Rights are viewed as vehicles of efficiency. These values or virtues of rights are not always viewed separately. However, one can detect two motivations. An action not consented to by an affected agent would be an 'externality' (interdependence sense) in the intrinsic-characteristic view. On the consequentialist view, consent is not critical. If efficiency can be attained without consent, no externality (inefficiency sense) is present. The crucial factor is not that the victim of an unconsented act is compensated, but that the perpetrator is punished by an amount that would hypothetically compensate the victim. The virtue of consent is that this function is achieved. In order that an individual can take certain actions affecting others, he/she must have the consent of those individuals. Consent will be given only if the acting agent compensates (or is 'punished' by) the affected agent.

6.2.3. Some Examples of Contrast between Consequentialist and Intrinsic Views

It is important to distinguish between the existence, or not, of some institution, and the efficiency consequences of some institution being present or not. This contrast is brought out in the two motivations that underlie the notion of externality. The economy could allocate resources efficiently in cases where consent has not been offered by some directly affected party, in cases where private-property rights have not been defined, as in cases where the market is not present. Having to compensate individuals or firms for acts that were not consented to may be efficient, but they would remain unconsented to. A firm may have to compensate those affected by the effluent it pours into some river. This may lead to an efficient amount of effluent and production, but it may still be singled out as a departure from some legitimate process, because it occurred without the prior consent of the affected parties. Private-property rights may not be defined for some fishing ground, yet some rules of exploitation of common resources may lead to efficient allocation. This could still be interpreted as activity outside the institution of private property and thus be afforded some special status on grounds other than efficiency. A similar argument can be made for activity not mediated by the market.

A particularly strong contrast between the consequentialist and intrinsic feature motivation comes out with Sen's (1970) Pareto-liberal paradox. Sen shows how a conflict can arise between the principle of Pareto-efficiency and the liberal principle that individuals should have full control over certain decisions that are considered very personal. In certain cases where individuals have extended preferences these two principles are irreconcilable. For a consequentialist, if the outcome were Pareto-optimal there would be no issue, since the concern is with efficiency. The intrinsic-characteristic approach may view it as illegitimate activity by emphasizing the importance of control that individuals should exert over certain actions. Sen's Pareto-liberal paradox has forcefully uncovered the tension between an unrelenting pursuit of Pareto-optimality and the need to protect some private domain for the individual.[25]

7. CONSEQUENCES, INTRINSIC CHARACTERISTICS AND EXISTING VIEWS OF EXTERNALITY

In the literature on externalities one cannot find the two approaches presented here in their 'pure forms'. However, most conceptualizations of externality contain elements of both these views. Most conceptualizations of externality make reference to a specific institution, whether it be consent, property rights, or the market.[26] Also there is no conceptualization that does not refer, at least implicitly, to the consequences (inefficiency) as one of the defining attributes. Their differences can be found in the different institutions they specify or the different emphasis they place between consequences and institutions.

A glance at the possible definitions considered for the intrinsic-characteristic view, reveals their similarity with the definitions of externality in the literature, the difference being that in the literature the 'unconsented-to activity', or the 'lack of property', or the 'non-existence of the market', are meant to imply the resulting inefficiency (this is often stated). The use of 'consent' in Meade's (1973) definition of externality signals an intrinsic-characteristic

[25] Riley (1988) offers a way of relieving this tension within a utilitarian framework: 'Sen's paradox demonstrates that Paretianism (the democratic principle that society's choice rule should respect unanimity of consensus) is logically incompatible with respect for absolute libertarian rights, *given unrestricted domain*. In order to harmonize rationally the democratic value of consensus with the liberal value of liberty, therefore, "utility in the largest sense" must connote a suitable moral domain restriction. That is, only suitable "ethical" patterns or profiles of individual preferences can be admissible for social choice' (1988: 2). See also Wriglesworth (1985) and Suzumura (1983) for similar discussions.

[26] Baumol and Oates's definition does not make reference to specific institutions, however, as the discussion in Ch. 3 reveals, they are implicitly referring to property rights.

vantage point, similarly for Baumol and Oates's implicit emphasis on property rights, or Heller and Starrett's reliance on the market. It's difficult to justify the inclusion of an institution in a definition of externality without affording it some intrinsic value. Because economists are trained as consequentialists, the introduction of intrinsic elements is conducive to some of the confusion surrounding externality. The sanctity of institutions such as consent makes it easy to slip into methodological inconsistency. Institutions could be valued intrinsically within consequentialist reasoning, but this is another matter.

This tension between concern with inefficiency on the one hand, and the need to specify an intrinsic characteristic on the other, exudes a sense of circularity in the characterizations. The consequentialist approach brings out fully the issue of institutional and behavioural choices for resource allocation. It probes for a fuller understanding of the technology of institutions, and the need for such an understanding in order to make institutional comparisons. It also offers a way to evaluate the impact of behavioural assumptions on efficiency. It leads us to a new notion of efficiency where organizational costs are incorporated in the calculation of an optimal allocation, as well as a reconceptualization of market failure, where market failure is relative to other institutions. By confining a consequentialist approach to a specific institution, like the market or property rights, one avoids the central issues underlying institutional choice, which is at the heart of a consequential analysis. On the other hand, by treating certain intrinsic characteristics as a causal element in explaining inefficiency in the space of utilities, i.e. the lack of a market, or some private-property right, as a cause of market failure, one first faces the kind of difficulties raised in the discussion on causal explanation of failure (Chapters 5 and 6), and secondly loses sight of the potentially important issues raised by the intrinsic-characteristic approach (importance of control that an individual attaches to certain activities). The combined use of intrinsic features and consequences has seemed to rob the concept of externality of some of its more powerful and interesting implications by not fully developing the logic inherent in each motivation.

One can say that there has been a tension in the characterizations of externality. At one end the emphasis has been on the resultant inefficiency propitiated by 'external' activity, where action deviates from mutually benefiting action. At the other end the emphasis has been on control, some notion of 'private domain', where action unconsented to is external, forced. At one end there has been efficiency, at the other control. As was said before, these are not unrelated; however, it is important to disentangle the two so that one knows what is at issue. The consequentialist view helps us in this endeavour by concerning itself only with one end of the 'string', efficiency. Control is a variable in the calculus, to be defined according to the prescriptions of efficiency. How agents are allotted control over actions/resources, is determined by this single all-engulfing objective. Externality is not understood by the structure of control. It becomes equivalent to institutional deficiency or rule deficiency. It is a broader concept than market failure, and there has lain its motivational strength. It is this aspect of the notion that has led to the development of institutional economics (e.g. Coase 1960; Alchian and Demsetz 1972). It draws us towards an economics where institutions are treated as variables much as prices are.

At the other end of the 'rope' is the intrinsic-characteristic view. Emphasis is placed on control. 'In the part which merely concerns himself, his independence is, of right absolute, over himself, over his own body and mind, the individual is sovereign' (Mill 1985: 69). A protected 'private domain' is envisaged for the individual over which no one can interfere without the individual's consent. This may derive from the Kantian position that individuals should not be treated as means but as ends. The individual is in control, 'the individual is sovereign'. In several definitions of externality there is reference to actions for which consent has not been granted by an affected individual. In a sense, the individual's private domain was invaded. External activity is that activity which invades a private domain, or activity over which no private domain has been defined, possibly pointing to the need of assigning a 'private domain'. It is not a deficient rule, but lack of a rule or violation of a rule that characterizes the 'externality'.

The intuitive sense of externality that most economists have is a mixed bag of the two generic senses of externality along with the two motivations that underlie these senses. The more the emphasis falls on the intrinsic-value view, the more distinct as a concept it becomes, the greater the cutting edge.[27] Also, the more it lacks analytical power, the less it tells us about what is to be done or what to look for. The pure consequentialist view has powerful implications. It has a driving force. It tells us that institutions are variables in our analysis. It beckons us to focus on the links between norms, institutions, behaviour, and technology in order to find why certain activities or consequences have escaped our view. In a world that is becoming increasingly interdependent the consequences that flow from our actions follow an ever more complex path. The consequentialist motivation, that has underlied attempts to understand 'externality', signifies our persistence to trace out this path. It is the key to understanding why what we do leads to what it does. Importantly both views necessitate a much richer understanding of institutions, whether they are treated purely as instruments for furtherance of some social-welfare objective, or as processes or entitlements with some intrinsic value.

The discussion in this chapter points to the need to recognize a class of concepts involved in the apparently homogeneous notion of externality. For fruitful use of the set of ideas it is necessary to be aware of (1) their respective motivations, (2) their distinctions which don't make them exactly equivalent (in the absence of special assumptions), (3) their combined use of intrinsic features and consequences, and (4) their avoidance of central issues underlying institutional choices. Ultimately, an understanding of the complex notion of externality will help clarify some central methodological issues and notions of economic theory (optimality, market failure, etc.), and place at centre stage institutional and behavioural choices for resource allocation.

---

[27] Actually the difficulty in defining institutions qualifies this statement, e.g. it is not that easy to say what activity occurs outside the market.

APPENDIX

Fishing for an Illustration of Institutional Failure

A discussion of externality of fishing in open-access sea will provide a way to elucidate the notion of institutional efficiency by contrasting it with the standard notion of market failure in neoclassical economics. The basics of the fishery problem can be captured with the help of a simple diagram (Fig. 7.1, taken from Anderson 1986: 239) depicting the difference between open-access and efficient levels of fishing effort in a given period. The average-revenue and marginal-revenue curves are defined for a particular stock size. The open-access equilibrium level of effort is E_2, where average revenue intersects the marginal (static) cost of fishing effort. This occurs for two reasons: First, fishermen treat the average-revenue curve as a marginal-revenue curve since they do not take into account the reduction in revenue of other fishermen due to the more intense extraction effort from a common stock, i.e. the discrepancy between the average- and marginal-revenue curve could be seen as the opportunity cost of using the common stock resource which normally should command a positive rent. This is the standard inefficiency associated with the Tragedy of the Commons. Second, in a dynamic context there is an additional source of socially inefficient activity as individual fishermen ignore the effect that their extraction from a common stock has on the future productivity of the stock. As fish are extracted from

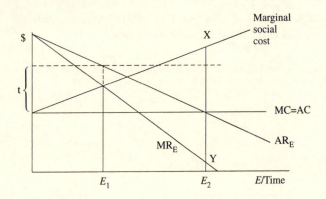

FIG 7.1.

the sea the reproductive capacity of the stock will fall and the costs of searching and catching fish will increase. The cost that reductions of the fish stock imposes on future extraction is shown diagrammatically as a discrepancy between marginal cost and marginal-social cost. This discrepancy is known as a 'user cost', or 'scarcity rent', in the literature. Because fishermen ignore these static and dynamic costs when they have open-access to the fishery, there will be too many fishermen putting too much effort into extracting too few fish.

If fishing could be regulated costlessly it would be optimal to induce the fishery to operate at E_1, where net social benefits are maximized. The literature on the theory of regulating fisheries (see Anderson 1986, Hartwick and Olewiler 1986, Dasgupta and Heal 1979, and Clark 1985) reveals numerous institutional means of attaining socially optimal levels of fishing activity in a world where institutions can be set up, defined, and enforced costlessly:

- A tax on the fish harvest, e.g. pounds of lobster, equal to the marginal social damage associated with extraction of fish at the optimum level of extraction. (The diagram shows effort in a given time on the horizontal axis, but one could draw a corresponding axis for catch, or harvest, levels and appropriately redraw and reinterpret the cost and revenue curves.)
- A tax on 'effort' (it is assumed that one can costlessly gauge some appropriate index of inputs used in extraction) equal to the marginal social damage associated with 'effort' exerted at the optimum level of extraction (tax level t in Fig. 7.1).
- Single owner of the open-access resource (sea), renting its use so as to maximize rents (rent level t in Fig. 7.1). If the owner controls a large share of the resource then one must allow first-degree price discrimination[28] to ensure socially optimal use of the resource.
- Tradable individual output quotas, where the total number of quotas are determined by the government at the Pareto-optimal level of catch.
- Tradable individual 'effort' quotas, where total number of input quotas are determined by government at the Pareto-optimal level of effort (total quotas equal to E_1 in Fig. 7.1). This is the mirror image of output quotas where each quota specifies the maximum inputs that fishermen can use.

These are the standard theoretical remedies discussed in the literature that have the same outcome in terms of efficiency (although not in terms of distribution) when there are no costs of defining and enforcing the

---

[28] The conceptual counterpart to the tax on 'effort' would be a single owner of 'effort'.

relevant instruments or property rights. In each of the examples above, entitlements are being redefined: a tax on effort represents a redefining of the right to the value of a certain kind of activity, the tax on output represents a redefining of the right to the value of some good, an individual harvest quota represents a right to some percentage of a resource, an individual quota on effort represents a right to a certain activity level, etc. However, the number of institutional remedies to this fishery problem in a world where there are no organizational costs are limited only by our imagination of alternative incentive and entitlement structures. Some of the insights of Coasean neutrality of property rights can easily be extended to institutions (and institutional structures) in general. In this context it is helpful to view institutions as attenuated property rights. As long as property rights are appropriately defined, the outcome of agents' interaction will be Pareto-optimal in a world where rules can be defined and enforced costlessly.[29] Recall that in the Coase Theorem it is assumed that bargaining can take place costlessly and thus all that is needed is that property rights are defined for all relevant resources (or activities). In the fishery example we need not assume that bargaining is costless but simply that the particular institutions considered are costless. That is why markets in 'named' vessels would not provide a solution since interaction is through parametric-prices rather than bargaining. Many remedies to the fishery problem can be envisaged with appropriate redefinition of the entitlement space. The following examples are a sample:

- cooperative ownership of fish industry with appropriate rules (incentive mechanism, e.g. shares of joint profits) for co-owners;
- costless bargaining and 'named' vessels;[30]
- private-ownership of divisible plots of sea, assuming that there is a

[29] Note, one need not assume a world where all kinds of interaction are costless, since in such a world institutions would lose their *raison d'être*. Such a world, though hard to imagine, could be likened to the rat-race story in Ch. 6, above, where agents could costlessly transmit all relevant information and instantly achieve an allocation that is in the core. In this respect the Coase Theorem should read: in a world where property rights can be defined costlessly and bargaining among agents is costless, Pareto-optimal allocations will ensue (as opposed to: in a world of zero transaction costs if property rights are well defined Pareto-optimal allocations will ensue). It is the combination of costless bargaining and well-defined property rights that generates the Coase Theorem. I use the term 'appropriately defined' to emphasize that what matters in generating Pareto-optimality is how the different property rights (and institutions) are combined.

[30] As discussed in Ch. 5, above, if markets in 'named' vessels could be established costlessly, this would not provide a solution because of the non-convexity of the firms' extended production space which would prevent competitive equilibria in the Lindahl markets.

way to 'fence in' the ultimate resource[31] (model becomes conventional; in Fig. 7.1, fishermen will have to pay for access to the sea so that they will perceive the marginal-revenue curve as their actual marginal revenue, the sea-plot rents will incorporate user-cost);
• state ownership of fish industry with appropriate rules for state functionaries.

While there might be a certain elegance to these various incentive mechanisms, none of these institutional remedies may be very useful in a world where valuable resources have to be used in organizing economic activity. It is through an investigation of the organizational costs associated with these alternative institutional schemes in the real world, that one can start getting to grips with their relative merits. A very cursory list of some of the advantages and disadvantages of a number of these institutional mechanisms in a world where organizational costs matter are presented below for illustrative purposes and give examples of different costs that need to be compared when looking at the effectiveness of alternative institutions and rules:

1. *Tax on catch*
   (a) costs of acquiring information on the biological characteristics of fish and extraction technology so that 'optimal' tax can be set;
   (b) costs of wrong tax level;
   (c) cost of adjusting tax to changes in demand, tastes, biological characteristics of fish, and other 'exogenous' factors;
   (d) cost of enforcing payment of tax: fishing firms may find it easy to evade payment;
   (e) the tax may interfere with governments' ability to form good fishery policies (if fish firms under report output to minimize tax burden the government may lack good harvest information when forming policy, including optimal tax policy);
   (f) cost of unemployment created by tax;
   (g) costs of lobbying against tax.

2. *Tax on fishing effort*
   Cost of defining, monitoring, and enforcing effort levels; it is difficult to tax an index of inputs (if the tax is applied to certain kinds of inputs there is danger of inefficient substitution away from this input, e.g. if tax is on number of boats, fishermen may alter the size of boats; if it is on size and number, fishermen may alter the nature of equipment to fit more sophisticated smaller equipment for more intensive fishing, etc.).

---

[31] This would deal with the problem of fish being a 'fugitive' resource.

3. *Total catch quota*
   (*a*) A total allowable harvest is set for the industry and then firms are
        allowed to enter up to the point where the harvest limit is reached.
        A problem is that in the dynamic setting, the same harvest level
        could be reached with a different underlying biomass (stock of
        fish), i.e. we could have a large stock of fish with a lower rate of
        reproduction equal to the allowable harvest level, or a small stock
        of fish with a high reproduction level equal to the level of allow-
        able harvest. Too many firms may enter the industry, increasing
        the effort level and harvesting the same quantity of fish (at a
        higher cost per fish) from a lower stock of fish;
   (*b*) resources wasted as fishermen compete for a larger share of the
        total quota, e.g. fishermen might prefer following others to a
        located colony of fish and try to outfish others, rather than spend-
        ing resources in trying to locate a new colony;
   (*c*) costs of enforcing quota;
   (*d*) costs of finding 'optimal' quota level.

4. *Tradable individual catch quotas*
   (*a*) Open-access problems could be overcome since firms will not be
        allowed to increase their catch beyond the level assigned by the
        private catch quota, i.e. they are no longer scrambling for a larger
        portion of a total quota;
   (*b*) cost of finding total allowable harvest level (if the total is high rel-
        ative to the stock, firms may again use excessive effort levels to
        attain their private quota level);
   (*c*) alternative administrative costs of allocating quotas, i.e. allocate
        according to historical 'rights', use auction mechanism, etc. (this is
        a problem rife with political conflict).

Anderson (1986) provides a very neat discussion of the kinds of issues
raised with the incorporation of organizational costs in the choice of
optimal regulatory regimes.

It is important to realize that, although it is possible . . . to describe an
approximation of the economically efficient intertemporal harvest plan
for a particular fishery, an agency cannot directly force a fleet of individual operators to follow this plan in the same way a corporate executive
can plan the activities of his or her firm.[32] The only thing that agencies
can directly control is type of regulation, the monitoring procedure, and
in some cases the type of penalty for noncompliance, as well as the levels of each of these activities or instruments. The actual level of effort

---

[32] Although Anderson (1986) draws this distinction, there are probably more
similarities in the two problems than are implied.

produced in any period of time is determined by the way individual firms react to market conditions, given the control instruments used and the way in which they are implemented. Therefore, fisheries agencies only indirectly determine the level of effort. (Anderson 1986: 234)

Three agency variables are considered by Anderson. First, the choice of governing instrument or regulation type and the level at which this instrument should be operated, e.g. licences, harvest quota. Second, the choice of monitoring and enforcement procedures and the extent of monitoring and enforcing, e.g. boat inspection, marine police observance of actual fishing, auditing of firms' financial records, etc. Third, the choice of a penalty structure for deviant behaviour and the level of penalties, e.g. forfeiture of catch, jail term, boat-confiscation, etc. Profit-maximizing firms will avoid adhering to the rules set down by regulators whenever the gains of such avoidance are greater than the (expected) costs of being detected and penalized for deviant behaviour. The success of alternative government regulatory mechanisms will depend in part on the ability and cost of detecting prohibited behaviour.

The essentials of an economic framework for forming optimal regulation can be captured with the help of a diagram (Fig. 7.2, reproduced from Anderson 1986: 239). Figure 7.2 is the familiar picture showing the difference between the open-access and the efficient levels of fishing effort in a static framework. The average revenue and marginal-revenue curves are defined for a particular stock size. The open-access equilibrium level of effort is E_2, where average revenue intersects the marginal cost of fishing effort. This results because fishermen only perceive the average revenue they get from expending more effort, they do not take into account the reduction in revenue of other fishermen due to the more intense extraction effort from a common stock. If fishing could be regulated costlessly it would be optimal to 'force' the fishery to operate at E_1, where net social benefits are maximized. But if regulating fisheries is a costly activity, then a better objective would be to establish regulating rules that achieve maximum potential benefits, net of all costs. 'This involves the selection of the proper combinations of governing instrument, enforcement activity, and penalty structure and the optimal level at which to operate each of these control variables' (Anderson 1986: 240). For simplicity the problem can be restricted to that of choosing between two instruments called types A and B (which could be taxes, harvest quotas, access times, etc.).

The difference between these two instruments is captured in Fig. 7.2*b* and *c* by the curves labelled actual marginal gain and marginal-enforcement cost. The curves labelled potential marginal gain represent the potential net benefits from costless regulation, i.e. the difference between the marginal social cost and the marginal revenue in Fig. 7.2*a*. The

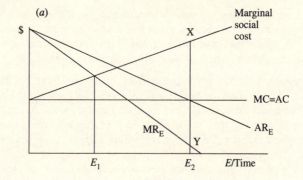

(a)

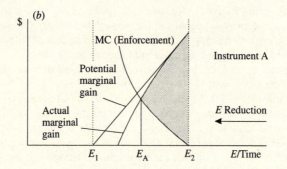

(b)

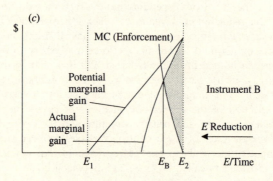

(c)

FIG 7.2.

actual marginal gain differs from the potential gain because: (1) some types of regulation cause effort to be produced inefficiently, e.g. restrictions on gear may lead to inefficient input combinations; and (2) regulations can encourage firms to engage in avoidance activity which is socially wasteful. The extent to which actual gains and costs differ between regulatory regimes will depend on the nature of these regimes (incentives they create for avoidance activities or inefficient input use, etc.).

The marginal-enforcement-cost curves in Fig. 7.2*b* and *c*, represent the marginal cost of getting firms to comply with reductions in effort levels. The greater the reduction in effort level sought out by the regulatory agency, the greater the resources required to enforce these reductions. Depending on the costs of detecting deviant behaviour and the actual cost of the particular enforcement activity, the cost of reducing effort may vary between regulatory regimes, e.g. it may be easier to detect use of an unauthorized type of vessel than unauthorized extraction of fish of a certain size.

In terms of this simplified example, the regulatory instrument type A is the optimal regulatory regime since it maximizes the net social benefits of regulation as compared to the alternative type B. The net social benefits attained by regulation is indicated in the diagram by the shaded area. Note that each regulatory regime may imply a different level of socially optimal effort. The diagrams assume that the two instruments have been applied at a specified level (e.g. a certain tax level, or a certain degree of gear restriction). If the instrument level were allowed to vary, the marginal benefit and cost curves would vary. Although this enhances the complexity of determining the optimal regulatory regime the reasoning behind this choice process is unaltered. Even the incorporation of time, while increasing greatly the complexity of the task, will leave unaffected the rationale of seeking a regulatory regime that maximizes social benefits that incorporate the cost of regulating.

Anderson's (1986) model suggests that there is nothing special about the optimal-effort level in a transaction-costless world, in fact it may well prove to be a highly misleading target. Is not abstracting from resource costs of organizing economic activity just like abstracting from production costs of economic activity? If there were no costs of extracting fish then the intertemporal socially efficient level of extraction would equal the maximum sustainable yield of fish harvests, i.e. the extraction rate that would maximize fish output through time. But economists rightly insist that there is nothing inherently special about the maximum sustainable yield because it abstracts from extraction costs, and once costs of producing fish are incorporated into one's model, one is likely to derive a different socially optimal level of fish extraction. It is in this spirit that incorporation of organizational costs is likely to lead to yet another socially efficient level of fish extraction. In fact, the zero-transaction-cost level of fish extraction is most likely not the socially optimal level of output.

COMPARING MARKET FAILURE AND INSTITUTIONAL INEFFICIENCY

The fishery example I have been discussing provides a good basis for comparing the standard notion of market failure with the alternative notion of institutional failure. One of the standard approaches to market failure in neoclassical economics could be described as follows:

1. Focus on some activity (e.g. fishing, oil-extraction) and determine a Pareto-optimal level of activity in a world of zero organizational costs.
2. Discern whether a costless private-ownership market economy with a given set of property rights defined (e.g. in the case of fishing all private-property rights are well-defined except for the resource sea) will generate the Pareto-optimal level of activity. If the market attains Pareto-optimality and no market exists for the activity in question, then the government should support the formation of a market. If a market already exists, then there is no reason for government intervention. If the market does not attain Pareto-optimality, then some government action is required.
3. Diagnose the cause of failure, e.g. non-convexity, public-good nature of good, too few agents, etc.
4. Consider and compare alternative remedies, mostly in the form of 'market-improving' or 'market-correcting' government intervention, e.g. improving the definition of private-property rights, taxation, regulation. It is usually at this last stage that transaction costs are considered when comparing alternative remedies.

The problems with this standard approach are the following:

1. It sets up an ideal of a Pareto-optimal allocation in a world where there are no costs of organizing the economy. Attempts to achieve such an ideal may be counterproductive.
2. It assumes that if a market attains a Pareto-optimal level of some activity that has been determined in a transaction-costless world, then there is no problem of inefficiency. That is, it does not consider the case where markets may be relatively costly means of achieving some end; for an extreme example, it could be that property rights for private plots of sea are set up and enforced at great expense, and while 'optimal' fish extraction is achieved, the organizational costs are not warranted (nor for that matter may the level

of extraction be warranted).

3. If 'market failure' is discerned for some activity, then a relatively small sample of remedies are compared. Most remedies considered tend to be in the form of 'market correcting' remedies, with the underlying presumption that 'tampering' should be minimized. Furthermore, the comparisons often focus more on which remedy will come closest to reaching the ideal Pareto-optimal activity level, rather than, *inter alia*, which remedy will require less resources to instigate. Finally, there is an implicit assumption that the institutions in the rest of the economy are efficient and that the problem activity can be tackled independently of the general institutional environment. This raises the question of second-best, but at the level of general institutional structures rather than market structures alone.

The alternative notion of institutional efficiency would lend itself to a different kind of economic enquiry of the fishery problem. I will assume for the moment that there is no particular social-welfare objective and that instead there is an interest in finding a set of institutional structures that would allocate resource in ways that are least wasteful in the space of utilities, i.e. Pareto-optimal.[33] The starting-point for the model would be to have: (1) a behavioural function for agents in the model (for simplicity it can be assumed that agents are utility-maximizers); (2) a production function representing the state of technology (it would be important to understand the underlying physical relationships of the resource inputs, not just the inputs as recognized by the agents);[34] and (3) an institution function representing the state of institutional technology (this would entail an understanding of the resource requirements of alternative institutions). Having specified these three components of the model, one would generate a set of allocations and institutional structures that were Pareto-optimal (some kind of mathematical optimization procedure may be used). Presumably one would get an array of institutional structures that are effective in dealing with the fishery problem, and different structures might be associated with different distributional concerns. One would also be able to compare the existing institutional structures with alternative ones, acquire a better understanding of the efficiency and distributional ramifications of existing institutions, and

---

[33] I will argue in Chs. 8 and 9 that one can no longer rely on a clear distinction between efficiency and distributional concerns. It is not likely that one can rely on a specific set of institutions like the market to generate all Pareto-efficient allocations, and use a specific set of tools like lump-sum taxes, to deal with distributional concerns. It is more likely that different distributional concerns will be more efficiently catered to by different institutional structures.

[34] In Ch.5, above, it became apparent that production functions would take on different shapes according to how the input space was defined.

gain insights about the nature of changes required. Note that the question of improving existing institutions is quite different from that of hypothetically setting up institutions from scratch. Once organizational costs are incorporated in models, history matters, in the sense that the cost of transition from one set of institutions to another may be very great. These transitional costs would have to be incorporated in models concerned with policy prescription.

Important advantages of such a modelling procedure would be:

1. The standard for comparing existing institutions or alternative institutions is not an unattainable world where there are no costs of organizing the economy.
2. This approach demands at the outset a modelling (and thus deeper understanding) of organizational costs and their implications for resource allocation.
3. The entire array of institutional means of resource allocation are evaluated and compared, i.e. there is no arbitrary restriction on what institutions can be used for resource allocation. Furthermore, although the complexity of the task is daunting, one can ultimately approach the question of optimal management of fishing resources from a general-equilibrium-type framework of institutions. The organizational costs of the various institutions in managing the allocation of resources in fishing effort will depend in large part on the institutions in place in the rest of the economy. A system, for instance, that already spends many resources on defining and enforcing private-property rights, which has a legal and administrative structure attuned to the requirements of private-property rights, may find that tradable individual quotas are a more efficient means of resource allocation than cooperative ownership of fisheries.

PART II

INSTITUTIONAL ANALYSIS

8
Evaluating Institutional Change

1. INTRODUCTION

Externality has proven to be a rather poor and often misleading classificatory principle. Attempts to define a certain class of events or phenomena, or a special cause of market failure, floundered as distinctions were made that were not differences. The few clear and consistent understandings, or characterizations of externality, do not seem to warrant a special distinction as 'externality'. The generic sense of externality as general interdependence should be called just that: general interdependence. Likewise the generic sense of externality as activity escaping the purview of institutions could be called institutional inefficiency. This way also they are not confused for one another. Efforts to narrow these broad categories, either by trying to form a special kind of interdependence, or a subset of causes of market failure, ultimately lacked a good criterion demarcating external and internal activity, or associating this 'external' activity with causes of market failure.

Of more lasting importance are the motivations implicit in the endeavours to unravel the illusive notion of externality, and the impact these motivations have been having on economic thinking. I suggested that two central concerns can be found behind the notion of externality, which I called the consequentialist and intrinsic-characteristic approach. The intrinsic-characteristic approach finds certain non-consequentialist reasons to distinguish between different kinds of interdependence. Distinctions between coercion and consent, or legitimate and illegitimate processes, become an important concern. This concern, the effects of which can be seen in much economic thinking, is much less prominent a motivation than the underlying consequentialist concern, primarily because economists are trained as consequentialists. It is this latter concern that I will develop in the following chapters. The consequentialist motivation has been the driving force behind the changing notion of market failure. The attachment, however, to the Arrow–Debreu general-equilibrium framework, prevented a full understanding of how organizational costs effect the notion of market failure. The 'Institutional' school of thought, by making institutions central to their analysis, are able to offer important insights into the function of institutions and the reappraisal of notions like market failure, optimality, causality of failure, etc. Many of their explicit characterizations of externality tend to be less ambiguous since they are closer to the generic senses, i.e. externality is seen as general interdependence (or coercion), or institutional inefficiency (however, some institutional economists intermingle many senses, and this can be misleading). For that reason, I will not delve further into the meanings of externality as such, but pursue their notion of institutional efficiency. Specifically, I am interested in bringing out more fully the implications of incorporating organizational costs into economic models. By critically discussing some of the models in 'Institutional' economics, I would like to call attention to the problems of institutional evaluation.

In this chapter I will consider some of the theories of institution formation in what might be called the Neo institutional Economics literature. The focus will be on the relationship between institution formation and the efficiency of institutions, and on the extent to which models of institution formation allow us to believe that the institutions that will emerge will be efficient.[1] Institutions will be called 'efficient' to the extent that they propitiate, or are directly associated with, Pareto-optimal resource allocations.[2] I will argue that many economic models of institution formation do not provide good theoretical grounds for the belief that efficient institutions are likely to evolve from the self-seeking activity of individuals. I will also reject a claim made by some models of institution formation that the institution of private property is (in general) the most efficient institution. A more general objective of mine in presenting models of institution formation is to gain some insights into ways of integrating institutions into economic analysis, and the kinds of problems such an endeavour might face.

---

[1] This corresponds to a fuller appraisal of Heller and Starrett's (1976) private-economy failure.

[2] A more critical appraisal of what it means to call an institution efficient will be left to subsequent chapters.

Explanation of institution formation has taken several forms. I will present, and critically discuss, four types of explanations. In section 2, I discuss what is known in the literature as the Property-Rights view[3] on institutional formation. According to proponents of this view, any Pareto-gains available through institutional innovation will be tapped by wealth-maximizing agents, ensuring that in equilibrium institutions will be optimal. In section 3, I consider a more sophisticated property-rights model presented by B. C. Field (1986) which suggests a process by which a community of individuals select optimal institutions. A noteworthy feature of Field's model is that it offers a framework for comparing the efficiency of alternative institutions. Section 4 looks at an approach that emphasizes the role of power in the formation of institutions. Section 5 considers a game-theoretic explanation of institution formation offered by Schotter (1981). The merit of his model is that it attempts to explain how agents may overcome Prisoners' Dilemma-type situations inherent in the formation of organizations. Finally, in section 6, I make some general points on the relationship between institutions, efficiency, and distributional concerns.

2. THE PROPERTY-RIGHTS VIEW OF INSTITUTION FORMATION

Demsetz (1967) is concerned with forming a theory of property rights; explaining the function and formation of institutions. Moreover, Demsetz is trying to explain how markets or a market economy may evolve historically. His analysis is meant to explain institutional change, whether this be the transition from feudalism to capitalism, or from a hunting-gathering community to one based on animal husbandry.

Changes in knowledge result in changes in production functions, market values, and aspirations. New techniques, new ways of doing the same things, and doing new things—all invoke harmful and beneficial effects to which society has not been accustomed . . . the emergence of new property rights takes place in response to the desires of the interacting persons for adjustments to new benefit-cost possibilities . . . property rights develop to internalize externalities when the gains of internalization become larger than the cost of internalization. (Demsetz 1967: 350)

[3] Demsetz and Posner are the main proponents of this school of thought.

As an example Demsetz discusses the evolution of private-property rights in land among American Indians.

Before the fur trade became established, hunting was carried on primarily for purposes of food and the relatively few furs that were required for the hunter's family. There externality was clearly present. Hunting could be practised freely and was carried on without assessing its impact on other hunters. But these external effects were of such small significance that it did not pay for anyone to take them into account. There did not exist anything resembling private ownership in land. (1967: 351–2)

With the advent of the fur trade the value of furs increased and as a consequence the scale of hunting increased. These factors meant that the value of 'externalities' associated with free hunting increased. Property rights started to change. At first the Indians would 'mark off the hunting ground selected by them by blazing the trees with their crests so that they may never encroach on each other' (Demsetz 1967: 352).[4] It became economic to husband fur-bearing animals and this meant that poaching had to be prevented, making greater demands on the enforcement of property rights. Private-property rights evolved as the new conditions meant that the gains associated with creation and enforcement of private-property rights outstripped the gains of letting hunters roam freely.

Demsetz asserts that 'no harmful or beneficial effect is external to the world' (1967: 348). In effect the world is one of general interdependence and all actions are internal to the world. He then defines externality[5] as that activity for which 'the cost of bringing the effect to bear on the decisions of one or more of the interacting persons is too high to make it worthwhile' (ibid.). It would seem then that externality poses no efficiency problems, since taking beneficial and harmful effects into account where transaction costs are too high would lead to efficiency losses. In fact, at any given time, the economic system would seem to be tautologically efficient since he implies that where transaction costs permit, private exchange will insure that any potential

---

[4] Quoting Eleanor Leacock (1954), *American Anthropologist*, 56/5, pt 2, memoir no. 78.

[5] Demsetz's idiosyncratic definition of externality is discussed in Ch. 2, above.

Pareto-improvements will be made.[6] If transaction costs are too high (greater than the potential gains from trade) then private exchange will not take place and this is consistent with efficiency. The system seems to be immune to inefficiency.[7]

Anderson and Hill (1975) extend Demsetz's property-rights theory by taking explicit account of exclusion costs. They are concerned with explaining the evolution of exclusive rights to the utilization of land, water, and cattle on the Great Plains of the American West in the latter half of the nineteenth century. The benefits of forming and enforcing property rights over activities increase when there is an increase in the value of some asset as well as an increase in the probability of encroachment from outsiders. However, exclusion is a costly activity, e.g. fencing, protecting borders, and punishing intruders, and the forming of property rights should consider both the benefits and the costs of such activity. In Fig. 8.1, reproduced from Anderson and Hill, the equilibrium level of defining and enforcing activity (Q_e) is determined by the maximization of net private benefits associated with such activity.

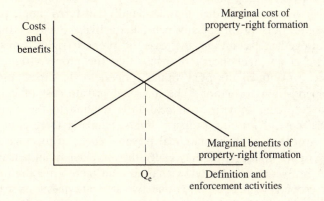

FIG 8.1.

[6] When incorporating transaction costs into microeconomic models there is a certain sense in which the equilibrium outcomes are tautologically efficient. I investigate this issue in Ch. 10, below.

[7] Demsetz actually does make room for a kind of dynamic inefficiency which is a lag in the time it takes to adjust to the set of efficient institutions. This issue is taken up in Ch. 10, below.

2.1. Private Versus Social Benefits

While under certain circumstances such a model may be able to provide a reasonable explanation of how institutions evolve, it certainly does not justify Demsetz's faith that the institutions that evolve will be efficient.[8] The fact that agents may form institutions by maximizing their net private benefits tells us nothing about the efficiency of the resulting institutions; at most it tells us something about the behaviour of agents. For an efficient level of property-right formation to take place it must also be shown that the private benefits and costs of forming property rights are no different from social benefits and costs.[9] In a perfectly competitive private-ownership economy, a firm produces a Pareto-efficient level of some productive activity because the prices of the inputs and outputs that the firm confronts ensure that the private benefits and costs will be good indicators of social value. The prices of inputs that the firm uses and the price of the output(s) produced, have been determined by an elaborate structure of universal markets (along with a list of conditions for the proper functioning of these markets). It is this elaborate structure (otherwise known as the 'invisible hand') that turns simple profit-maximization into a socially beneficial activity. Such a structure is altogether lacking in the case of property-right formation. There is no 'auctioneer' to ensure that the property-right producer will attach the right values (prices) to the inputs used in property-right formation. The marginal private cost of defining and enforcing activities will bear little relation to the marginal social cost of forming property rights. Similarly there is no reason to expect that the marginal private benefit of forming property rights will appropriately gauge the marginal social benefit.

A problem with Demsetz's analysis, and more generally that of the property-rights school, is that two separate questions seem to be conflated: How do property rights evolve? What determines

---

[8] Eggertsson (1990: 254) points out that such a 'model works well for situations in which formal political processes are relatively unimportant, such as in the case of the settlers of the American Great Plains, who, for various reasons, partly bypassed the formal decision-making apparatus of the United States, which was centred in the East'. This implies that more sophisticated modelling of institution formation would be needed when political processes are important.

[9] Social benefits and costs being determined by the requirements of Pareto-optimality or the maximization of some social-welfare function.

the efficiency of a property-right structure? Efficiency is seen as the locomotive of institutional change. If institutions are not efficient they will change. Stability will be attained when institutions are efficient. Yet, in Demsetz's model, it is not efficiency that leads to change, but the maximization of net private benefits by individuals; these are not the same. It is by positing individuals within a specific institutional structure that efficiency is guaranteed. It isn't enough that individuals are wealth-maximizers to ensure efficiency, they must be exchanging within a well-specified framework which channels individual self-seeking activity towards collective ends. When considering institution formation, individuals are functioning within an incomplete institutional framework (or no institutional framework: anarchy). Individual wealth-maximization is insufficient to explain optimal formation of institutions, just as it is insufficient to bring about optimality in a market with too few agents or too few markets. Historical evidence that institutions change and there is an increase in economic yield is dire support to the thesis of efficient institutions. In fact it would be surprising if individuals seeking personal gain in a highly unstructured environment came up with an efficient set of institutions.[10]

Bromley's (1989) simple model of the evolution of money from a Hobbesian state of nature helps illustrate some points concerning the likelihood of efficient institutions. He assumes that there are no institutions of property rights, contract, and market.

Assume that the onset of exchange is seen to be impeded, first of all, by the lack of a common currency. Because there are different interests to be served in this decision, because the various members of society have differential gains and losses depending on the currency decision, there is no unanimous decision possible. To pick one medium of exchange over the *n* other possibilities is to serve the interests of some, and to impinge upon the interests of others . . . But a common currency is required and so a coercive decision is necessary. (Bromley 1989: 68)

[10] It has sometimes been argued that the mechanism that provides the link between efficiency and institution formation is similar to evolutionary models in biology. The fittest institutions survive, the inefficient being weeded out. There is a danger here of equating efficiency with survivability and making the vacuous statement that the institutions that survive are the most efficient. This deprives the concept of efficiency of any semantic content. One need only to consider models such as Akerlof's (1984) market for lemons to be convinced that survivability is not a prerogative of efficient institutions. Inefficient markets or property rights could very well be stable.

Now that a currency has been established and it starts circulating it becomes clear that further advances can be made by the establishment of property rights in physical objects. Again the decision of forming and delineating property rights is not universally supported, some will lose. Through coercion, property rights are established which enhance the aggregate well-being of the community although it is not in the interests of some. Is there any reason why the institutions that evolve out of this process will be, on some definition of the term, optimal? Is there any reason why among the n possible currencies the most efficient will be selected, or, among all the possible property-rights structures, an optimal one will evolve? Especially given the lack of a structure that helps people intermediate with each other, one does not expect decisions taken concerning the formation of institutions to be optimal. Rent-seekers may be able unduly to influence decisions on institutions precisely because transaction costs prevent large groups of individuals, who may be adversely affected, to make an impact. It is not enough to posit the presence of potential gains to expect institutions to change optimally. The presence of potential gains in a Prisoner's Dilemma is insufficient for prisoners to act optimally by not confessing. While the prisoners may avoid the worst consequences, they fail as a totality to select the most efficient strategy. Institutional change may be motivated by potential gains, and gains there may be, but this does not imply that the gains are realized to the hilt.

Much as Arrow and Debreu have offered a detailed account of how markets may allocate resource efficiently, a similar theory would be required to show the necessary conditions for optimal institution formation, and sadly, this may bear little relation to evolution. Whatever is the case, the burden of the proof that institutions evolve optimally lies with the proponents of such a view.

2.2. Private Property and Efficiency

Demsetz (as well as many property-rights theorists) not only believed that profit-seeking sufficed for efficient institution formation, he also held the belief that progress on the economic front entailed a move towards private-property rights. By focusing too much on transaction costs associated with jointly held assets he discounted transaction costs of forming and protecting private-property rights. Bromley (1989: 15) points out, that 'by failing to understand the concept of property and therefore being unable to comprehend the notion of common property as a constellation of rights for the co-owners—including the most fundamental right to exclude non-owners—Demsetz is led to elevate private property to the status of a major institutional defence against resource destruction'.

The logic of the property-rights school can be captured in an expression such as the following:

$$\text{economic yield} = f(\text{property rights}). \qquad [8.1]$$

That is, as property rights evolve toward exclusive private rights, the economic yield attainable from a piece of land will increase. An alternative model of institutional change in land might be formulated as

$$\text{property rights} = g(\text{economic yield}). \qquad [8.2]$$

This captures the idea that the appropriate structure of property rights in productive assets is a dependent variable, as opposed to an explanatory variable as suggested by the property-rights school . . . The idea in [8.2] is simply that different forms of property rights (institutions) will require different levels of supporting infrastructure to define rights and duties, to demarcate boundaries, and to enforce that structure of rights; and that therefore the economically appropriate structure, whether private property, state property, or common property, is a function of the economic surplus available to support those differential costs.

Under current technology, the economic surplus available from the summer pastures of Switzerland is insufficient to make it economically feasible to divide those pastures into privately held parcels. To do so would require extensive fencing and water development so that each small parcel would be self-contained. As it stands the several farmers who jointly own a summer pasture are able to share the cost of a single herder to move the animals around to water, and to select those areas for grazing where the vegetation is particularly lush. If the summer pastures were owned in severalty, it might then be possible for one strategically located owner to prevent all others from gaining access to water . . . The current level of economic surplus from the summer pastures makes common property the most efficient property arrangement (Bromley 1989: 15–16).

Interestingly Bromley's quote reveals that even if it were inexpensive to establish private ownership of parcels, this may still be a less efficient property-right structure than common-property rights; inefficiency arising from the behaviour of the 'strategically located owner'. It is not just the cost of establishing property rights but whether the specific property-right structure is the most efficient given the conditions (number of agents, technology, demand, etc.).[11] In this sense the property-right school is correct in specifying the economic yield as a function of property rights although there is no justification in their belief that economic yield will increase with a move towards exclusive private-property rights. That would depend both on the cost of establishing and protecting private rights, as Bromley asserts, and on their effectiveness as an allocational mechanism. The property-right structure is both a dependent and an explanatory variable; it seems that both [8.1] and [8.2] in Bromley's quote are at least partially correct. Rejection of either equation would obscure our understanding of the function and evolution of property rights.

3. THE OPTIMAL COMMONS

B. C. Field (1986)[12] provides a model of changes in property-rights institutions which is also based on agents seeking to maximize net gains from institutional innovation, only this time it is the community of individuals pursuing the profitable activity rather than individuals separately seeking to profit from institution-building. His model also offers further testimony that private-property rights have no prerogative to being the efficient institutional form. Field assumes that a community of N families (or individuals) have acquired R units of natural resources which can be divided into any number of equal-sized plots. The community wants to maximize the rent from the combined use of natural resources and variable inputs; land and labour inputs are assumed homogeneous. Importantly, it is assumed that 'political' struggles over the distribution of these rents have no effect on the rules that evolve or the behaviour of the individuals. That is, the

---

[11] In the Law and Economics literature it is well known that the determination of 'efficient' legal rules entails not only accounting for the costs of forming and enforcing rules, but whether the rules elicit the most 'efficient' behaviour on the part of the agents. This issue will be taken up in Ch. 9, below.

[12] In presenting Field's model I have relied heavily on Eggertsson's (1990) nice summary and simplified version of Field's model.

community of individuals, who are the institution-builders, are the 'ideal' government concerned solely with the welfare of the community as a whole. One of the decisions the Group has to make concerns the optimal size of the plots. For instance, if the natural resource in question is agricultural land, then N could be kept intact and all families could work on the commonly owned land sharing the returns. Alternatively, the land could be subdivided and ownership rights could be given to smaller groups of families, or at one extreme, each of the N families could be given exclusive rights over $1/N$th equally sized plots.

There are three kinds of cost functions in the model: a standard neoclassical-production cost function, an internal governance cost function, and an exclusion cost function.

In the model, governance costs are solely caused by the commons problem, namely the incentive to overutilize variable, individually owned inputs when several families share the ownership of a resource. The dissipation of the rent from the shared resource can be reduced by collective action, but such measures are costly and give rise to internal governance costs, costs that are justified if the limits on overutilization increase *net* output. It is assumed that governance costs vary directly both with the number of families on each commons and with the curbs on the use of variable inputs (Eggertsson 1990: 257).

Exclusion prevents outsiders from dissipating rents but results in costs associated with defending boundaries from outsiders. The greater the length of overall boundaries, i.e. the larger the number of plots, the greater the overall exclusion costs.

The problem for the community of families is to find the number of commons, the quantity of exclusion resources, as well as the level of variable input used on the representative commons. 'Assuming the latter to remain optimally adjusted, [we get a] reduced-form version of Field's model' (Eggertsson 1990: 257), shown in Fig. 8.2.

The forces that determine the optimum number of commons, m are channelled through two functions—$m = m^*(e)$ and $e = e^*(m)$—and can either change the slope of the functions or shift them. The $m = m^*(e)$ function *defines the optimal number of commons for each level of exclusion expenditure*, $\hat{m}$, and the function $e = e^*(m)$ *maps the optimal level of exclusion expenditure for each number of commons*, $\hat{e}$ (Eggertsson 1990: 257–8).

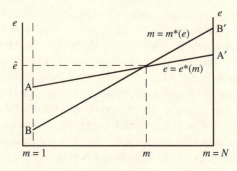

Fig 8.2.

Governance costs are likely to be lower the more homogeneous the population or the more that the families adhere to a common ideology. Changes in the formal voting procedures such as a move from a unanimity rule to a simple majority rule will have a similar effect on governance costs. Lower governance costs will lead to an equilibrium outcome involving fewer and larger commons. For a given level of exclusion expenditure, governance has become a relatively cheaper means of restricting rent dissipation, so resources should be shifted away from exclusion and towards governance. Optimal adjustment will entail a reduction in the number of the commons (reduction in protected borders) so that at the margin, the return on expenditure on governance is equal to the return on expenditure on exclusion. This would be shown in Fig. 8.2 as a shift up in the $m = m^*(e)$ function, indicating larger optimal commons for any given level of expenditure.

An improvement in exclusion technology, e.g. better weapons or advancements in ways of apprehending intruders, would mean that resources could be saved by having a greater number of smaller commons, since governance has become relatively expensive. This would correspond to a shift up in the $e = e^*(m)$ function, indicating a higher level of optimal (the now more productive) exclusion expenditure for any given number of commons. If there was an exogenous increase in the amount of trespassing, this would mean that exclusion is less productive and thus the e function would shift down, and fewer commons would be optimal.[13]

[13] Naturally this assumes there is no correlation between trespassing and factors that affect governance costs.

3.1. Private Property Versus Governance Rules

B. C. Field's (1986) model shows that an increase in the value of the natural resource R does not necessarily mean that optimal adjustment will be in the direction of greater exclusion. The higher the value of the natural resource the greater the rents lost from dissipation, and thus the greater the returns on preventing dissipation. There are higher returns associated with both governance and exclusion expenditures so both e- and m-functions shift up. However, trespassing, as well as breaking of internal governance rules, will become more profitable, thus increasing the cost of exclusion and governance. This means that the e- and m-functions shift down. Unless there is far more detailed knowledge of exclusion and governance technology, there is no way to say what the overall effect of a higher valued natural resource will be on the optimal commons. In general there is no reason why, under certain circumstances, governance may not be a more effective means of institutional control over production than private-property rights.

Eggertsson (1990: 260–1) points out that Field's analysis concentrates on

only one of several dimensions of property-rights institutions: the *size* of the optimal commons. Another important margin of the rights structure is the degree of *precision* with which the rules are defined. For example, if rights are not clearly defined, it may be difficult for a proprietor to prove to a third party (e.g., the courts) that his rights have been violated. Posner and others have advanced the thesis that property rights will be made more precise as resources become more valuable'.

While it seems a reasonable thesis that control over resources will become more precise as these are more highly valued it is not at all clear that this will entail a preference for private-property rights over more detailed and precise governance and monitoring rules.[14] On close scrutiny the very dichotomy of exclusion–

---

[14] I have already pointed out the difficulty in defining private-property rights. Here it could be argued that a hierarchic structure which has a set of rules and monitoring procedures to ensure that agents are complying could be viewed as a kind of property-right structure, where the rights are being defined over activities. Also, it is not inconceivable that the costs of setting up more precise rules of control over natural resources outweigh the new potential gains. Again more needs to be known about the transaction technologies.

governance looks problematic. Governance entails a structure of authority with rules for agents that prescribe which actions agents are allowed to take, or which actions are proscribed. In essence governance rules 'exclude' agents from certain activities. How does this differ from the way that private-property rights exclude agents from taking certain actions? In fact exclusion is likely to be a characteristic of all forms of entitlements. If one is to distinguish between private-property rights and other rules of governance one has to delve into the specific detailed content of rules. The exclusion–governance dichotomy falsely narrows the scope of institutional choice by placing all authority structures under the label 'governance' and treating private-property rights (or wrongly 'exclusion') as a natural alternative, when it should be treated as one particular kind of 'governance' rule along a continuum of governance rules.

3.2. Institutional Efficiency

Having established that private-property rights should have no a priori special status among institutions that promote efficiency, let us return to the question of whether B. C. Field's model provides hope that efficient institutions will evolve. On the surface, the community is both the 'unit of account' and 'the unit of action'[15] and thus the community's net marginal benefit associated with alternative institutions (as valued by the community itself) is maximized, so the institutions selected are optimal. But for the institutions selected to be optimal a very strong assumption needs to be made: that the very process by which decisions are made by the group is optimal. That is, in order to have faith that the institutions selected by the community are efficient, one needs to believe that formal voting procedures and information-gathering procedures[16] followed by the community will ensure community-welfare-maximizing choices. For the community to be

---

[15] I discussed in Ch. 7, above, that if the activity being evaluated happens to coincide with the activity of a single actor, then if the actor is assumed rational (in the neoclassical sense), the action will be optimal (by definition). Of course, the 'unit of action' in this model is the entire group, but in fact the group is made up of many individuals who are the ultimate units of action. If the group is to make efficient decisions it must be shown how the individuals are induced to make efficient decisions for the group.

[16] Naturally these are not completely separate procedures.

taking decisions that reflect the welfare of the community, assurances are needed that interest groups are not able unduly to influence decisions, or similarly, that the representatives making the decisions are not basing their votes on their own self-interests. Furthermore, even assuming that decision-makers for the community have the community's interest in mind, the information on which they base their choices may be highly distorted; members of the community may not reveal correct information. Essentially, Field's model explains how certain institutions may evolve optimally by assuming that the far more sophisticated political institutions of community decision-making are already optimal. The collective action problems (free-rider, preference revelation, strategic behaviour, etc.) at the level of the smaller subgroups are solved by assuming away the collective-action problems at a higher level where decisions are taken for the entire community.

4. INSTITUTIONS AND POWER

Several authors (see Bush and Mayer (1974), Bates (1983), and Umbeck (1981) have presented theories of how property rights may evolve from an initial state of anarchy, i.e. a state in which no prior institution exists. Given the lack of institutions to coordinate individuals' actions it is surprising to find that some of the models suggest that the institutions that evolve from anarchical interaction are efficient. An important contribution of these models is that they delve into the role and nature of power (or force) which is a fundamental element in understanding transaction costs and institutions.

Umbeck (1981) presents a pre-institution model in order to explain the establishment of a stable system of private-property rights in California during the Gold Rush years. While there was a massive inflow of gold-seekers into California, and there was no real system of law in place (most US government employees abandoned their posts to participate in the search), excessive violence was avoided and a fairly stable system of private-property right over land evolved. Umbeck proposes 'to use the orthodox theory of competition to explain the formation and distribution of property rights among individuals' (1981: 38). He starts by

explaining the fundamental role of force in entitlement formation.

Ownership rights to property can exist only as long as other people
agree to respect them or as long as the owner can forcefully exclude
those who do not agree. If the individuals agree to respect each other's
ownership rights, they may do so either implicitly, in which case they are
usually called customs or traditions, or explicitly through contract, in
which case they are called laws or rules . . . However, even if all individuals enter into an explicit agreement to assign and respect each other's
ownership rights, some force or threat of force will still be required. This
follows from the postulate of individual maximization. If one person can
violate the terms of the agreement and deprive another of his assigned
rights he will do so if the gains exceed the costs. Therefore, the contracting group must agree to impose costs upon anyone who would take
someone else's property. This would involve the forceful exclusion of
would-be violators. *Ultimately all ownership rights are based on the abilities of individuals, or groups of individuals, to forcefully maintain exclusivity.* Force also underlies all allocative systems. (Umbeck: 1981: 39)

If an individual can gain by force more than is allotted to her
by some allocative system, then rationality[17] dictates that she vio-
lates the rationing device.[18] This does not imply that 'force or
even the threat of force will be the actual rationing system used
by individuals. However, potential force is the relevant constraint
underlying any initial agreements (and subsequent agreements)
which allocate wealth among competitors' (Umbeck 1981: 40),
i.e. no one will accept less than they can gain by the use of force.
Umbeck considers a simple model where there is a group of
individuals on an island which contains a single scarce resource,
namely gold buried in the land. There is no government or law
to constrain individuals. Individuals are endowed with some initial labour power which can be put to use either in productive
activity, in this case gold-mining, or in violence, the forceful
acquisition of land. Labour will be exhausted in these two activities; there is no labour–leisure trade-off. He assumes 'that the
exclusive rights to a miner's labour and the gold he extracts from
the ground belong to him and are costlessly enforced private

[17] Rationality here is defined in the narrow neoclassical sense.
[18] Any way in which resources are allocated and distribution is determined can
be called a rationing system whether this is an elaborate system of legal rules,
contracts, and markets; a centrally planned system; or a system of behavioural
norms in a primitive society.

property' (1981: 41).[19] The cost of entering into contractual agreement is prohibitively high.[20] Individuals can spend their labour either mining for gold, or acquiring land, or both. Their decision on whether to allocate labour to violence or mining will depend on the relative benefits and costs of each activity. The opportunity cost of fighting for a piece of land is the lost marginal-value product of labour in mining (VMP_L). For someone who has a large plot of land, the VMP_L will be high since land and labour complement each other and thus the productivity of labour will be high. Likewise, someone who has a small plot of land will have a low VMP_L as labour is not as productive in

[19] Umbeck points out 'that the nature of the traditional economic model places an interesting constraint on the selection of assumptions. *We must assume initially that each individual has the right to some resource.* Without this assumption, the individual's decisions could not affect the allocation of anything and there would be no behavior to explain. This suggests that economic theory will never be able to examine anarchy as a state in which no one has the rights to anything.' (Umbeck 1981: 41) In particular he says that his model could not explain slavery, or the control of one's labour by another, implying that a model would have to allow that individuals may start with zero endowments in order to explain such phenomena. But the limitation Umbeck points to is not confined to economic theory. It is important to note the definition of right that Umbeck uses: ownership rights are 'the expectations a person has that his decision about the uses of certain resources will be effective' (Alchian and Allen 1969: 158). With such a definition of rights no theory could examine 'anarchy as a state in which no one has the rights to anything,' since if we can't surmise anything about individuals' expectation of the effect of their actions, there is no way to explain behaviour. In effect if individuals are not endowed with anything, they will be unable to produce anything, whether for themselves or for others. Even a slave has some initial endowment which makes her valuable to a slave owner, and ultimately provides a last resort to survival as labour is 'exchanged' for food. There is some problem, however, with a definition of private property that strips it of any institutional context. The fact that someone can 'forcefully exclude someone who does not agree' should not be sufficient to label some resource private property. Private property implies a legal institution, a set of relationships among agents, it cannot be distilled to some abstract concept of control or power. While an individual may be able to exclude others forcefully, this does not mean she has the right to do so. While Umbeck states that miners have exclusive rights to their labour and the gold they extract, and this fits his definition of private property, all that is needed is to state that miners have control over these resources, they have some initial endowment of force or power. Likewise it might be wrong to assume that the equilibrium whereby agents tacitly recognize each other's claim over some land, constitutes private property. Nevertheless it offers insight into a mechanism whereby private property institutions may evolve.

[20] This is an important assumption since it greatly restricts the set of allocations that are considered Pareto-efficient, e.g. an agreement between two individuals that the more skilled gold-miner specializes in extraction while the more skilled gun-slinger specializes in protection so that overall production of gold is increased, is made inefficient by the high cost of forming such an agreement.

mining. The marginal benefit from fighting will depend on the value of an additional unit of land put to productive use (VMP_H). The larger the plot of land, the lower the marginal-value product of an additional unit of land.

Umbeck's first illustration considers only two persons, X and Y, inhabiting the island with identical skills in mining and violence, where land is homogeneous in terms of gold deposits. At the start individual X has all the land, and Y shows up and claims a unit of land. X must decide whether to protect the threatened unit of land by allocating some of his labour to violence. Given he has all the land, the opportunity cost of labour used for violence will be high (high VMP_L), while the benefits of fighting will be low. In fact the ratio $(VMP_H/VMP_L)^X$, which is the marginal rate of substitution of land for labour, indicates the amount of labour that X is willing to use to protect a marginal unit of land. For instance if the VMP_H is three gold nuggets while the VMP_L is one gold nugget it makes sense to transfer up to three units of labour from mining to fighting for one unit of land. Since X has all the land, the marginal rate of substitution of land for labour will be low, indicating the relatively low productivity of the marginal unit of land (and thus violence). Y on the other hand, who has no land, will have a high marginal rate of substitution of land for labour $(VMP_H/VMP_L)^Y$, suggesting that she will be willing to put many units of labour into fighting. Furthermore, X has full knowledge and is thus aware that Y is going to win the land since she will spend more labour fighting than he is willing to allocate to a fight.[21] X will thus let Y take the first unit of land without putting up a fight. In fact X will allow Y to take half his land since at that point there will be equality in the marginal rates of substitution between land and labour, and beyond that point X will be willing to spend more labour in protecting his remaining land than Y is willing to increase her holdings (see Fig. 8.3 where equilibrium is H/2).

A kind of private-property rights (mutual recognition of each other's claim on a portion of the land) has evolved from an initial state of anarchy. This is based, *inter alia*, on the underlying

[21] The implicit assumption here is that the person who puts relatively more labour in violence will win the fight. Also, full knowledge includes knowledge of what the potential outcome of a fight will be. It is this knowledge that prevents any violence from actually occurring.

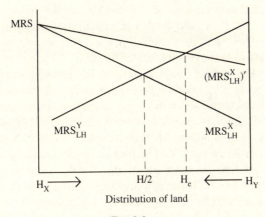

FIG 8.3.

distribution of force or power. In this case it also happens that the distribution of land that results is efficient. That is, given the initial allocation of skills in force and mining, a Pareto-optimal allocation of labour and land has occurred. Umbeck extends his model to one with more individuals and even allows for heterogeneity of land in terms of gold deposits, and shows that under certain assumptions (full information, constant returns to scale in violence, prohibitively high costs of contracting), an efficient distribution of land occurs.

From an essentially institutionless world there has come an efficient allocation of resources. While Umbeck has assumed 'private property' of certain resources (labour and extracted gold) one can assume some initial allocation of force rather than entitlements and therefore model a truly institutionless world. While all allocative systems require force or depend on some underlying structure of force, in this model force itself is the allocative mechanism. There is a direct correspondence between the structure of force and resource allocation, willingness to pay has given way to willingness to fight. Individuals maximized their utility subject to their endowment of force (control they exerted over labour, land, and gold), and the outcome of their interaction was an efficient allocation of resources.[22]

---

[22] While this model offers a possible explanation of the emergence of private-property rights, it also reveals a sort of redundancy of an entitlement system in the specific example, at least with regards to efficiency concerns.

The efficiency result of Umbeck's model goes well with Demsetz's belief in individual maximization of utility as a road to progress. However, Pareto-efficiency is achieved with very strong assumptions: homogeneity of land, equal distribution of skills, complete knowledge, constant returns in the technology of force, and, importantly, prohibitively high costs of contracting.[23] It would be easy to show how an inefficient allocation of land occurred if these assumptions were weakened. In Fig. 8.3, I show an equilibrium outcome H_e which would result if X were more skilled in violence than Y. The higher MRS^x could be interpreted as resulting from a lowering of the VMP_L, since an additional unit of land can be forcefully acquired with a smaller sacrifice in labour diverted from mining (and thus gold nuggets) now that X is more powerful. The equilibrium outcome H_e means that X will now possess more than half the land even though he is equally productive with Y. Given decreasing returns to labour in mining this means that the total production of gold from both X and Y is lower than when both possessed half the land. This is clearly Pareto-inefficient in the standard neoclassical sense which abstracts from transaction costs. The question that comes to mind is: Why don't the two individuals contract away from this equilibrium since there are potential gains for both? The answer is that the costs of coming to some agreement (and enforcing the agreement) are too high; at least this is the assumption made by Umbeck. If that is the case, then what initially looks like an inefficient outcome (H_e in Fig. 8.3) may not be since the losses from transacting would be greater than the gains. With this kind of reasoning all equilibrium outcomes will be efficient since the costs of contracting away from them will be prohibitive. Since I confront this rather disturbing feature of what looks like tautological efficiency in Chapter 10, I will not pursue this matter here. Instead, I will note that whether we call the equilibrium outcome H_e efficient or not, it still does not appear to be a particularly appealing outcome. This is especially so if the reason that the two individuals are not coming to some agreement is because of mistrust or strategic bargaining, and not because there are some

---

[23] Umbeck believed these assumptions to be good approximations for the conditions that individuals faced during the California Gold Rush.

'material' costs of getting information about the productive potential of land.[24]

In general, a loosening of the assumptions made in Umbeck's model, like allowing for different levels of skill in violence and mining, or imperfect information, or increasing returns in the technology of violence, would lead to equilibrium results which would leave little to be desired. Heterogeneity in the levels of skill in violence and mining would lead to the kind of result that I have just described (H_e in Fig. 8.3). Imperfect information would lead to wasteful violence and bargaining problems. Non-convexities in the technology of violence could lead to natural monopolies in violence as groups of individuals form coalitions to increase their power. In essence, it is the structure of Umbeck's example that aligns individual maximization of utility with an efficient collective outcome.[25] Alter the structure and there is no reason why inefficiency will not result from individual maximization, or the atomized calculus of costs and benefits.[26] While the model suggests how individuals seeking to maximize their utility could generate an optimal set of private-property rights, unlike Demsetz, it at least recognizes (implicitly) that individual self-seeking behaviour needs to be channelled by a clearly specified structure of interdependence for efficient institutions to ensue.[27]

An important issue illuminated by models of anarchy like Umbeck's is that while property rights are treated in most mainstream economic models as variables that can be freely altered to bring about different allocations, here the allocation is dependent on a distribution of force which is prior to entitlements and by its nature unalterable without cost. If entitlement systems are grounded on some underlying structure of force then there are

[24] Note that the assumption of full information contrasts rather starkly with the assumption of prohibitively high costs of contracting. If agents are fully aware what the outcome of a fight will be before they actually fight, would it not be natural to expect them to know what the outcome of a contractual agreement would be on the basis of knowledge of each other's bargaining strategies?

[25] Note that the equilibrium in Umbeck's model where individuals are identical and 'own' equal-sized plots happens to be the Pareto-efficient outcome even when there are zero costs of transacting.

[26] Again I am abstracting from the view that prohibitive transaction costs make all equilibrium outcomes Pareto-efficient.

[27] It is almost ironic that a model of anarchy should demand so much structure.

clear limitations to how entitlements can be varied to alter allocations. The cost of enforcing entitlement systems will depend on this underlying structure of force. This is a far cry from the 'Coasean neutrality' of property assignment (when transaction costs are zero).

These models of anarchy are important not only for the insights they offer on the emergence of property rights, but in that they deal explicitly with the concept of force (or power, coercion, and influence). No doubt the concepts of power or coercion are in many ways obscure, but similar problems with a concept like transaction costs have not hindered its currency. Power has been a taboo word in mainstream economics, probably because of its Marxist overtones, but recent microeconomic analysis makes an explicit understanding of power, or some correlate concept, long overdue. As Bowles and Gintis (1988: 145) say, 'a consistent application of the axioms of rational self-interested individual action does not support the neoclassical view of the apolitical economy but rather . . . provides the microeconomic basis for the study of economic power'. In earlier chapters my investigation into notions of externality raised questions about actions taken without entitlement. In order to evaluate these actions it was necessary to refer to costs of forming property rights (and more broadly, entitlements) and this includes enforcement costs. But models of anarchy suggest that in order to understand such costs, one needs to investigate the technology of coercion. After all, as I quoted earlier: 'Ultimately all ownership rights [or more generally entitlements] are based on the abilities of individuals, or groups of individuals, to forcefully maintain exclusivity' (Umbeck 1981: 39). It is in this sense that 'a consistent application of the axioms of rational self-interested individual action' makes imperative an analysis of power (and not just political power).

5. A GAME-THEORETIC MODEL OF INSTITUTIONS

The property-rights theorists avoid confronting a key ingredient in explaining how institutions may evolve efficiently: How will self-interested individuals be able to generate institutions that cater to the interests of the community? Stated otherwise, they avoid dealing with the problem of collective action. Umbeck's model of anarchy dealt with this problem by setting up a structure of interaction that channelled individual action towards efficient collective ends. However, the assumptions required for efficient formation of institutions were very stringent and unlikely to be present in most real-world situations of anarchy. An alternative theory advocated by Schotter (1981) tries to confront the collective-action problem directly. It is based on what he calls organic explanations which have institutions emerge as the unintended or undesigned consequence of individual action;[28] in particular, *'how individual economic agents pursuing their own selfish ends evolve institutions as a means to satisfy them'* (Schotter 1981: 5). The novel element of Schotter's analysis, *vis-à-vis* earlier models presented, is his discussion of various game-theoretic ways that institutions may evolve when individuals face coordination problems, Prisoners' Dilemma problems, inequality-preserving problems, or cooperative-game problems, i.e. exactly those situations that one usually cites as a cause of inefficiency of collective action, and which one expects agents forming institutions to confront.

I only intend to give a very intuitive exposition of Schotter's models of institution formation. In all Schotter's models agents find themselves confronting a particular collective action problem repeatedly. For instance, if no property rights have been established over land that is being farmed or used as hunting ground, neighbouring individuals (or groups of individuals) may be constantly fighting each other to establish some claims over commonly used land. Each individual associates some expected pay-off from making a claim to a plot of land and excluding

---

[28] Organic refers to the point that none of the agents set out consciously to create an institution. Institutions are a kind of byproduct of individual action rather than a conscious result of a group of individuals or some government representing the collective. In many respects 'organic' explanations are no different than the models already represented in this ch. And in fact there are some interpretational problems with the term organic when associated to human agents whose behaviour is, to a large extent, intentional. Is Umbeck's explanation of private-property rights intentional or organic? Schotter acknowledges that institutions may be created through deliberate action as well, he simply focuses on 'unintended' institution formation. There are also organic explanations of institutions that consider the emergence of institutions from the unintended consequences of groups of individuals, e.g. Marxian class analysis, or interest-group theories, etc. The subject or agent of the institutional model need not be the individual.

others from its use. As some individuals decide to fight and others not, over time expectations of each other's reactions are adjusted and expected pay-offs of alternative actions change accordingly. In some cases, an equilibrium occurs where individuals' expected pay-offs are such that there is mutual 'acceptance' of a particular distribution of land (or at least an implicit acceptance not to start a new round of fighting), i.e. given expectations, the utility-maximizing strategy for individuals is to acknowledge a certain set of property rights. The basis of such an equilibrium is that everyone has to gain by the formation of property rights as effort can be spent on mutually beneficial trade rather than wasting it in a purely redistributive Hobbesian fight.[29]

The fact that the rights assignment may be arbitrary and preserving of an unequal distribution of income merely reflect the fact that the equilibrium achieved with property rights is preferred by all agents to the state of conflict that would result if all property rights were removed, but not necessarily preferred by all agents to the state that might result under another set of property rights. The existence of property rights determines a noncooperative equilibrium to a social coordination problem but not necessarily the only one. (Schotter 1981: 44)

A more concrete example of organic creation of institutions provided by Schotter is a simple game-theoretic model that could explain the evolution of the week. The main function of the week in this model is to determine the interval of time in which farmers will converge to a predestined location to trade goods. It is in all farmers' interests that such a time-interval be established and adhered to by all, as it maximizes the number of consumers for each farmer's goods at a minimum transportation cost.

The preferences of the players are . . . identical in establishing the existence of the week, but their preferences are conflicting in determining its length . . . The exact form of any social institution can be specified only probabilistically. The development of the week will be greatly influenced by the coincidence with which people start to converge on the city and

---

[29] Such equilibriums are called inequality-preserving since they may be largely arbitrary and based on some initial unequal distribution of land, which, however, is established because agents prefer this to a new round of war. This process of institution-formation does not seem too far removed from Umbeck's model. One added element here is imperfect knowledge which is improved through experience in recurrent interaction.

		Farmer 2		
		Every day	Every 2 days	Every 3 days
Farmer 1	Every day	6, 5	3, 4	2, 3
	Every 2 days	5, 5	8, 10	0, 0
	Every 3 days	3, 2	0, 0	9, 6

Fig 8.4.

see each other. What develops is a snowballing effect in which people come to the city in a particular pattern, see other people are also following this pattern, and continue to return or not, according to whether their pattern is popular. Eventually, a universal pattern is established and institutionalized, but the exact pattern that is institutionalized is actually randomly determined . . . As we will see in our formal model, the history or path of the game will have a dramatic influence upon the type of institution that is created, and to the extent that different coincidental paths occur, different institutions are possible . . . .Finally, it is clear that the size of the week that finally evolves from a given society may not be Pareto-optimal [consider Fig. 8.4 reproduced from Schotter (p. 35)] . . . Notice, however, that there exists a length of week—the 1-day week—that is Pareto-inferior to the 2- and 3-day weeks but may still evolve as an equilibrium pattern. Consequently the efficiency of the institutions that evolve from a given situation may be rather low. (Schotter 1981: 34–5)

Schotter's analysis can be applied in explaining the formation of any institution. The state itself, that ultimate of institutions, can be given an organic explanation:

According to Nozick [1974] the state emerges as the agents in society form protective associations to adjudicate disputes they have with each other and protect each other from outsiders. If there are any increasing returns to group size in the formation of these protective associations, one stable 'grand protective association' will be formed to which all agents will belong and that has the power to adjudicate all disputes. This grand protective association is what Nozick calls the 'minimal state.' Consequently, the agents need not sit down together with the explicit purpose of creating a state in order for it to emerge. It can be created unintentionally as the equilibrium outcome of individual protective behaviour. (Schotter 1981: 46)

In all Schotter's models the presence of gains for individuals when faced with some kind of coordination problem provides the incentive for the formation of an institution. A further prerequisite is that the problem be one that the agents face repeatedly;[30] this provides an opportunity for individuals to try out cooperative forms of behaviour and also be 'punished' when acting 'non-cooperatively' by the fear of dissolution of the institution.[31] The mechanism by which conventions become formed is a stochastic one where agents form strategies (and act) on the basis of the others' previous actions (this is the only information they have). Schotter's model illustrates how agents' behaviour converge to some equilibrium point where a regularity in behaviour (institution) is established. What affords staying power to certain patterns of behaviour is that once regularities are established, if anyone deviates, 'it is known that some or all of the others will also deviate and the payoffs associated with the recurrent play of [the supergame] using these deviating strategies are worse for all agents than is the payoff associated with [the regularity]' (Schotter 1981: 53).

The salient points distilled from Schotter's models concerning the efficiency of the institutions that are formed, are the following:

1. There are multiple equilibrium points in the models, i.e. many possible institutions can evolve. Equilibrium points may or may not contain Pareto-optimal points, while there may be several Pareto-suboptimal points. So while the models can be used to explain how an 'optimal' institution has evolved it can just as easily explain how 'suboptimal' institutions may emerge.

[30] The function of repetition in games is that of altering the perceived expected pay-offs associated with alternative strategies that individuals face. It can be shown e.g. that individuals can overcome the quagmire of a one-shot Prisoner Dilemma if the game being played is repeated enough times and with a low enough discount rate so that future outcomes count. The intuition is simple: if the prisoners know that they will be playing the game many times and they are concerned about the future then it may pay to avoid non-cooperative behaviour which could set a very costly pattern of retaliation. Alternatively it may pay to risk cooperative behaviour given the potential benefits gained if the opponent follows suit. There is substantial literature on the role of repetition in Prisoners' Dilemma games; see Taylor (1990) and Hechter (1990).

[31] 'A social institution is a regularity in social behavior that is agreed to by all members of society, specifies behavior in specific recurrent situations, and is either self-policed or policed by some external authority' (Schotter 1981: 11).

2. Although not explicitly stated, one can derive from the analysis that suboptimal institutions can have staying power as deviant behaviour will be punished once regularity has been established.

3. Even if a Pareto-optimal institution finally prevails, the dynamic process of reaching such a point may be long, and thus a source of inefficiency; 'the question is not only which equilibrium convention will be established but how long one could expect to wait until a particular one is' (Schotter 1981: 80).

4. The stochastic nature of the process of institution creation means that the institutions that evolve are an 'accident of history and what exists today could have evolved in a very different manner' (1981: 79).

6. INSTITUTIONS AND EFFICIENCY

Although institutions are poorly defined abstract entities in neo-classical economic models, they provide the structure through which individual action is channelled towards collective ends. Without a universal set of markets and private-property rights (as well as parametric prices and certain convexity assumptions for utility and production functions), the Pareto-optimality of competitive private-ownership economies would not be possible.[32] Adam Smith's 'invisible hand' is invisible only to someone who is blind to the function of institutions. Importantly, the achievements of private-ownership economies also require that there are no costs of forming markets and private-ownership rights. Once this assumption is dropped (and that seems necessary if one is to model the real world), then it becomes important not just to consider the efficiency of alternative resource allocations, but also the efficiency of the institutions themselves. They can no longer be treated as exogenous elements in models of resource allocation. When modelling the formation of institutions rather than just the allocation of resources, one can no longer completely rely on institutions to provide the structure for channelling individual activity towards efficient formation of

[32] See sect. 3.1, above, for a fuller account of the conditions for Pareto-optimality of competitive markets.

institutions. One can assume some initial institutional structure that helps individuals form new institutions that are efficient, but the question then becomes: How did the initial institutional structure become formed? A problem of infinite regress seems to be in the making. In order to have an optimal allocation of resources we need an optimal set of institutions. In order to have an optimal set of institutions we need an optimal system of interaction that will insure the formation of optimal institutions.

Demsetz's (1967) reliance on wealth-maximizing by individuals to bring about efficient institutions is clearly unjustified. There is no market[33] for institutions to insure that the net private benefits maximized by individuals when forming institutions will bear any relationship to the social net benefits of forming institutions. To make a case that institution formation is efficient one has to provide a framework conceptually similar to the general-equilibrium framework that is able to forge a link between individual behaviour and collective outcome. B. C. Field's (1986) 'optimal commons' model of institution formation manages to give rise to efficient institutions only by assuming that some governing group will set up institutions on behalf of the collective. Institutions are formed by a direct maximization of net social benefits by some governing institution. But unless an explanation is offered as to how this government body is formed, and how the governing body actually arrives at the correct decisions about which institutions should be implemented, there are no grounds for expecting efficient institutions to evolve.

Anarchy models of institution formation like Umbeck's (1981) have the advantage of addressing the problem of initial institution formation, thus forcing a better understanding of notions

---

[33] It seems that the presumption that efficient institutions will emerge as individuals try to maximize their utility, derives from a view of institution formation as a kind of market for institutions. Even if one accepts such a broad understanding of the term market, it would be a very different market from the commodity markets. It might be that institutions are formed through a bargaining process among agents, but this process would bear little resemblance to market exchange (as Arrow (1969) defines it), even when market exchange is defined quite broadly: 'Exchange involves contractual agreement and the exchange of property rights, and the market consists in part of mechanisms to structure, organize and legitimate these activities. Markets, in short, are organized and institutionalized exchange' (Hodgson 1988: 174). One doesn't have to accept this definition of market exchange to recognize the vast difference between market exchange processes and bargaining for institutions. In the latter there is no structure defining the bargaining process.

like power or coercion which must be a fundamental element in any economic theory of institutions. As in Demsetz's model, institutions evolve through private net-benefit maximization by individuals who decide, *inter alia*, how to allocate their ability to fight. While Umbeck suggests how there might be a kind of general-equilibrium of force which corresponds to an optimal resource allocation, he achieves this result by making rather stringent demands on the initial conditions of the model (homogeneity of land, equal distribution of skills, complete knowledge, etc.). In many cases such strong initial conditions are not likely to be present in the world, and thus the likelihood of the evolution of efficient institutions seems small. Finally, Schotter's (1981) game-theoretic model of institution formation which confronts the collective-action problem head on, raises some hope that institutions may evolve in the direction of greater efficiency, but not that the institutions will be optimal.

7. INSTITUTIONS AND DISTRIBUTIVE JUSTICE

Thus far I have argued that many models in the economic literature on institution formation do not provide good theoretical grounds for a belief that efficient institutions are likely to evolve through the interaction of self-seeking individuals (whether these institutions are market institutions or not). Another point that needs to be made about economic models that endogenize organizational costs, is that the neat division between distributional and efficiency matters, enshrined in the two Welfare Theorems, is lost. Dahlman (1980) sees the function of property rights as:

determining income or wealth distribution, on the one hand, and also serving as signals for behaviour, thereby guiding incentives, on the other. If we accept the view that institutions are really nothing but specific collections of attenuated property rights, then it follows that institutions are also tied up with both income distribution and incentive formation . . . (T)he relative efficiency of various institutions now becomes dependent upon our ability to rank various income distributions. For if every set of institutions is associated with a certain distribution of income, and if we wish to ascertain which set of institutions is the most efficient with respect to transaction costs, then we are also, implicitly or explicitly, comparing various distributions of benefits associated with particular institutions. (1980: 213–14)

Our ability to say that a certain set of institutions is efficient requires a ranking of income distributions; in effect we have to start with a social-welfare function in order to determine what institutions we consider efficient. If one is to use the term efficient it has to refer to some welfare target, unlike allocation of resources in a world where institutions are costless and one can consider an allocation Pareto-efficient with respect to some initial endowment. In this case the initial conditions are a given and not subject to change the way endowments are in the general-equilibrium model. In the general-equilibrium model one can alter the endowments by costless lump-sum taxes, in effect changing the starting-point from which the market process initiates. When considering institutional change one is starting from some fixed point defined by the technology of force, technology of production, agents' utilities and behavioural characteristics, spatial allocation of agents, etc. These initial conditions are not variables, they form the underlying conditions from which institutional formation can take place. Any choice of institutions will not only be limited by this initial distribution of power, but will also entail an implicit distributional choice. In Chapter 9 I confront this issue more rigorously. An example, however, will help illustrate the point.

North (1981) has argued that the abolition of the institution of slavery could be comprehended on economic grounds. In particular, he believes that the changing structure of transaction costs made slavery an inefficient institution. Efficiency gains could be made by owners if they changed from slave labour to wage labour. The essentials of the argument were that as farms grew, the enforcement costs required to ensure a high work-effort on the part of the slaves became prohibitively high. By shifting to wage labour the farm-owners could drastically reduce enforcement costs. However, efficiency gains may have been latent in the system for a long time, at least long before the transformation from slave to wage labour, and the problem was whether the landlords could ensure the gains for themselves. It may be the case that efficiency gains would entail an absolute decline in the landlords' income despite an overall increase in the income of the economy. A true property-rights economist would retort that if such gains were possible then the landlords would have negotiated a Pareto-improvement with the slaves. But that would work only if transaction costs permitted, undoubtedly they would be large. The point is that institutional change does not require efficiency gains to be initiated, it requires gains to the initiators of change, which may or may not coincide with an overall increase in wealth, and would surely leave many potential efficiency gains untapped. Furthermore, whatever efficiency gains are made they are intimately tied to a distribution of wealth. North's discussion of the abolition of slavery makes the implicit assumption that slavery may at one time have been an efficient institution. If so, it was efficient in achieving a specific welfare goal, one that favoured the slave-owners and not the slaves. One could form a rather sophisticated argument that the true dictates of efficiency could never lead to espousal of slavery,[34] but it is likely that at least under certain conditions, slavery could be considered efficient given some initial distribution of power. Surely there are instances where individuals will produce more of certain goods under duress than voluntarily and that for a given social-welfare function (one we would consider repugnant), slavery would be an optimal institution.

An institution can be said to be optimal if it best attains some welfare goal. If one were to have a different welfare goal a different institution would be likely. Surely slavery would not be a very efficient system if one wanted to have a more equal distribution of income, or even a system that would be sensitive to slaves' desires (utility) at a minimum.

The intuition of this argument can be put in very simple terms. Imagine a world with two individuals: one is powerful and the other weak. The powerful individual is able to use violence, or the threat of violence to get more resources than the weak individual, whether this is through direct acquisition, or by forcing the weak agent to part with some of the fruits of her labour. Now assume that there exists some governing body which has a police force. The police could be used to enforce alternative property-right regimes (different entitlements over resources and labour power), and the more enforcement required the less they can be used for 'productive' activity. Clearly, property-right regimes that favour the less powerful will require more enforcement activity. The powerful are in a better position to defend their acquisitions and will put up a more forceful fight to hold on

---

[34] See Hare (1979) for a philosophical account of why a utilitarian would never support slavery.

to what they can. It might be argued that the governing body need only to use the threat of coercion and thus not divert any resources. But this is unlikely unless one is considering a highly idealized world with complete information, since at least some additional resources will be required to make the threat viable. This illustrates the intimate link that is forged between distribution and productive efficiency once organizational costs are part of the calculus of resource allocation.

8. CONCLUSION

The externality literature has always focused on those areas where institutions had not been formed, and it was initially believed that lack of institutions was a cause of market failure. The advent of transaction costs in economic analysis made it clear that lack of an institution was not a cause of failure, and more importantly, that it was necessary to acquire a fuller understanding of the implications of endogenizing organizational costs in order to evaluate the efficiency of institutions (market and non-market). Interestingly, some of the strongest advocates of models with endogenous organizational costs (Demsetz, Posner), took the view that a pre-market economy left on its own, would gradually generate market institutions, and these would be optimal. In this chapter my main aim was to dispel this notion as well as the notion that the institution of private property has any a priori theoretical claim to efficiency. I have argued that it is false to assume that the mere possibility of cooperative gains through institutional innovation will ensure that the best institutions will evolve. In an Arrow–Debreu framework we can rely on an auctioneer and well-defined private-property rights, and still need to make certain assumptions in order that the market outcome is optimal; in a pre-market environment there is no structure to provide an 'invisible hand'. There is no reason to believe that the institutions that evolve will be efficient, or for that matter to seek inefficiency in those activities for which no institutions have evolved (e.g. activities where there is open access, or over which private-property rights have not been formed), since the institutions that exist deserve equal attention as potential sources of inefficiency.

While I discussed how the pre-market economy could lead to inefficient institutions, it is still unclear what it means to call an institution efficient. It has not become clear how the very notion of optimality is to be reinterpreted once institutions have been incorporated endogenously. In Chapter 10, I consider this question, and the problems that a revised notion of optimality raise. In the next chapter I critically examine one of the more prominent views in the Law and Economics literature on what an 'optimal' institutional structure entails.

9
Wealth-Maximization

1. INTRODUCTION

The dominant notion of efficiency in the Law and Economics literature is that of wealth-maximization. According to Posner (1977: 10) 'Efficiency means exploiting economic resources in such a way that value—human satisfaction as measured by aggregate willingness to pay for goods and services—is maximized'. While this criterion has been used primarily on issues of property-rights assignment and protection in common law, Posner has promoted its use as a guide to all questions of resource allocation. Even such basic entitlements as the entitlement to one's labour could and should be derived according to this principle.

In this scheme of things entitlements are simply incentives, and their efficiency is judged according to what allocation of resources they engender. In particular if the allocation of resources is wealth-maximizing, then the allocation along with the institutional structure that supports it is deemed efficient.

Posner forms a rather elaborate thesis in support of wealth-maximization as a general ethical principle to be used as a guide to action. Accordingly, Wealth-Maximization provides a mix between Utilitarian and Kantian ethics. Rather than looking at some of the grander claims that Posner has made on behalf of wealth-maximization, I want to consider some apparently more modest claims that seem to have accounted for its resilience in the Law and Economics literature and have bolstered it as a guiding principle of 'efficient' legal structures; essentially the belief that wealth-maximization somehow mimics a well-functioning market, thereby imbuing it with the virtues of the market, that resources are not wasted in the sense of Pareto-optimality.

A part of the debate over the normative value of the wealth-maximization principle has turned on the question of whether it could in fact endorse repugnant institutions such as slavery.

Dworkin (1980) constructed an example (to be discussed presently in section 3) to show how wealth-maximization could espouse slavery. In the example, a wealthy nobleman, Sir George, would like to purchase the right to own Agatha who is a talented novel-writer, but is not wealthy. Dworkin points out that if the right to Agatha's labour is to be determined by wealth-maximization, Sir George will be assigned the right since he will be able to pay more for it. Posner (1983) countered. In a more recent article, S. E. Margolis (1987) clarifies some misconceptions about the precise meaning of wealth-maximization and takes the view that slavery would not be endorsed by a correctly applied wealth-maximizing principle.

S. E. Margolis's treatment of the slavery question is twofold: first, if the right to one's labour is treated as an individual case, then it is possible to construct an example which would lead to an ethically repulsive institution, although he believes that this does not apply to Dworkin's example; secondly, that legal rules such as the right to one's labour, should be treated as a class, in which case wealth-maximization will be a good guide to property-right assignment, and ethically repulsive outcomes will be avoided. In short, he believes that a correctly specified notion of wealth-maximization will provide a guide for efficient legal structures. On S. E. Margolis's first point I argue that even with Dworkin's specific example it is likely that slavery will be espoused, but that generally it is all too easy to construct examples which will lead to ethically unsound outcomes. On the second point I argue that when legal rules or institutions are treated as a class, wealth-maximization becomes an incoherent objective, affording no determinate outcome.

These points reflect bigger questions underlying the slavery example, and which are the main themes of this chapter. First, in so far as wealth-maximization provides guidance for policy, will it lead to results that can have an ethical plausibility in terms of usual norms? The discussion of Dworkin's example indicates that when considering specific entitlements in isolation, policy could be seriously defective. I also discuss a less colourful example of driver–pedestrian accidents, which helps show that distributional concerns must be incorporated in the concept of efficient legal rules once transaction costs have become endogenous, if the term 'efficient' is to retain any meaning. Secondly, is the idea of wealth-maximization a coherent and complete objective? I argue that in many cases, when institutional adjustments on a broad scale are being considered (or when entitlements should be treated as a class), it is an unattainable and incoherent objective. Even when property-right assignment is confined to isolated instances, its claim to forming 'efficient' institutions is highly tenuous.

My objective is threefold:

1. To clarify the notion of wealth-maximization.
2. To show that in so far as wealth-maximization provides guidance for policy, it will lead to results that cannot be ethically defended; either because they will be distributionally unsound, or they will violate other strong ethical principles, or they will not even attain Pareto-optimality.
3. To show that in the most important cases, wealth-maximization offers no policy guidance since it becomes an incoherent objective.

2. WHAT IS WEALTH-MAXIMIZATION?

There are some interpretational difficulties regarding the precise form the wealth-maximization principle should take, and a discussion by S. E. Margolis (1987) may help to clarify the problem. Margolis has argued that two definitions of efficient legal systems can be found, either implicitly or explicitly, in the literature of Law and Economics, and that sometimes inconsistent use of these has been misleading:

Definition 1. An efficient legal system is one in which property rights are assigned and liability rules are formulated so as to duplicate the allocation of rights obtained by a market in a world in which transaction costs are zero. (1987: 472)

Definition 2. An efficient legal system is one in which property rights are assigned and liability rules are formulated so that the value of the things present in society, as measured by willingness to pay, is maximized over all alternative legal environments, given the costs of transacting. (1987: 473–4)

The best way to illustrate the differences between these definitions as well as the weaknesses of the first is by reproducing an example from Margolis.

Chuck and David are neighbours. Chuck is a medical student; he owns his house but is mortgaged to the hilt. He is a decent fellow who will pay all his debts, but only the omniscient reader and writer know this. Because of this information problem, he is unable to borrow further. If he could borrow at the riskless rate and buy life insurance at the actuarially fair rate in order to protect his creditors, he would rearrange his income stream extensively. Dave wants to put up a brick wall. After he does, there will be no taking it down. Dave values the right to build the wall at $2,000. Chuck opposes the wall, and, even given his limited access to capital, he would pay $1,000 rather than have it go up. If he were able to rearrange his consumption stream fully, he would be willing to pay $3,000 to avoid the brick wall. But given his real world difficulties in borrowing, if he were assigned the right to avoid the wall, he would sell it to Dave. Regardless of which party has the right, it would cost $100 to draw up a contract to transfer the right.

Given all this, which vesting of rights would we regard as efficient? By definition 1, efficiency awards the right to Chuck. In a world devoid of transaction costs, Chuck could bind himself to contracts that would insure repayment of debt. There are no costs of enforcement, of monitoring, or of executing contracts that specify every contingency. Using Kronman's metaphor, the hypothetical auctioneer would serve as Chuck's banker, Chuck would rearrange his income stream, and he would buy the right. In a frictionless world, Chuck, not Dave, places the highest value on the right.

An efficiency rule that acknowledges the prospect of transaction costs would, on the other hand, award the right to Dave, given the true difficulties that Chuck will face once he walks out of the courtroom. If Chuck won the right through litigation, he would promptly sell it to Dave. So the court can save society the $100 cost of the transaction by awarding the right initially to Dave. Of course, it might be objected that this improperly constrains the purview of the court, that, if the court could take a more complete view and rearrange Chuck's portfolio, Chuck would retain the right when it was awarded to him. But the constraint is not arbitrary; the court would not have the opportunity to rearrange income streams in this way. Dave's right to build a wall is being contested, not the bank's right to refuse to lend at a riskless rate. Nor is this a matter solely of institutional competence or jurisdictional restriction. The costs of lending are real costs. If Chuck were allowed to borrow, some lender—perhaps the court—would have to watch him to be sure that he worked hard at his studies, that he took proper care of himself, and that he did not leave the country. Although the cost of proclaiming, Dave can build the wall if he wants to, is no higher than that of, He'd better get Chuck's permission, attempts to rearrange Chuck's income stream impose real costs, costs that no court could abolish by proclamation.

This example does not hinge crucially on the difficulty in borrowing against human capital. The assumption of zero transaction costs affects valuations of the rights being contested. The values that dictate allocation in a hypothetical costless auction do not apply to real agents in real markets. These real agents have reason to transact away from any such initial allocation. (Margolis 1987: 476–7)

This discussion reveals bluntly the problem with the first definition, or, what is otherwise known as mimicking a costless market. In a costless world the wall would not be built; Chuck must retain the right to the wall if the costless-market allocation is to be duplicated. In the real world of ubiquitous transaction costs the costs of attaining such an allocation may far outweigh any gains. Clearly wealth is not maximized. If the object is to maximize social wealth, and organizational costs are real, they must be incorporated in the evaluation of property rights. It seems that definition 2 is the correct form that the wealth-maximization principle should take. The question that must be considered now is whether this is a desirable principle for the formation and assignment of property rights. More specifically, the question is whether actual costs and benefits as proxied by the existing institutional structure should be the guide to decisions about entitlements.

3. DOES WEALTH-MAXIMIZATION AVOID ETHICALLY REPULSIVE INSTITUTIONS?

Given the somewhat non-intuitive nature of the subject, part of the debate about the value of the wealth-maximization principle has turned on the question of whether morally repulsive outcomes could result from an unflinching application of the rule. The celebrated debate which Dworkin began is about a woman named Agatha who has a great talent in writing mystery novels, but who would rather spend her time interior-decorating. Sir George, a wealthy nobleman, has a keen eye for talent, and would like to lay claim to Agatha's labour to put it to lucrative use. The question is, Who would be given the right to Agatha's labour under a rule of wealth-maximization? Dworkin claims that slavery would be condoned by such a rule, as Sir George would be the highest bidder, his willingness to pay amply backed by his wealth. Despite the boundless utility that Agatha attaches to ownership of her person, she lacks the wealth to outbid Sir George. Posner (1980: 243) responds that were Agatha to face a perfect capital market, she could borrow on the basis of her talent in book-writing and outbid Sir George, on the basis of her saving on any monitoring costs he would have to bear if she were his slave. From this, Posner argues that monitoring costs will be minimized, and wealth maximized, if Agatha is given the right to her labour from the start.

The debate continues. Even accepting Posner's reasoning of a perfect capital market, the institution of slavery hinges on the relative effectiveness of self-monitoring as compared to external monitoring. Will Agatha be more motivated if she is repaying her debts of freedom, or working for Sir George? Some would argue that slaves work harder because the costs of shirking are unthinkable. Maybe if Sir George is a lenient slave-driver Agatha would work harder on her own. Whatever is the case, there is at least a possibility that the institution of slavery would be selected even with a perfect capital market, and that is not comforting.

S. E. Margolis points out that Posner 'invokes elements of both definitions' aforementioned.

On the one hand, the cost of monitoring Agatha's output, judging whether she is being as clever as she can be, is the reason that her talents are more valuable to her than to someone else. But on the other hand, her cost of contracting for a loan is assumed away. Posner assumes that Agatha faces no limitations in borrowing, necessarily placing her in the world of zero transaction costs. Persistent application of the costless auction metaphor would seem to be inconclusive. Sir George and Agatha seem to be equally qualified to exploit her talent if information is perfect. Agatha might buy some limited levels of autonomy, or she might choose to buy her freedom from slavery altogether. Wealth maximization in the first sense would seem to be neutral with regard to slavery. Posner's position can be defended by explicit use of definition 2. Monitoring costs are real costs, which means that Agatha is more valuable to herself than she is to someone else. Borrowing also imposes real costs, which are avoided if Agatha starts out free. (Margolis 1987: 477)

Margolis goes on to point out that Dworkin is only concerned to show that we could construct some example where slavery would be selected by wealth-maximization principle, and in this respect he is correct. But Margolis argues that while this may be so when considering individual cases, this is not the way institutions of this sort would be addressed by law.

> To consider the efficiency of slavery, however, we could not ask whether some one person would sell herself into slavery. Because the law does not address each individual separately, the question is more general. What is efficiency of slavery for some definable class of individuals?
>
> Assume that some Agathas would borrow to buy their freedom if born as slaves and that an equal number would indenture themselves if born free. The transaction costs imposed by the possible starting-points are not equal. Borrowing against future earnings to buy one's freedom is very difficult. Entering a long-term labour services contract is less difficult. Thus a rule of slavery for some class would impose greater costs than a rule by which members of that class start out owning their human capital. (Margolis 1987: 478)

I will argue first, that even with use of definition 2 Dworkin does not need to search for another example to defend his position, in fact it is all too easy to construct examples that would support his view. Secondly, treating these kinds of entitlements as a class rather than individually does not provide an escape from morally repulsive outcomes.

3.1. Slavery Treated Individually

There is something fundamentally wrong with the way this example has been presented and used. The point of determining entitlements according to wealth-maximization is that resources, whether organizational, productive, or natural, are put to their most efficient use (as defined by wealth-maximization theory, the most wealth-maximizing use). When considering the ownership of labour, the question is which entitlement structure will make most efficient use of labour (including organizational costs). Agatha's claim to her labour is to use it as she wills, she demands the right to dispose of her person as she likes. Sir George is interested in her labour for its productive value to society: his claim of ownership is a claim to this use, much as a polluter claims ownership of air for its use in the production process of some other good. It is alternative uses of the resource in question that are being determined simultaneously with institutional costs. When we say that the willingness to pay by the polluter outweighs the willingness to pay by the soiled-laundry owners, we are making a statement (in this system of evaluation) that air is more efficiently used by the polluter. The ownership of labour is not disputed for the sake of ownership, but for the right of use. If Agatha is given the entitlement to her person because she can better monitor herself in writing novels, the decision is based on the premiss that she will use her labour to that end. But that defeats the purpose. If she is really entitled to her labour she may well spend her life interior-decorating which we know does not maximize wealth. The entitlement to ownership of one's person is fundamentally an entitlement to appropriate the fruits of use and to have power of choice over how the entitlement will be used. In effect it is partly an entitlement to veto the dictates of wealth-maximization.

What seems to be problematic about the arguments, at least in the case of labour allocation, is that Agatha's willingness to pay is being based on a potential entitlement, the proceeds of her use in novel-writing which is precisely what she is contesting. She is using the willingness to pay that derives from her use in novel-producing to acquire a right not to produce novels. The correct willingness to pay is the income she could attain from a bank on the basis of her future work in interior-decorating.

The choices to be made are the following:

1. Sir George owns Agatha and makes her churn out books incurring some monitoring cost. One might add the cost of Agatha attempting to get a loan to buy her freedom, but if she is well informed she won't even attempt, since the banks' monitoring costs may make it clear that she won't have enough to bribe Sir George for her freedom.

2. Agatha gets a loan to buy her freedom and pays off debt by selling books; the bank incurs some monitoring costs. Agatha cannot do what she wants to.

3. Agatha is free and she may either publish some books and spend the rest of the time interior-decorating, or she may spend all her time interior-decorating, or just idle away her free time. No doubt monitoring costs are an important element in deciding institutions, but while Agatha may be more efficient in her spending of time on novel-writing when she is the direct beneficiary of the proceeds, she may also produce fewer books because of her pleasure in deco-

rating or idling (recall the backward-bending supply curve). This could entail a net wealth loss for society precisely because she does what she would prefer to do.

The principle of wealth-maximization would pick the one that maximized wealth; given that Agatha is likely to put her labour to use in interior-decorating if she is free, the wealth-maximizing principle is likely to pick (1) or (2), depending on whether Sir George or the banks are better slave-drivers. If Agatha gains the entitlement on the condition that she has to publish books, then she is still in principle a slave. The point of the principle is not to minimize any monitoring (or transaction) costs, but to maximize wealth. Those transaction costs should be minimized that help maximize wealth, that's where willingness to pay comes in. The fact that the banks incur monitoring costs does not mean that these should be avoided altogether by giving Agatha the right to her freedom, it depends on whether Agatha will actually produce more wealth this way.

Given that it seems likely Agatha will be a slave there are two implications of wealth-maximization in this example. First, it has a powerful distributional impact in that Agatha will not get the proceeds of her labour. To this one might say 'tough luck', society is better off because it is wealthier (keeping in mind that this is a peculiar 'better off' since total utility may not have increased). This response may be prompted by the belief that income could be redistributed to Agatha through taxes, but that defeats the point of slavery, since she will be able to live off fewer books thus reducing overall wealth. And why not avoid the problem of possibly costly redistribution by making the distributional goal explicit in one's assessment of 'willingness to pay'. Of course this would no longer be wealth-maximization. Secondly, an entitlement to freedom is an entitlement to use one's labour against the dictates of wealth-maximization if one so pleases. To the extent that one places value on such notions as liberty, wealth-maximization does not seem appropriate, we might call this the wealth-maximizer–liberal conflict.[1] Yet Posner may reply that if agents value liberty highly they will be willing to pay for it

---

[1] This is in reference to Sen's Pareto-liberal Paradox, see Sen (1970). In Sen's story 'entitlements' that are determined by the Pareto-principle clash with those determined by a libertarian principle, and this is a powerful result precisely because the Pareto-principle is often seen as the protector of individuals'

and thus wealth-maximization would account for this; it's clear from Agatha's story that however highly she values liberty, wealth-maximization is insensitive since liberty is not a wealth-earning activity.

According to the story it has been assumed that Agatha prefers interior-decorating to novel-writing; in fact, a very similar conclusion to the one we arrived at could be attained even if Agatha did not prefer interior-decorating to novel-writing. All that is needed for slavery to become a possibility, is that Agatha have a higher preference for leisure than what society has for Agatha's leisure. If Agatha had it her way she would spend some time writing novels and a lot of time basking in the sun. If she had to outbid Sir George using her novel-writing resources, she would effectively lose the choice between work and leisure, whether a slave to Sir George or to the banks. It is clear that wealth-maximization would have Agatha labour hard and long. Furthermore, it is not even necessary that Sir George be a Sir, a simple George would do. George could get a loan from the bank, convincing them that Agatha would be valuable as a novel-writer and not an interior-decorator, and that as a slave-driver he could put her to profitable use. George may even have competition from other would-be slave-drivers. Wealth-maximization would give the right to the most proficient slave-driver (this could even be Agatha). Whatever arrangement results, Agatha will be the loser.

When considering the assignment of a specific isolated entitlement, where the rest of the entitlements of an economy are taken as given, wealth-maximization can all too easily condone ethically repulsive institutions. Willingness to pay depends on ability to pay, and that must be determined by the competing uses of the resource in question, and not simply the monitoring costs attached to alternative owners of the resource when put to the same use. In the case of Agatha, the question is whether wealth is maximized in novel-writing or in interior-decorating, not whether Agatha is a better monitor of her novel-writing activity. It is on this basis that wealth-maximization does not provide

liberty. In the case of wealth-maximization which can be seen as a Kaldor–Hicks compensation principle (hypothetical Pareto-improvements), any link with liberty is highly tenuous so there is no difficult paradox involved. See Jules L. Coleman (1988: ch. 3), for an attack on Posner's position that wealth-maximization preserves liberty.

Agatha with effective ownership of her labour. These points may apply independently of the initial wealth distribution (Sir George need not be wealthy) or of Agatha's preference for interior-decorating.

3.2. Slavery Treated as a Class

Are matters different if entitlements are determined by considering a class of individuals rather than treating individuals separately, as S. E. Margolis suggests? If one is to use individuals' willingness to pay on the basis of how much they could produce when put to the most 'efficient' use, wealth-maximization will be redundant as before. The potential slaves' willingness to pay must be determined by the wealth they could attain when applying their labour as they wish. As free agents, individuals may prefer to spend more time at leisurely activities or other activities than those that maximize their material wealth. With this wealth they may not be able to outbid the slave-owners. The 'efficiency' of slavery is that it puts individuals to that use (and possibly more intensively) that is dictated by the demands of wealth-owners. Furthermore, if one were to treat slavery as an institution for a large class of individuals there are many other enforcement costs involved that have to be considered before one is able to judge whether wealth-maximization would condone it. If the other institutions in the rest of the economy are well attuned to monitoring and enforcing slavery, then surely slavery could be wealth-maximizing.

Another serious problem that arises when considering a class of slaves is that the wealth-effects are overwhelming.[2] Deciding to give labourers the right to freedom and selling of their labour, has a decisive impact on what is deemed efficient use of their labour. Such a large transfer of wealth will affect the constitution of the wealth-maximizing allocation of resources. Who has the right, determines what allocation is wealth-maximizing. It may now be wealth-maximizing to construct workers' dwellings as opposed to grandiose monuments or mansions, potato produc-

---

[2] Note that wealth-effects are not the issue in the case of entitlement for a single individual, as the transfer of wealth is hardly going to have an impact on the optimal amount of novel-writing: Agatha's demand for novel-writing is a drop in the ocean.

tion may outbid diamond extraction. In the case of Agatha wealth-maximization determined simultaneously the specific activity which maximized wealth (novel-writing) as well as the property-right rule that supported the activity at the least cost, since giving Agatha the right to her labour would only barely affect the overall evaluation of her novel-producing activity. When treating slavery as a class, the wealth-transfer is so great that it has a substantial impact on what activities are deemed wealth-maximizing. The wealth-maximization principle cannot be used on a large scale, or for entitlements that should be treated as a class and not individually, since it becomes indeterminate: that is, changing rights alters the wealth-maximizing allocation.

Unless entitlements are formed on some other principle besides wealth-maximization, there does not seem to be any a priori reason to expect that the institutions formed will avoid ethically repulsive outcomes, whether institutions are treated as a class or individually. On the contrary, it seems frightfully easy to arrive at an ugly institution. Wealth-maximization is not the reason for 'giving a worker the right to sell his labour and a woman the right to determine her sexual partners', as Posner (1986: 71) would have it.

4. WEALTH-MAXIMIZATION AND DISTRIBUTIONAL CONCERNS

Agatha's tale revealed that when wealth-maximization is applied to a specific property right it can lead to morally repulsive outcomes. According to the principle of wealth-maximization, slavery could be an efficient institution. But what is meant by efficient? In the Arrow–Debreu general-equilibrium models, where transaction costs are not present, an allocation can be called efficient without reference to distributional concerns; a distributional goal can be attained by picking one of the many efficient solutions through a costless change in the initial endowments. Once organization costs are endogenous in the model, redistribution may itself be a user of resources, making the efficiency of an institution dependent on the distributional goal. The problem is that distribution of income is not only the starting-point from which efficiency gains are judged, but it is also the dependent variable in determining 'optimal' institutions. I will consider a less dramatic example to show the link between matters of distribution and efficiency in the assignment of entitlements, and why calling wealth-maximizing institutions 'efficient' can be misleading.

A discussion on pedestrian–driver accidents offers some insights into the relationship between distributional concerns and wealth-maximization when considering the efficiency of legal rules. In the general case, there are two matters of concern for the assignment and protection of entitlements: (1) the optimal amount of driving (total hours of driving) must be determined, and (2) the optimal level of precaution by drivers and pedestrians must be determined. This particular example, for simplicity, concerns itself solely with the optimal level of precaution; rules have already been specified for the amount of driving. It is assumed that drivers have the options to drive fast, moderately, or slowly, while pedestrians can walk fast or slow; i.e. they both have an impact on costs associated with driving.[3] The driver's net expected benefit from driving is the benefit[4] the driver attaches to driving at a certain speed, minus the amount the driver is liable to pay in an accident times the probability of an accident. The pedestrians' net expected benefit equals the benefit from walking at different speeds minus the cost of an accident multiplied by the probability of an accident.

Alternative legal rules will affect the incidence of costs faced by the driver and pedestrian in association with their preventive activity. A strict-liability rule on the driver will insure that the driver will take into account the expected costs inflicted on the pedestrian associated with different speeds of driving.[5] The driver will behave 'efficiently' by choosing a speed that incorporates the social costs of driving as reflected in the liability rule. If the increase in expected costs (private and social as gauged by the

---

[3] Some further assumptions should be made on issues such as the risk-aversity of the agents, availability of insurance, etc., but I leave these out for simplicity, and their inclusion while complicating the specifics of the ex., will not alter the conceptual points.

[4] By benefit, meaning how much the driver is willing to pay to drive at a certain speed.

[5] It is assumed in this ex. that the authorities have the appropriate information required for the application of the rules. In the case of strict liability they must know the damage function of the injured, and in the case of negligence they must know the efficient level of preventive activity.

estimated damage function) associated with driving fast is greater than the gain from driving fast, the driver will drive at a slower speed. The pedestrian, on the other hand, will not take into account all the costs associated with walking fast, since the driver is strictly liable and will compensate the pedestrian fully. That is, even if walking fast imposes greater costs than the benefits the perambulator gets, she will have no incentive to internalize them since the driver will foot the bill. A negligence rule imposed on the driver would insure efficient speeds by both driver and pedestrian; the driver is liable for damages only if she does not meet some standard of care, therefore, since the driver will be taking care, the pedestrian will bear any costs associated with walking too fast (in this case not being careful).

The following quotes from Polinsky (1983) will help motivate the discussion on the meaning of efficiency when transaction costs are of concern:

> Under a negligence rule, the pedestrian will bear his own losses because the driver will choose to meet the standard of care—to drive moderately—whereas under a strict liability rule the driver will have to compensate the pedestrian for his losses. Since there is no contractual or market relationship between the parties, there is no contract price or market price that can be adjusted when legal rules change.[6] Thus shifting from one liability rule to the other will redistribute income by the amount of the expected losses. (1983: 109–10)

Polinsky then goes on to argue that given that we know the kind of distributional effects legal rules can have, we can decide whether to use taxes or legal rules to redistribute income according to the relative cost of either method.

> Legal redistribution may be costly in the sense that *inefficient* [*my italics*] rules may have to be chosen in order to achieve the desired result . . . But if drivers are wealthier than pedestrians, strict liability may be preferable to negligence on equity grounds. The loss of efficiency from using strict liability rather than negligence is a 'cost' of redistributing income from drivers as a class to pedestrians as a class. (1983: 111)

---

[6] Wherever legal rules concern contractual disputes (breach of contract, liability rules) the redistributive power of the rules are circumscribed since the contracting parties can eliminate any redistributive elements through contract price. Alternatively, where disputes concern strangers—or agents unable to contract because of transaction cost (pollution, nuisance law, automobile accidents)—legal rules have a redistributive impact.

It is interesting to note the way the term 'efficiency' is used. It is presumed that even if taxation is a more costly method of redistributing income than by use of legal rules, the use of legal rules while correcting for distributional goals will still be 'inefficient', albeit less inefficient than taxation. Let me regress for a moment; three options are being compared: (1) an 'efficient' level of preventative activity by drivers and pedestrians and an undesirable distribution of income; (2) taxation which leads to a desirable distribution and 'efficient' activity, but has other costly repercussions; (3) legal rule that leads to a desirable income distribution but an 'inefficient' level of activity.

What is interesting in the way the term 'efficient' is used, is that it seems to imply that there is some level of preventative activity that is efficient, independently of the community's goal.[7] There are two interpretations: the strict-liability rule may be considered inefficient either because it does not bring about that level of preventative activity that could be attained in a transaction-costless world, or because it diverges from the legal rule that maximizes wealth. The former reason harks back to S. E. Margolis's definition 1, as it labels efficient a rule that would maximize wealth in a world where transaction costs are zero. As we saw, transaction costs are real and should be incorporated in wealth-maximizing. It is important to realize that the level of preventative activity is a dependent variable, to be derived by finding that level that maximizes wealth. The way Polinsky's example is formulated it happens that the level of preventative activity that maximizes wealth is the same level that would have been attained if transaction costs were absent, but this need not be so. If it were less costly to get information about the pedestrians' damage function than to discern the drivers' benefit function, then a strict-liability rule would be wealth-maximizing despite it being a departure from the 'efficient' level in a transaction-costless world. Let me reiterate: a negligence rule would be wealth-maximizing if the costs of enforcing the rule were not high, but if information about the drivers' benefit function is

---

[7] It almost seems to be referring to a level of preventative activity in a transaction-costless world. Although this cannot be attributed to Polinsky, one can easily forget that the inclusion of transaction costs often alters what is considered an efficient level of activity, and not only an efficient entitlement rule.

costly to attain, then these costs have to be considered when deciding which rule to impose.

According to Margolis's definition 2, one should call efficient any level of activity that happens to maximize wealth, even if this implies levels which are not at the intersection of the marginal-benefit and cost curves of the involved parties. There is no inherently efficient level of preventative activity, there is that level which maximizes wealth, and that is efficient by virtue of maximizing wealth, and nothing else. Going back to the three options, the negligence rule is efficient because it maximizes wealth, strict liability is inefficient since it does not maximize wealth (but caters to another objective), negligence plus taxation is even less efficient since presumably overall wealth is reduced even more than strict liability.

This reveals the particularly restrictive nature of wealth-maximization as a characterization of efficiency.[8] What imparts the epithet 'efficient' to an entitlement, or to a given level of activity, is that they are the best instruments to guide actions and the best action given one's objective respectively. As long as wealth-maximization is one's objective then there will be some rule(s), and some actions by the agents, that best attain this objective. I emphasize rule and action, because these have to be co-determined, an action cannot in itself be efficient if it requires a costly rule to materialize. When it is said that a level of activity is wealth-maximizing, it is meant that the level of activity, along with the legal rule, are wealth-maximizing.

If one were to have a different objective, say the maximization of some social-welfare function, then it is likely that another set of rules, and other actions, will best attain this objective. If it is the case in Polinsky's example that the authorities would like to promote a more equitable distribution of resources among drivers and pedestrians, then strict liability is the most efficient rule given that objective. There is no sacrifice of efficiency to attain a distributional goal, the negligence rule was efficient simply because wealth-maximization was the objective; now that it is not,

[8] I am assuming that wealth-maximization is actually attainable. While it is plausible that a specific activity can be wealth-maximizing when other activities are taken as given, this tells us little about whether the entire legal structure supports a wealth-maximizing allocation of resources. I will turn to this problem later.

negligence would be an inefficient rule. One might say that wealth-maximization has been sacrificed for distributional reasons, but this departs a legitimacy to wealth-maximization that is independent of any value system.

The discussion of pedestrian–driver accidents has shown that the authorities must compare policy instruments in their effectiveness to redistribute income before deciding whether to incorporate distributional concerns in legal rules. There is an additional reason, however, in making legal rules sensitive to distributional concerns. One of Dworkin's criticisms of wealth-maximization is that it is circular because of wealth-effects. The assignment of an entitlement that is meant to lead to a wealth-maximizing allocation, alters the wealth of the involved parties and by so doing alters the wealth-maximizing allocation. The authorities discern the wealth-maximizing allocation by considering agents' willingness to pay (as well as transaction costs). The assignment of entitlements by virtue of changing the wealth of the agents, is liable to change the willingness to pay for the activity in question. The wealth-maximizing allocation is constantly shifting. Posner countered this argument by saying that the impact of the entitlement assignment on the agents' wealth will be minimal, since in most cases it will represent a small proportion of their wealth. None the less, it does restrict the scope of wealth-maximization to entitlements that do not represent a substantial part of the income of the agents. But more importantly, as long as income-distribution concerns have not been incorporated when forming entitlements, any income-redistribution policy would potentially make all the existing entitlements inefficient. A strict-liability rule will penalize the driver by the cost that the pedestrian associates with different levels of the driver's activity: this has been set at a specific level by the courts. A redistribution of income is likely to alter the pedestrian's evaluation of costs, as well as the driver's evaluation of benefits, making the damage function that the driver has to face under the strict-liability rule inappropriate to maximize wealth. Entitlements that maximize wealth will do so, for a given distribution of income, but will no longer maximize wealth if the income distribution changes. Property rights, unlike prices in a competitive economy, do not readjust after income changes to realize a new efficient allocation of resources, unless courts were to readjust property rights every time income were redistributed.

Margolis's second definition of an efficient legal system, looks like a needless restriction of possible legal systems. Whether a legal system is efficient must depend on whether it offers the best legal environment, among feasible alternatives, in achieving some social-welfare objective. For the sake of contrast I will propose another definition of an efficient legal system:

> Definition 3: An efficient legal system is one in which property rights are assigned and liability rules are formulated so that some desired social-welfare function is maximized. (The organizational costs required to further this objective should be minimized.)

This definition is nearly tautological, it doesn't have the neatness of wealth-maximization. It doesn't offer some clear rule that judges can follow in their endeavour to specify property rights. But it does not obscure the fact that, with the endogenizing of organizational costs, distributional concerns are no longer separable from efficiency concerns. And it avoids covering up the complexity of the problem of forming a desirable legal system.

To summarize, wherever legal rules are more efficient, with respect to some social-welfare objective, in redistributing income than other policy instruments, distributional goals should be incorporated in legal rules. Furthermore, even if it is the case that distributional aims can be better achieved by other instruments, there remains the question of whether distributional goals should be anticipated in legal rules.

5. WEALTH-MAXIMIZATION, INDETERMINACY, AND SECOND-BEST

Until now I have been looking at a very localized level at the question of entitlement formation, enforcement, and assignment. Even at this level it was shown in the case of Agatha, when entitlements were treated individually, that an undesirable institution may be supported, or that in the driver–pedestrian case wealth-maximization was unduly restrictive. If wealth-maximization is to be used as a tool of policy it must be shown to be effective on a broader scale of entitlement formation. I turn to this question now.

In the literature there is some ambivalence as to whether wealth-maximization should be confined to common law, or whether it provides a general principle to be followed in the formation of institutions. Posner tends to treat these on an equal footing. What function should be given to the legal system, and what rules it should follow, is itself dependent on the broader question of what roles should be distributed among the governing institutions of a society, that is, how best these institutions share responsibilities. It is from this broader vantage point that one should determine what function and rules common law should adhere to. Seen in this light the arguments for what rule the common law should follow may be different from the more general question of rules for the formation of institutions. The coherence of wealth-maximization as a principle depends on its scope. If it is used as a general rule for institution-formation wealth-maximization becomes an unattainable objective.

A problem of indeterminacy may arise, however, if rights are being assigned when a society first comes into existence. In the Agatha–Sir George example it was easy to obtain a determinate rights assignment, because only one good in society was unowned—Agatha's labour. With every other good having a market or shadow price, one could compute, in principle at least, the effects on aggregate wealth of assigning Agatha's labour to herself or to Sir George. But suppose no goods are yet owned: land, labour, sexual access—everything is up for grabs. How can each good be assigned to its most valuable use when no values—no market or shadow prices—exist? This is the problem of wealth-effects with a vengeance. All rights have yet to be assigned; assignment of rights on so massive a scale is bound to affect prices; and prices in turn will affect the question of whom the rights should be assigned to. (Posner 1983: 111)

This shows a recognition by Posner that the wealth-maximization principle cannot be used as a rule to form initial institutions for an economy. It must be presumed that institutions have in large part been formed already for wealth-maximization to provide a basis; Posner is not explicit about how many institutions should be defined, in order that such a procedure be fruitful. But, as Jules L. Coleman suggests, if wealth-maximization is limited to those cases where alteration of entitlements will have a minimal effect on prices (and this means not only that the specific instances entail minimal wealth-effects, but that the activities needing entitlement formation are few in number), 'the principle would have been stripped of its power in helping to frame or shape the common law' (Jules L. Coleman 1988: 110).

Unfortunately the system of wealth-maximization has its fair share of drawbacks—many of which arise because of the conceptual or logical connection of wealth-maximization to the existence of prices. First, because the reliance on prices is necessary and not merely contingent, the system of wealth-maximization cannot tell us anything about right conduct where no prices exist. Second, prices are in part the result of demand, demand the result of prior entitlements. Consequently, wealth-maximization cannot generate an initial set of entitlements. Rearrangement of entitlements, once assigned, may be further restricted by the feature of wealth-maximization that applying it both requires and affects prices—and, therefore, value.[9] (Coleman 1988: 111)

The purview of wealth-maximization as a principle of entitlement formation has to be very limited if wealth is to be a guide to determinate solutions at all. It is not just a question of forming entitlements in a world where no institutions have been formed, but a question of the scope of rearrangement, in a world where entitlements exist. The broader the scope of entitlement formation or rearrangement, the greater the wealth-effects, making wealth-maximization indeterminate. In a piecemeal approach one could get determinate wealth-maximizing entitlements at the time of formation of the specific entitlement, but if piecemeal policy is widespread the aggregate wealth-effects will make nonsense of the overall objective of wealth-maximization.

For wealth-maximization to be coherent as a rule it must be applied on a very limited scale and on entitlements that should not be treated as a class (it is not clear how one determines when entitlements should be treated as a class). Under these circumstances, in its limited purview, wealth-maximization can be attained, but will it be ethically defendable? We saw how it may not be if there are distributional concerns[10] or libertarian ones, but even if distributional goals can be better attained by other policy instruments, there is another reason why

[9] This point became apparent when treating the entitlement of slavery as a class.

[10] Most pointedly when these distributional concerns take on the spectre of individual liberty as with Agatha.

wealth-maximization may be undesirable. Individuals' willingness to pay is a function of the existing entitlement regime and the transaction costs associated with that regime. If the rest of the economy's institutions are not efficient (in either Margolis's sense of definition 2, or my sense of definition 3), then willingness to pay is a poor indicator in the formation of a new entitlement rule. If shadow prices are to be good guides, it is not enough that entitlements exist, but that they also be efficient entitlements. The problem then is not wealth-effects with a vengeance, but second-best with a vengeance. Forming efficient entitlements on the basis of willingness to pay, presumes not only that institutions already exist, but that they are efficient. Wealth-maximization uses the incentives provided by the existing system as a guide to efficient entitlements, when the object of entitlement formation is to create an efficient incentive structure.

An initial institutional structure will determine simultaneously the marginal-benefit and cost curves associated with activities, as well as the transaction costs associated with alternative entitlement structures. If a firm exists because hierarchy provides efficiency gains over a market organization of some activity, by virtue of the resources saved, certain agents in the economy will have more to spend. It also determines a new set of transaction costs. The specific institutional structure determines the wealth of agents and therefore their willingness to pay for alternative activities. The existing marginal-cost and benefit curves may be good indicators to determine new entitlements only if the initial institutions are efficient, otherwise any inefficiencies in existing institutions will simply be transmitted to new ones.

In a country with a highly imperfect capital market the agents' willingness to pay will be highly distorted, i.e. it will not reflect their productive potential. When discussing Chuck and Dave it was seen that wealth-maximization was a good rule precisely because it took into account imperfections of the capital market. These imperfections were those of a real capital market as opposed to some ideal, unattainable, or perfect capital market. Even in the real world there is some capital market that is most efficient given transaction costs. While Margolis emphasizes that these imperfections, these real costs, should be incorporated in one's appraisal of entitlements, he must presume that these are costs unavoidable in the best of feasible worlds. If a capital market is the best possible in the real world, then there is good sense in expecting that it will reflect agents' productive potential, but if a capital market is highly inefficient even by real-world standards, surely it would be a sad predicament to take agents' willingness to pay at face value. And while the capital market is an important institution in determining agents' wealth, all institutions affect agents' wealth, and if these are inefficient, they will further devalue the informative content of willingness to pay.[11]

One of the important contributions of Coase (1960) was to dispel the belief that resource allocations and institutions should be judged according to how far they depart from an unattainable utopian world (see also Demsetz 1969). Institutions should be selected so that they best promote some welfare objective given the real-world limitations, the costs of organizing human interaction. The strength of this position is precisely that 'imperfections' are taken into account (no world is perfect). But when deciding to form institutions one has to discern which 'imperfections' are unavoidable in the best of all worlds and which are imperfections that can be done away with. The real difficulty arises when one tries to translate these notions into operational rules; rules that common-law judges can apply, or other institution-forming actors in the system. The costs of walking on a street may not be a good indicator if streets are without pavements because the local public authorities are inefficient investment planners. Common-law judges must be able to discriminate between 'avoidable' and 'unavoidable' transaction costs. In other words, the benchmark for transaction cost should not be those deriving from existing institutions but those deriving from hypothetically better institutions. Of course there is a danger of falling back on the problems of definition 1, since Chuck and Dave will transact away from any entitlement not based on existing institutions, however imperfect.[12] But often transaction costs prevent agents from any transactions so this may not be a problem.

---

[11] This issue should not be confused with the point about Agatha's enslavement; slavery will be espoused under the wealth-maximization principle even if the capital market is perfect.

[12] The real difficulty of forming institutions more generally, is that when forming an institution at a local level one does not know whether other institutions are likely to improve. If one forms an institution that is well suited to the existing institutional environment, it may function well but contribute little to global improvements, or will be out of place if the institutional environment is

Posner (1977: 79) points out that 'it is easier to guess people's market preferences in areas where the market cannot be made to work than to guess what policies will maximize happiness'. While this may be true, it is hardly a reason to use market preferences as a guide to the formation of new institutions, unless one has good reason to believe that the existing markets are 'optimal' institutions. The problem is that the formation of efficient entitlements that determine where market mechanisms should function and where other mechanisms should be relied on, is prior to the market; to use the implicit market evaluations to form entitlements presumes that the existing market institutions are the most desirable.

Entitlements are highly interdependent entities, they are devices that guide actions, and the success of an entitlement in attaining some objective depends on how it interacts with other entitlements in the economy. An entitlement structure is like a price vector, in that a price is efficient only if the entire price vector is efficient; likewise an entitlement's efficiency is related to that of the entitlement structure. At least with prices we could rely on an auctioneer (or an underlying entitlement structure) to coordinate prices. With institutions we cannot rely on an auctioneer to establish an efficient institutional structure, but the greater the scope of institutional rearrangement the more likely it is that we can form an institutional structure that will advance societal goals. In pedestrian-accident rules we are likely to make better decisions about precautionary measures if we also consider optimal levels of driving, even better if we consider conditions of roads, even better if we consider alternatives to private transportation. This is not to say that decisions should not be taken at the micro-level, but only that they should be sensitive to the interdependencies involved and the complexity of the issues.

improving. One needs a mechanism that coordinates the micro-level institutional interventions so that the aggregate effect is good, much as an ideal market coordinates the utility-maximizing activities of agents. It's not as simple as telling lawmakers to minimize a given set of transaction costs, whether the benchmark be the existing institutional environment or the best possible institutional environment.

6. CONCLUSION

Wealth-maximization is indeterminate when institutional changes or property-right changes are considered on a broad scale, or for entitlements that should be treated as a class (it is not clear how one determines this). As a piecemeal approach and on a small scale, wealth-maximization affords far too much legitimacy to agents' willingness to pay, being insensitive to distributional concerns, the lessons from second-best theory, and the liberty of the individual. Agatha's tale offers a strong warning about the value of wealth-maximization as a rule for rule-formation. Dealt with as an individual case (which makes it much more practical as a guide to policy), wealth-maximization can severely curtail liberty, it carries an implicit distributional choice, and makes unreasonably strong demands on the existing entitlement structure (that it be somehow 'optimal') in order to approximate 'efficient' entitlements. Dealt with as a class of entitlements, the objective of wealth-maximization is incoherent and incomplete.

10
Transaction Costs, Efficiency, and Counterfactuals

All places that the eye of heaven visits
Are to a wise man ports and happy havens
Teach thy necessity to reason thus;
There is no virtue like necessity

Shakespeare, Richard II

If one wants to pass through open doors easily, one must bear in mind that they have a solid frame: this principle, according to which the old professor had always lived is simply a requirement of the sense of reality. But if there is such a thing as a sense of reality—and no one will doubt that it has its *raison d'être*—then there must also be something that one can call a sense of possibility.

Robert Musil, The Man Without Qualities

1. INTRODUCTION

The traditional concept of optimality or efficiency found in welfare economics has come under strong criticism from institutional economists[1] for using as its reference point a world of zero organizational costs.[2] A real-world market is said to fail when the allocation of resources it engenders diverges from that attainable

---

[1] While this criticism is closely associated with Demsetz (1969), who has been variously labelled as a Property Rights and Transaction Costs economist, there are very different economists, such as Bromley (1989), who espouse this criticism. By 'institutional economists' I am not referring to a specific school of thought but a number of diverse economists who advocate an enriched institutional analysis in economics. For descriptions of various schools of institutional economists, see Samuels (1988), Langlois (1986a), and Eggertsson (1990).

[2] I use the term organizational costs interchangeably with transaction costs, generally preferring the former since it does not elicit a sense of physical transaction. For the purposes of this chapter the very broad working definition of transaction cost suggested by Arrow (1970) is appropriate: 'transaction costs are costs of running the economic system' (enforcement cost, monitoring cost, information cost, etc.).

in a frictionless world of zero transaction costs. A monopoly would by definition represent a suboptimal state of affairs since in a world of zero transaction costs the foregone consumer surplus associated with the smaller monopoly output could be tapped by a price-discriminating monopolist. A missing market or 'externality' would represent market failure since a complete set of markets is needed for transaction-costless Pareto-optimal allocation to ensue.[3]

Many institutional economists advocate a notion of efficiency that incorporates organizational costs,[4] the focus of such a notion being whether there exists some feasible reorganization of the economy that would afford Pareto-gains when the institutional costs of reorganization are incorporated in the evaluation of economic outcomes.[5] A monopoly would be inefficient only if there existed some alternative institution that could better exploit the untapped resources without at the same time imposing transaction costs that outweigh the 'efficiency' gains. Likewise a missing market, in this case, would represent inefficiency only if the imposition of a market were not too costly. Rather than chasing an unattainable utopia, sights should be set on achieving the best of worlds given the presence of real transaction costs.

While the critique of the traditional notion of efficiency has been well taken, the ramifications of incorporating organizational costs in the notion of optimality remain far from clear. A particularly discouraging feature of such models, when combined with the behavioural assumption made, seems to be that they lead to the unpalatable conclusion that any institution that exists must be optimal otherwise wealth-maximizing agents would have exploited any 'attainable' improvements.[6]

[3] There are some exceptions such as non-paternalistic altruism, see Winter (1969), and Archibald and Donaldson (1976).

[4] This notion, sometimes referred to as 'transaction-cost-constrained optimality', is implicit throughout the Law and Economics literature. Explicit advocates of such a notion have been Coase (1960), Demsetz (1969), and Dahlman (1979). Bromley (1989) also advocates a kind of organizationally inclusive notion of efficiency although he emphasizes the need to specify a welfare function for efficiency to have meaning. Samuels (1972) and Schmid (1987), however, have strong reservations whether any notion of efficiency or optimality is meaningful once transaction costs are incorporated in models.

[5] Coase (1960) has been influential in turning economists' attention to organizational costs (see Ch. 2, sect. 11).

[6] As Dahlman (1979: 154–5) puts it: 'If you do not like the smell of the air, seek comfort in the knowledge that it would cost you more than it is worth to

In section 2 of this chapter I will illustrate how models of the economy that treat transaction costs endogenously arrive at the conclusion that what exists is optimal. The crucial feature is the particular deterministic form that these models take so that the actual outcome is the only possible outcome.[7] In section 3 I describe two different attempts to make the models less deterministic so that inefficiency is possible, and therefore policy intervention can have meaning. Both attempts lead to internal contradictions. In section 4 I describe two ways to generate a set of counterfactuals in microeconomic models so that alternative outcomes are possible. I emphasize the need to reconceptualize the behavioural model of individuals in order that some notion of 'attainable' optimality is salvaged. In particular, I argue that the behavioural model must allow that agents are in some sense free to choose alternative courses of action and not just utility-maximizing actions. Finally, in section 5 I suggest that the problem of determinism that afflicts the neoclassical notion of rationality characterizes other models of rationality as well, and that the challenge is to form a behavioural model that is both explanatory of behaviour but also makes room for alternative courses of action.

2. WHAT IS, IS OPTIMAL

Staten and Umbeck (1986) argue that it is logically impossible to derive Pareto-inefficient outcomes from microeconomic models

you to do away with the stench, for, otherwise, would you not do it? . . . If we include transaction costs in the constraints, this appears to be the unavoidable conundrum we end up in: externalities are irrelevant, monopoly problems do not exist, public goods present no difficulties, and so on.' Dahlman (1979: 157–61) believes, however, that this problem derives from incorporating transaction costs in a general-equilibrium framework and that a partial-equilibrium approach envisioned by Coase would not give rise to such a conclusion. I don't think this is correct. There is no reason why a partial equilibrium analysis should offer opportunities for improvement that are not already present in the general-equilibrium framework.

[7] Importantly, this problem does not afflict just those models that aspire to show that what exists is optimal, or that the 'market' should be left alone, but any model that attempts to incorporate organizational costs endogenously. More generally it is a feature of models that attempt a causal explanation of resource allocation and institution formation. It thus seriously threatens the value that such models can have on questions of policy.

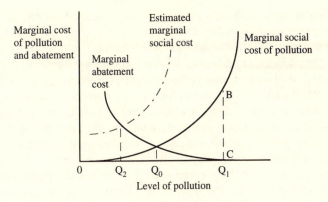

FIG 10.1.

with agents that behave according to the postulate of constrained maximization. This point is illustrated in Fig. 10.1 above which shows the marginal social cost associated with different levels of pollution emitted by a factory as well as the marginal cost of pollution abatement. If the factory were free to pollute, no effort would be expended curtailing pollution and an excessive amount of pollutants would be emitted (point Q_1) as indicated by the discrepancy between the marginal social cost of pollution and the marginal cost of abatement (segment BC). In traditional neoclassical models any such discrepancy (any point other than Q_0) would be treated as Pareto-inefficient, but Staten and Umbeck (1986) stress that it is logically impossible to derive such a discrepancy between social benefits and costs from a microeconomic model. At any point beyond Q_0 in Fig. 10.1, the damage inflicted on the community is greater than what it costs the factory to reduce emissions. So why don't those members that are suffering pay the factory-owners to lower pollution to level Q_1? The answer must be that the model is misspecified, that some constraint is missing, such as the costs of collective action or any other transaction cost preventing the members of the community from 'bribing' the polluter. As long as the model is fully specified (all organizational costs are incorporated) the equilibrium outcome must, by definition, be Pareto-efficient.[8]

---

[8] Cheung (1974: 71) says that 'in a world where each and every individual is asserted to behave consistently with the postulate of constrained maximization,

Staten and Umbeck's argument can be pushed further. Taking the perspective of policy formation one might not be daunted by their result. While it might be true that an equilibrium outcome of agents interacting within a fully specified institutional environment (all organizational costs are incorporated in the model) will be Pareto-efficient by definition, policy-makers, it would seem, are able to alter institutions (the constraints faced by the agents) and thus bring about new outcomes. In the case of the factory emitting deleterious substances, for example, policy-makers could limit allowable emissions by the factory, or apply a Pigouvian tax. Alternatively, they could set up a market for pollution permits with a limit on the number of permits.[9] The factory-owners, potential polluters, and those who suffer from the factory's emissions, could purchase permits (and/or bid up the price) for the right to use the atmosphere. Given this new institutional framework air would be allocated to those agents most willing and able to pay.[10]

Seen from the eyes of the policy-makers there seem to be several alternative rules among which an 'optimal' one can be chosen.[11] However, if one is to be consistent in avoiding comparisons with utopian worlds where some constraints have been left unspecified,[12] one should consider the constraints faced by the policy-makers. Suppose the policy-makers wish to maximize wealth[13] (or maximize aggregate benefits minus costs as measured

economic inefficiency presents a contradiction in terms. Even outright mistakes are traceable to constraints of some type. The world is efficient, if the model describing it sufficiently specifies the gains and costs of making it so.'

[9] Of course the total number of permits issued is itself a policy control variable to be determined by the government's objective.

[10] This does not ensure that we will arrive at Q_0. If the government initially set a limit to the number of permits at Q_1, we may find that, due to the free-rider problems given the public-good nature of atmosphere, this newly formed market for permits may bring about insufficient increases in abatement (leftward movement from Q_1).

[11] Policy-makers may have greater ambitions than simply to exhaust potential Pareto-gains. They may wish to form an institutional environment that maximizes a social-welfare function. This would mean that among all the tools at the policy-makers' disposal (manipulation of legal rules: emission charges, quotas, pollution permits, etc.), they would choose that set of rules that attains their social-welfare objective at the least organizational cost.

[12] Whether you compare the real world to a transaction-costless world or to a world with some transaction costs left unspecified ('missing'), you are subject to the nirvana criticism of comparing the real world to unattainable utopias.

[13] See Ch. 9 for a discussion and critique of wealth-maximization.

by willingness to pay) but lack the information on the factory's abatement cost and are unable to calculate the 'theoretical' wealth-maximizing level of pollution (Q_0 in Fig. 10.1). The policy-makers may be able to access information more easily on the social damage of pollution and find that they could better achieve their objective by making the factory liable to damages. If the policy-makers overestimate the damage from pollution[14] the resulting liability rule would induce the factory to take excessive abatement measures. But this would be wealth-maximizing given the government's informational constraints. Given their objective and the constraints they face, they are doing the best they can; the outcome is determinate and no other outcome is possible within the constraints of the model. The illusory freedom of action initially gained when looking through the policy-makers' eyes is further eroded as additional 'hidden' constraints are specified in the model. This would be the case if policy formation were seen in the context of interest groups, rent-seeking, disparate objectives of governing officials, etc.[15]

Whatever reassuring sense is left in this model that we are at least in the best of all possible worlds, is quickly shattered when we realize that we are in the worst of all possible worlds as well. The outcome is Pareto-optimal because the model is determinate and no other outcomes are possible to allow comparisons. A simple multiple Prisoners' Dilemma will propitiate a more acute sense of both the 'power' of such reasoning as well as its stifling consequences. Consider the well-known audience example where everyone is standing even though everyone would be better off if all sat, although it is in each person's interest to stand up if others are sitting.[16] No one has an incentive to sit down given others are standing. It would seem that our audience is stuck in a suboptimal outcome. But is it suboptimal? Is the alternative of all sitting down feasible given the specific constraints faced by the agents as well as the fact that agents are 'rational' in the narrow sense of constrained maximization? Surely for the agents to be

---

[14] It could be either that the government believes this to be the correct damage function, or that it believes that further research would cost more than the gains from a better estimate.

[15] Any attempts at partial exogenizing of the government are susceptible to the nirvana criticism since one may be allowing government actions which would not be feasible in a fully specified model of organizational constraints.

[16] Standing is the dominant strategy.

standing it must be that if we look hard enough we will find 'hidden' constraints that could only lead to this outcome. If the 'sitting-down' outcome is not feasible (given the constraints) why compare the existing outcome with a 'nirvana'?

What if some members of the audience could act as enforcers (or hire an enforcer) and penalize anyone standing up, wouldn't this bring about the optimal outcome?[17] It would depend on the enforcement costs. If the enforcement costs are small enough to make it individually rational to penalize, then we can expect the sitting-down outcome to be attained. Otherwise, given large-enough enforcement cost, the sitting-down outcome is unattainable and possibly undesirable.[18] Standing is optimal given the lack of feasible alternatives.

By knowing all the costs an individual perceives, her utility function and behavioural rule, one can fully predict what the agent will do.[19] If this information was known for all agents one could figure out the outcome of their interaction; the outcome would be determinate.[20] Given the constraints of the model the outcome that is attained is the only feasible one. We are in the best of all worlds and in the worst of all worlds.[21] In order that

[17] Cheung (1983) discusses an interesting ex. of self-imposed policing by river-boat pullers in pre-Communist China. A large group of workers, who had to tow a good-sized boat, agreed to the hiring of a monitor to whip them. I don't think this would go down well with our audience.

[18] Note that it is not necessary that the enforcement costs be greater than the gains accruing to all from sitting down, only that they be greater than the gains accruing to those undertaking the enforcement. It could be that many are willing to pay, but the enforcers are unable to tap into these resources, or ensure that they will be paid for their efforts. It is not enough that 'willingness to pay' is greater than the cost, 'actual pay' to those bearing the costs must be greater than the cost.

[19] 'Perceived' costs are relevant in explaining what actions an agent will take.

[20] A certain indeterminacy would exist when different actions (with different consequences) present the same pay-off to the agent taking the action. Models with multiple equilibria present this kind of indeterminacy. In some sense there are many possible worlds since agents may take different actions and thus inefficiency may be possible. But the alternative outcomes would be of little interest to us because agents would have no way of controlling the outcome. If I am conversing with my mother over the phone and the line goes dead, the most efficient response is that one of us calls back while the other waits. Lacking any conventions we have no way of ensuring this 'optimal' outcome. If the convention already exists, then, given the convention, the outcome will be determinate.

[21] This is surely not the kind of conclusion that Demsetz (1967) and Posner (1983) envisage when they argue that any inefficiency in the system will be eliminated by wealth-maximizing agents. They aspire to impart legitimacy to existing institutions as somehow being better than other possible institutions, yet a strict application of their reasoning does not make such comparisons meaningful.

optimality has more than rhetorical value, feasible inefficient outcomes must be possible; the models must show that there is at least a possibility of inefficiency arising and offer an explanation why such outcomes are avoided.

Since the outcome of microeconomic models with fully specified organizational costs are determinate, any efficiency notion based on comparison of feasible alternatives become meaningless, e.g. Pareto-efficiency, social-welfare maximization. Models with endogenous transaction costs could not provide insights for improving economic outcomes since, given the constraints of the model, no other outcome is possible.[22] Historical analysis of institutions would take the form of uncovering the transaction costs faced by the agents that generated the particular set of institutions. Discussion of the efficiency or inefficiency of the institutions would be meaningless.[23]

3. ATTEMPTS TO SALVAGE 'ATTAINABLE' OPTIMALITY

Most economists who advocate the need for endogenizing institutions in models do not take such a grim view of 'attainable' optimality. At least implicitly, it is assumed that inefficiency is possible. I will sketch briefly two ways that inefficiency is assumed possible in the models of Demsetz (1967) and Ruttan and Hayami (1984) and illustrate the inconsistencies that arise.

---

[22] Any freedom of action to change resource allocations, and/or institutions, seems to be present only when some organizational costs (constraints) have not been specified. The demand for greater realism leads to an unveiling of organizational costs which increasingly limit the space for policy, and eventually, when all action is 'explainable' there is no room for policy. Parallels can be found in the conflict between the Utopian's belief in change and the Pragmatist's cautionary note against unreasonable action.

[23] e.g. the very interesting debate about how certain 'inefficient' practices like the open-field system in the middle ages have managed to persist for long periods of time, could be nothing more than an exercise in 'digging up' hidden organizational constraints faced by the farmers at the time which made those institutional arrangements the only possible ones. Debate about whether the existing practices were efficient or not would be misleading. See McCloskey (1972), Dahlman (1980) and Fenoaltea (1986) for the debate. Eggertsson (1990) offers an excellent critical survey of this and similar literature.

3.1. A Lag in Rationality

For Demsetz (1967) the locomotive for institutional change is inefficiency. 'Changes in knowledge . . . production functions, market values . . . aspirations . . . New techniques,' (1967: 350) lead to a new set of costs and benefits. Property rights adjust to 'internalize' potential gains. Institutions evolve as a result of the interaction of individuals attempting to squeeze out gains from the new conditions. Overall this wealth-maximizing activity of agents will ensure an optimal set of institutions given the existing conditions at any one time.

Demsetz acknowledges, however, that these adjustments in property rights may often not occur by conscious endeavours to cope with specific externality problems.

These adjustments have arisen in Western societies largely as a result of gradual changes in social mores and in common-law precedents. At each step of this adjustment process, it is unlikely that externalities *per se* were consciously related to the issue being resolved. These legal and moral experiments may be hit-and-miss procedures to some extent but in a society that weights the achievement of efficiency heavily, their viability in the long run will depend on how well they modify behaviour to accommodate to externalities associated with important changes in technology or market values (Demsetz 1967: 350).

Inefficiency, to the extent that it exists, seems to be of a dynamic nature: a lag in adjustment to the new conditions. The duration of this lag depends on how rational agents are, the slowness of adjustment of social mores.[24] If there is a prescriptive message it seems to be that agents be more rational, that they

[24] There might seem to be a contradiction here in that Demsetz assumes individual rationality and yet talks of social mores. One might be able to reconcile these by reference to what Winter (1986) (following Blaug (1980)) calls the 'Classic Defense' of the rationality-as-optimization paradigm in economic theory, the central characteristic of which is: 'the willingness to concede that the rationality assumptions of economic theory are not descriptive of the process by which decisions are reached and, further, that most decisions actually emerge from response repertoires developed over a period of time by what may broadly be termed "adaptive" or "learning processes"' (Winter 1986: 244). So that rationality does not describe how agents actually make decisions, but provides a good approximation of what decisions will be arrived at through agents' 'response repertoires', in steady states. Social mores could be conceived as kinds of response repertoires. In which case, Demsetz might be interpreted as saying that the quicker agents acquire the 'repertoires' needed for the new conditions the quicker society will reach its socially optimal allocation of resources. For a discussion on

readjust their behaviour more quickly in line with their objectives, and avoid any lags in rationality.[25] But once a departure from rational behaviour is allowed, there is no guarantee that 'rational' behaviour is the socially optimal behaviour. We know that in a Prisoners' Dilemma if individuals could behave 'irrationally' they could achieve an optimal outcome, i.e. overcome the organizational cost associated with strategic behaviour. That is, a recognition that individuals might have more complex behavioural characteristics, like following social mores, allows for new feasible institutional alternatives. Optimality may no longer be a moot question, however, the prescription that agents be 'rational' is not justified.[26] Demsetz may not consider this departure from rationality as a control variable, but he would still have to justify the claim that greater rationality will necessarily entail efficiency. Morishima's (1982) and Dore's (1987) discussion of the Japanese economic 'success' story, offer convincing accounts of how 'irrational' or 'moral' behaviour may have an important function in internalizing potential gains in the system. As discussed in Chapter 4, section 6, one important efficiency-enhancing aspect of the Japanese Confucian ethos derives from the economic function of loyalty to one's superior.[27] Such loyalty

ways that norms might be reducible to some individual optimization process, and a view that they ultimately are not, see Elster (1989).

[25] Prescribing that agents adapt more quickly seems to assume a higher-order decision rule that is capable of selecting more quickly the best new social more or 'repertoire' for agents. Importantly if we accept that agents can deviate from the repertoires that simulate rational choices, there is no reason that rational choice repertoires would be the socially optimal decision rules for individuals to have. (I am ignoring the untenable argument that the repertoires that survive are the fittest and thus the optimal ones, with the further untenable link that these are also the rational-choice-simulating ones.) It might be argued that the only thing we have discretion over is the speed at which agents move from old repertoires to rational-choice-simulating new ones, and between old 'arbitrary' repertoires and rational-choice repertoires, the latter would always be better. Fred Hirsch (1977) offers an interesting account of how capitalism's success was based on social mores that were 'outdated', that the individualist calculus cultivated by capitalism would ultimately undermine the market system which requires a reserve of altruism. For the markets' need of a reserve of altruism see Arrow (1972).

[26] If efficiency is seen in terms of transaction-costs minimization, then agents should follow that behavioural pattern that minimizes organizational costs, and this may not be rationality. It has been argued that rationality would support the formation of social mores, see Gauthier (1986) and Frank (1986, 1989). For an interesting account of rationally formed social codes that lead to suboptimality see Akerlof (1984).

makes it possible for companies to invest in human capital without worrying that their investment will be 'poached', a problem which has often been cited as the cause of insufficient skilling of workers in advanced Western economies. It's highly questionable whether greater 'rationality' on the part of the Japanese people would bring greater economic gains.

The possibility that agents behave in ways that depart from rationality allows for other feasible trajectories for economic interaction. That agents may choose to act in a way that does not maximize their welfare, introduces a degree of freedom in the model. But if such alternative outcomes are possible then it is no longer clear that the best of feasible outcomes will be selected. Nor can it be said that rational behaviour would provide a recipe for optimality unless it was shown to be optimal among all alternative behavioural patterns. If such lags of rationality are simply aberrations over which there is no control, then it seems meaningless to offer any prescription (which seems to be the way Demsetz treats them). Prescription assumes that the authorities have control over some variables, either that they could promote certain behavioural patterns among the agents of the economy, or that they themselves could depart from the dictates of rationality.

3.2. Inefficiency of Institution Innovators

Some of the more sophisticated models of institutional change envisage political entrepreneurs as protectors of institutions, as well as instigators of institutional change (Ruttan and Hayami 1984; Davis and North 1970). These political entrepreneurs may be the government or even opposition forces in a democratic society applying pressures on the government. Accordingly, institutional change will be applied when the gains from such change outweigh the costs.

[27] A true believer in individual rationality can explain any behaviour in terms of rational choice. Becker and Murphy (1988) have even treated drug addiction as rational behaviour. Unless the analyst is able to have factual information of an agent's preferences there is no way of 'verifying' any behavioural model (see Sen 1970). I believe it to be methodologically preferable to at least consider alternative behavioural models than rigidly resist any departure from the rational-choice model.

We hypothesize that institutional innovations will be supplied if the expected return from the innovation that accrues to the political entrepreneurs exceeds the marginal cost of mobilizing the resources necessary to introduce the innovation. To the extent that the private return to the political entrepreneurs is different from the social return, the institutional innovation will not be supplied at a socially optimum level. (Ruttan and Hayami 1984: 213)

While this sounds like inefficiency, no mechanism is provided that could bring about a better state of affairs. If we say that the private and social returns associated with institutional innovation are out of 'sync', in a Coasean spirit, we would want to consider whether the cost of aligning social and private cost outweigh the gains. But there is no enforcer of rules over the political entrepreneurs or institution innovators. Since the political entrepreneurs are the ultimate 'rule-makers' the world can be no different than what they make it. Given the transaction costs they face, the system is 'efficient'. In effect, given the constraints of the model, no other outcome would be 'feasible', and the issue of efficiency is trivialized.

In both models of institutional change discussed, the presumed possibility of inefficiency, or other feasible worlds, seems to conflict with the deterministic nature of the models. In Demsetz's model, lags in rationality raise the spectre of other feasible worlds, but as long as these are uncontrollable aberrations, the economist can at best sit back and watch how institutions evolve. With Ruttan and Hayami's model we can hope that the transaction costs faced by the political entrepreneurs are conducive to good outcomes, but there is no room for prescription. As long as the institutions that evolve are the only ones that can evolve it seems senseless to make any reference to 'attainable' optimality. If some notion of optimality is called for, it will have to elicit counterfactual states. One could introduce counterfactual statements of the form 'if only individuals behaved differently', or 'if only the conditions under which agents acted were different', or 'if only the rules of the game could be changed', and all these ifs would represent different worlds to compare with the actual outcome. The problem is how to introduce these counterfactual states while avoiding the 'nirvana' criticism of comparing the real world to utopian ones.

4. GENERATING COUNTERFACTUALS TO SALVAGE 'ATTAINABLE' OPTIMALITY

Are we to choose between a utopian notion of optimality that abstracts from so many essential features of reality, and a realistic notion of 'attainable' optimality that makes a virtue of necessity? Can room be made in institutional models that allow for a non-trivial notion of feasible optimality? To compare our world with some paradise might enlighten us as to the shortcomings of our lot, but it might not do well as a goal to strive towards if it lacks any realism. We do need to incorporate aspects of reality that constrain possible worlds, but we do not want to constrain the model to such an extent that only the existing allocations are feasible. While we do not want to break up a monopoly if the costs of doing so outweigh the social gains (even given distributional objectives), there is little consolation in acquiescing to the monopoly's existence because no other world is possible.

In traditional neoclassical approaches there are no qualms about comparing outcomes of microeconomic models to counterfactual outcomes derived from models with zero transaction costs that are similar in other respects (technology, endowments, preferences, etc.). For instance, a resource allocation derived from an incomplete set of markets is compared to the resource allocation attained with a complete set of markets. The call to realism by institutional economists prevents comparisons with zero-transaction-cost outcomes, but more generally, it prevents comparisons with resource allocations derived from models with arbitrarily different organizational costs. In the audience example, we arrived at the 'standing-up' outcome by assuming rationality and having specified a certain set of preferences and transaction costs. We could derive a 'sitting-down' result simply by changing the incidence or level of transaction costs, but a comparison of the two outcomes would not warrant calling the 'standing-up' outcome inefficient since the 'sitting-down' outcome is not attainable given the 'actual' transaction costs we are modelling. We would be making a comparison with a world that has a different set of transaction costs and is thus irrelevant (and misleading) for the world we are modelling. It would be like comparing outcomes of models with different production functions and calling the outcome of one model inefficient because less output is produced than in the other. Since all exogenous changes of organizational costs seem arbitrary, there are no other 'feasible' microeconomic outcomes to compare to the determinate outcome of the model. The outcome of the initial model is the only feasible outcome.

4.1. Two Ways to Generate Counterfactuals

If some notion of attainable optimality is to be salvaged it would seem that microeconomic models would have to somehow generate alternative feasible outcomes, i.e. a set of counterfactuals. The problem is to decide what counterfactuals should be allowed. In general, there are two ways to bring about different outcomes of individual and collective action: either there is some alteration in the perceived pay-offs faced by some agents in the model (i.e. a change in the constraints or perceived constraints), or there is some change in the actions that individuals take without a change in the perceived pay-offs. The first way is familiar from game-theoretical attempts at 'solutions' to the Prisoners' Dilemma whereby individuals' perceptions of the expected pay-offs associated with alternative actions are changed, say by repetition, discounting, incomplete information, or some combination of these.[28] In fact a variety of ways to resolve the Prisoners' Dilemma have been developed which involve some kind of alteration in the environment within which agents act, like the addition of some activity so that the strategic interaction is changed, e.g. allowing enforceable commitments (Schelling 1960) and observing players interact with third parties so that reputations can be formed (Taylor 1976). While these 'solutions' may be good methods of providing a theoretical explanation or a historical account of the existence of certain kinds of cooperation, they are less well suited for showing how other feasible worlds are possible given a certain set of constraints (or when these remedies are not already available).[29]

The second way by which different outcomes of collective action can be generated is through changes emanating from the

[28] See Taylor (1990) and Hechter (1990) for a discussion of the effectiveness of some of these 'solutions' to the Prisoners' Dilemma.

[29] Furthermore, none of these 'solutions' would alleviate the sense of unsolvability of the simple one-shot Prisoners' Dilemma.

agent herself. In the rational-choice model an individual maximizes some objective function given perceived constraints; if these constraints are not altered, the action will be determinate and different outcomes are simply not possible. We often call the set of actions that are available to an individual at any given moment the agent's possibility set, and this is convenient because we can determine which action maximizes her pay-off function, and therefore which action the agent will take. Note, however, that all alternative actions are not really possible, since the individual would have to be irrational to take them, and irrationality is precluded from the outset. The agent does not 'choose' among the various possible actions, she simply computes the optimal actions and executes. In order for a change in the outcome of a microeconomic model to emanate from the individual as opposed to the environment, an agent would have to be able to renege the dictates of the rational-choice model by choosing actions within the possibility set that do not maximize her objective function. In the case of the Prisoners' Dilemma individuals could escape their sorry predicament by behaving 'irrationally'.[30]

In models that incorporate transaction costs the behavioural model of agents acts as a 'constraint' on the allocations that are organizationally feasible. The institutional rules and accompanying expenses required in revealing preferences for public goods, or the costs of enforcing contracts and legal rules (such as pollution permits), are fundamentally linked up to the behaviour of agents. The costs of enforcing a rule with a self-centred individual are likely to be different from enforcement costs if individuals were altruistic, or honest, irrespective of price. The rational-choice model is not just a description of individual behaviour, it

[30] Bromley's (1989: 86–9) discussion of the Prisoners' Dream highlights the institutional nature of the isolation problem. The authorities, in their attempt to extract confessions, set up an incentive structure whereby prisoners are induced to 'rat' on each other. (It is interesting to note that even if the prisoners have not committed a crime it is in their interest to confess to a crime they didn't commit.) Were the authorities not so clever in offering leniency in return for cooperation, the prisoners would no longer have a dominant strategy to confess and their dream (of less proficient authorities) would be fulfilled. But this is not the only dream the prisoners could have. In the spirit of my discussion on change originating from the agents' behaviour, the Prisoners' Dream might be that people were less rational (harbouring such 'irrational' thoughts as solidarity with their partners in crime) and did not confess despite the incentives to do so. It is the institutional structure coupled with individual rationality that makes the unhappy outcome inevitable.

also 'constrains' the set of feasible allocations or institutions. With this in mind my discussion on two ways of generating multiple feasible outcomes (a non-unique comparison set) can be reinterpreted as softening two kinds of organizational constraints: those that are environmentally determined (costs of defining property rights, availability of information) and those that emerge from the behavioural model (dishonest revelation of preferences).

An illustration may help clarify this distinction as well as suggest why focusing on the behavioural model to generate different outcomes is more appropriate. Someone looking back to the 1950s and 1960s may say that the installation of asbestos was suboptimal. This may be an unfair judgement since, given the state of knowledge at the time, it may have been the optimal thing to do. But we would also like to avoid the opposite extreme of saying it was the optimal thing to do since no other course of action was possible, given a full specification of the constraints faced by individuals in the 1950s. What we need is to generate a set of reasonable counterfactuals that were feasible in the 1950s and then judge whether among these counterfactuals the best action had been taken. The difficulty is to generate the reasonable set of counterfactuals. One way of doing this would be to slightly soften the information constraint faced by agents at the time, and compare the outcome of asbestos installation with what would have occurred if evidence of asbestos danger was a little more widespread. The problem is that such an alteration in the information set seems arbitrary. How would one decide what comparisons are allowable? Surely one wouldn't want to call the achievements of early entrepreneurs of the industrial revolution 'suboptimal' by comparing them with possibilities present in the computer age.

A more fruitful line of thought would be to consider what 'possibilities' were open to individuals given the information at their disposal, and consider whether their actions could have led to a better outcome without an exogenous change in their information set. Imagine there were some employees of asbestos companies that were knowledgeable about the risks of asbestos in the 1950s and 1960s but decided to conceal their knowledge for private benefit. In one sense, given these peoples' motives (behavioural model), this concealment could not have been otherwise and it would be logically wrong to call the installation of asbestos insulation suboptimal. However, it is not as if they were totally unaware of the danger and thus could not even perceive of another course of action; in this case, some people were aware of the dangers but *chose* to behave selfishly. Maybe in this case we are warranted in saying that this outcome was suboptimal if we assume that the behavioural model doesn't preclude them from selecting a non-selfish act, or any other act that is 'possible' but not behaviourally consistent. This seems to be a more plausible basis for generating counterfactuals than by simply assuming an alternative set of constraints on individuals. What I am saying is that if we are to allow for alternative outcomes we should do it by removing determinism from the behavioural model rather than 'arbitrarily' suggesting that the constraints on agents could have been different.[31]

By relying on comparison of alternative outcomes that derive from alternative actions within individuals' choice sets we can also avoid calling the 1950s suboptimal because of the ignorance of information present in our computer age. Given the information available in the 1950s, none of the options available to individuals could have brought about the acquisition of knowledge of electronic computers. Likewise, if the asbestos companies were not aware of the dangers of asbestos, and an understanding of that danger required at least five years of scientific research, we would be less apt to call asbestos use suboptimal. On the other hand, if information of the dangers of asbestos was attainable at the time and yet certain individuals chose to ignore or conceal this information, then we might be warranted in suggesting that asbestos insulation was suboptimal.

The reason I concentrate on the organizational constraints posed by the behavioural model as opposed to other transaction costs is that these seem harder to accept as unalterable con-

---

[31] Alternatively, if we are to say that the constraints could have been different this should be explained ultimately by reference to human agency (no *Deus ex machina*). Note that this includes outcomes derived from alternative choices of information gathering. That is, certain sorts of knowledge can be acquired by agents through actions within their possibility set, while other kinds cannot. In this sense it may be that knowledge of the truth about asbestos would have been accessible to agents had they behaved differently. It may have been that there were others unaffiliated to the companies who could have campaigned harder for the truth, etc.

straints.[32] A transaction cost in the form of the physical difficulty in defining and enforcing private-property rights over air, or apprehending a polluter, can be easily accepted as setting limits on what allocations are feasible within a system. To say that the audience will never sit down because rationality makes that outcome infeasible is harder to swallow. If scope is to be found for non-deterministic outcomes, it is natural to seek it in agents' ability to choose alternative courses of action. Yet the assumption of rationality sets limitations on ways to organize public-good provision, or enforce private property, and this is well taken. The challenge is to find a way to generate counterfactuals, allowing individuals a reasonable range of alternative courses of action, without compromising realism.

5. BEHAVIOURAL MODELS, DETERMINATE OUTCOMES, AND COUNTERFACTUALS

The narrow view of rationality offers a Sisyphian picture of agents perpetually stuck in a low-level trap when confronted by a Prisoners' Dilemma: unable to overcome the behavioural model

[32] In an interesting article A. J. Field (1984: 685) argues that 'if the behavioural principle of social science models is to be self-interest maximization, and one wishes to model stable social orders, one must posit logically anterior rules or norms that help define the arena within which such maximization takes place'. If all institutions, rules, norms, are taken as endogenous to be derived as outcomes of self-interest maximizing interaction, 'the analytical structure of microeconomic theory begins to unravel, in the sense that one is left with no consistent explanation of why the world does not degenerate into a war of all against all' (1984: 684). The implication is that if microeconomic analysis is to be fruitful one must assume some structure, some 'anterior rules or norms'. If microeconomic theory is to provide an analysis of institutional variation it must do this by 'comparative exercises where rules are varied and the impact on endogenous variables (such as output and prices) is investigated, but where adherence to basic rules in each of the cases compared is taken as given or as accounted for by forces outside the model' (1984: 684). However, the problem that I have been discussing in this chapter remains. While we can discuss hypothetical changes of rules and consider the merits of alternative outcomes (prices, outputs, institutions), if we have fully specified the constraints in our model there will be no room for alternatives, no way by which the rules can be changed (unless we treat the 'rule-makers' (government) as above rules and behavioural models). I think that if we are to explain the existence and change of institutions, and simultaneously provide room for the human agent as a source of change, we must ultimately seek out the answer in the behavioural model of the agent. We must ask what kind of behavioural model would make inefficiency (as well as institutions) possible.

that defines them. As long as the behavioural model is treated as a constraint, a solution to the problem is precluded as infeasible. There is no scope for alternative courses of action. The action an individual takes is fully determined by her utility function and the constraints on her action. So long as there is a determined course of action maximizing utility, choice is redundant. Any other action would be 'irrational'. In this framework the other courses of action are only possible when a lapse of rationality is present on the part of the agent. But such random lapses would be small consolation, since while the world may be less predictable, any changes from predicted outcomes would be random. Human agents could not 'wilfully' bring about other outcomes. Unless agents could somehow escape the dictates of their behavioural model, the 'sitting-down' solution is not a real possibility.

The problem at hand is not so much a result of a specific behavioural model (rational-choice model), but the causal or deterministic nature of the model. Any behavioural model that could accurately predict what an agent will do given the perceived pay-off function faced by the agent, would present the same difficulties. Many institutional economists who are critical of the rational choice model have espoused some variant of Herbert Simon's (1982) notion of bounded rationality which provides an alternative view of individuals' means-rationality.[33] Accordingly, agents have limited computational capacities and thus are unable to maximize some function.[34] Recognition of their inherent inability to maximize, or be consistent, leads individuals to seek out effective procedures or rules of thumb that do an 'adequate' job of guiding action towards desired goals (these procedures are sometimes seen as a kind of second-best optimizing). In order to be able to predict a boundedly rational person's actions, knowledge of the mechanism used to pick rules of thumb is required.[35] An understanding of these mechanisms would seem

[33] Means-rationality concerns the formal properties of decision-making and usually takes the form of consistency requirements on the ultimate decisions of individuals.

[34] If nothing else the time lost computing the 'optimal' action may be more valuable than the improved precision afforded.

[35] On one interpretation of 'bounded rationality', individuals set aspiration levels which they try to achieve but beyond which they do not attempt to improve. In this case to predict individuals' actions, information on how agents set aspiration levels would be needed.

to take us into the direction of physiological accounts of the function of emotions and intuition[36] which are equally if not more susceptible to deterministic accounts of human action.

More radical departures from the rational-choice model also give rise to determinate outcomes, whether these are models of endogenous preferences (changing the stable-preference assumption), habit formation, cognitive dissonance, commitment, subconscious processes, cognitive theoretical approaches, etc.[37] Although some of these models may be more capable of explaining successful collective action, the problem of determinism may still remain. For instance, even if agents manage to escape some Prisoners' Dilemma situations by acting out of a sense of duty, if we can predict when duty-guided behaviour will ensue on the basis of information at our disposal, then the outcome will be the only one possible given the behavioural model and the organizational constraints faced by the agents.[38] Alternative outcomes will not be possible and thus the notion of efficiency will be redundant.

The following quote from Nagel (1986) on the topic of autonomy captures the essence of the problem that confronts us:

From the inside, when we act, alternative possibilities seem to lie open before us: to turn right or left, to order this dish or that, to vote for one candidate or the other—and one of the possibilities is made actual by what we do. The same applies to our internal consideration of the actions of others. But from an external perspective, things look different. That perspective takes in not only the circumstances of action as they present themselves to the agent, but also the conditions and influences lying behind the action, including the complete nature of the agent himself. While we cannot fully occupy this perspective toward ourselves while acting, it seems possible that many of the alternatives that appear to lie open when viewed from an internal perspective would seem closed from this outer point of view, if we could take it up. And even if some of them are left open, given a complete specification of the condition of the agent and the circumstances of action, it is not clear how this would leave anything further for the agent to contribute to the outcome—

[36] See Simon (1983) for a discussion of the role of emotions and intuition.

[37] See Hodgson (1989: chs. 4, 5) for a critical overview of these behavioural models.

[38] In more complex behavioural models more information than individuals' preference orderings may be required to predict an agents' actions. See Sen's (1973) discussion on commitment where *as if* behaviour can drive a wedge between preference and choice.

anything that he could contribute as source, rather than merely as the scene of the outcome—the person whose act it is. (1986: 133–4)

The external view Nagel describes is precisely the kind of view I argue that the institutional approach is taking. By specifying all the constraints relevant to explain and fully determine an action it explains away alternative actions; they are infeasible given the constraints. Knowing the constraints and the behavioural model the agent will turn in one direction, say right, and no other action is possible. We may make evaluative judgements about the action, but not for policy reasons, since no alternative action could be taken. In order to be able to meaningfully say 'you should have turned to the left' it must be possible for the agent, within the constraints, to actually choose left.[39] We need to generate counterfactuals; alternative courses of action that agents can take.

Is it possible to construct a model that avoids the kind of determinism in Nagel's external view, but is also able to make sense of human action as willed and not random?[40] The enormous burden of such a model would be to find a vocabulary that

[39] 'Should', is not meant as a moral precept, but simply indicates that some other action may have on certain grounds greater merit. There is a separate issue of moral responsibility that some argue can be made despite a deterministic account of action, i.e. an agent may have no alternative act available to take and still be held morally accountable for her action. Frankfurt (1969) and Fischer (1986) present such views.

[40] The philosophical debate on determinism and free will has been rife with traps and pitfalls and any broaching of the issue, especially by one whose field of speciality is not philosophy, can be dangerous. The following quote from a dictionary of philosophy will help convey the sense of determinism that I am concerned with: '*Soft determinists*, by far the largest class in recent times, say that our actions are indeed caused, but we are not therefore any less free than we might be, because the causation is not a constraint or compulsion on us. So long as our natures and choices are effective as items in the causal chain, the fact that they are themselves caused is irrelevant and does not stop them being what they are. *Indeterminists*, however, insist that determinists, of whatever complexion, can give no sense to the sentence "He could have done otherwise", where this means something more than simply "He *might* have done otherwise (had his nature or circumstances been different)". Soft determinists often hold that what justifies praise and blame is solely that they can influence action. This, say indeterminists, misses the point of those concepts. Hard determinists are *incompatibilists*, i.e., think free will and universal causation are incompatible. Soft determinists are *compatibilists*. Indeterminists may be either, but are usually incompatibilists' (Lacey 1986: 79–82). When I invoke the problem of determinism or free will it is in the sense discussed in the quote, '"He could have done otherwise", where this means more than simply "He *might* have done otherwise"'.

can describe action as neither completely determined nor random. When we ask why an individual turned right and not left we feel compelled to provide a reason, to make sense of the particular action. We say that the individual believed that by turning right she would get to her destination faster, or that she believed that turning right is the proper thing to do and she wants to be proper. Now given her beliefs she could not have done otherwise. If we say that given her beliefs she could have turned right or left the actual decision to turn right seems unexplained; we remain with the impression that her actual decision to turn right as opposed to left must have been random.

If alternative courses of action, or alternative worlds are to be possible, these have to be built into our models of individual behaviour. It's far from clear how this can be done. It would be nice in the audience example to treat the sitting-down solution as a real possibility, allowing the judgement that standing up is not the best of all possible worlds. It is less clear that we want to treat as a real possibility the honest revelation of agents when confronted with contributions for a public good, and treat as inefficient the policy that cannot capture all the benefits that could be attained by costless honest behaviour, or that we want to treat as inefficient a policy that doesn't costlessly eliminate criminal activity because it is possible for potential criminals, even given the constraints they face, to avoid crime.[41] Can we build into our models enough scope for alternative courses of action to allow for many possible worlds, without setting up unattainable worlds?

6. CONCLUSION

The traditional notion of optimality in welfare economics has been criticized for comparing real-world outcomes with unattainable outcomes of a transaction-costless world. The alternative notion of 'attainable' optimality implicit in models with endogenous transaction costs, suffers in that by offering a causal explanation of economic interaction it precludes other feasible

---

[41] Becker (1968) offers an analysis of optimal levels of crime given organizational costs. All such optimal-enforcement models have an implicit notion of attainable optimality.

alternatives with which to compare the outcome of the model. By disallowing comparisons of the 'real-world' microeconomic model with microeconomic models that have different organizational costs, the set of feasible outcomes collapses to the outcome of the 'real-world' model. Accordingly, the outcome that exists is the only possible one. As the joke goes, an optimist will say that we are in the best of all possible worlds and the pessimist will agree.

Attempts to relax the deterministic nature of models that incorporate organizational costs by introducing 'lags in rationality', or political entrepreneurs with the ability to intervene, are self-contradictory. If some notion of attainable optimality is to be salvaged it must be shown that a model with a given set of organizational costs can generate alternative outcomes. One way that economists generate alternative outcomes is by altering the pay-offs (or perceived pay-offs) faced by agents, as is done in Prisoners' Dilemma games by assuming that the game is repeated. But, in a sense, this is just altering organizational costs which is what we want to avoid. Another way to generate alternative outcomes (that do not conflict with the spirit of disallowing comparisons of models with different organizational costs) is to reconceptualize behavioural models so that agents are allowed to take different actions even when nothing in their environment has changed. If asbestos insulation was inefficient it was because, with the organizational costs present at the time, there were actions that agents could have taken that would have lead to a better outcome. This is preferable to saying that insulation was inefficient because if more information had been available at the time, asbestos insulation could have been avoided.

The neoclassical notion of rationality envisages agents as maximizing some objective function so that any actions that do not maximize the objective function are, in a sense, not really available options to the agent. This kind of determinism prevents agents from being able to take different actions in a given environment. Yet this problem of determinism, in its narrow form, is not confined just to the neoclassical rational-choice model but seems to characterize most behavioural models. As long as individuals' actions are fully predictable from knowledge of their behavioural model and the information at their disposal, this kind of determinism cannot be escaped. If there are to be many possible worlds, models have to make room for counterfactual states. It is not at all clear, however, how counterfactuals can be meaningfully built into microeconomic models to salvage the notion of 'attainable' optimality.

Traditional welfare economics was rightly criticized for being too harsh in judgement of the real world by comparing it with utopian alternatives. More importantly such comparisons could seriously mislead policy prescriptions. There are clearly important advantages of comparative institution models that recognize the real organizational constraints of this world. Unfortunately relentless application of realism seems to leave no scope for prescription as the realist modeller comes to realize that her most accurate model of the world describes what is, or what will be, rather than what could be. If alternative institutions and courses of actions are to be possible the modeller must somehow build these alternatives into the models.

11
Conclusion

There has always been a strong sense that no good characterization of externality exists. I suggested in the conclusion of Chapter 2 that a temptation to avoid the problem of characterizing externality should be resisted because of the important insights a better understanding of the notion would provide for the appraisal of an economy and its institutions. In this book I have tried to show why characterizing externality has been such an intractable task. This has entailed a critical examination of many of the existing characterizations, and an attempt to understand and evaluate the many concepts, distinctions and motivations latent in the apparently homogeneous notion of externality.

In Chapter 3 I looked at what I called a 'phenomenological approach' to externality which entailed an attempt to separate out a special kind of interdependence without reference to institutions or consequences in terms of inefficiency. In trying to identify this special kind of interdependence, Baumol and Oates (1975) invoke the nature of the utility function and the kind, or degree, of control that an agent has over events. The difficulty of determining the degree of control over an activity to distinguish internality from externality, is overcome by implicitly treating it as a question of whether private-property rights have been defined over activity. Externality becomes synonymous with the non-existence of private property. The attempt to find a kind of interdependence without reference to institutions is foiled. More importantly, the apparent clarity of externality as non-existence of private-property rights is lost once an attempt is made to define the institution of private property. The two main problems confronting the phenomenological approach are first, how to offer a clear distinction between external and internal activity (or events) that is not consequence-dependent, and second, how to justify the need for such a distinction, i.e. what is the motivation.

In the general-equilibrium approach discussed in Chapter 4, the attempt was to better understand the causes of market fail-

ure, clarifying the role of non-convexities, public goods, externality, too few agents, etc., within the framework of a general-
equilibrium model. Despite the important insights gained from
this approach, the concept of externality remains vague and
imprecise, whether seen as equivalent to market failure, or as a
subset of market failure. The sense is retained that there are some
special kinds of phenomena that are behind market failure, but
no satisfactory means of identifying them are provided. In the
general-equilibrium approach there is a strong association of
externality with the non-existence of markets, non-universality of
markets being a central cause of market failure. While this association is meaningful within the confines of the Arrow–Debreu
model, it is problematic in a model which incorporates transaction costs. Yet transaction costs are essential if one is to explain
the existence or non-existence of markets in the first place. In
models with transaction costs, non-existence of markets is an
absolute concept that is inappropriate for an understanding of
failure. The question is not whether an ideal type of institution
exists or not, but whether imperfect markets do a better job allocating resources, relative to alternative imperfect modes of organization.

In their endeavour to fully specify the causal mechanism
underlying market failure and to establish externality's place
therein, the authors taking the general-equilibrium approach alter
the very notion of market failure. Arrow (1970) moves us from
'absolute' to 'relative' market failure as he attempts to take
account of transaction costs, and Heller and Starrett (1976) take
us from 'relative' to 'pre-market' failure as they try to incorporate the process of institution formation in their conception of
failure. However, the metamorphosis of market failure is incomplete as the full implications of incorporating organizational costs
into economic models have not been worked out.

Chapters 5 and 6 clarified and further developed some of the
issues raised by the general-equilibrium approach. Chapter 5
took a closer look at the relationship between externality and
non-convexity in transaction-costless general-equilibrium models.
The nature and degree of non-convexity is seen to depend largely
on how institutions are defined. Market failure in frictionless
models, and the role that non-convexity has as a cause of market
failure, is a function of the entitlement structure defining eco-

nomic interaction. In order to evaluate the entitlement structure, and the role of missing markets, missing property rights, etc., it is necessary to consider the factors that determine the size and function of economic units, i.e. incorporate organizational costs. If organizational costs are incorporated in our model we must leave the Arrow–Debreu framework.

In Chapter 6 I looked at one of the central themes of the general-equilibrium approach, that of determining the causes of market failure. I argued that one cannot treat the mere presence of organizational costs (or information costs) as a cause of market failure, nor for that matter do organizational costs explain all market failure. In fact treating transaction costs as a cause of failure is just another indication of the fragmented way that transaction costs have been incorporated in economic thinking. As long as organizational costs are endogenous to the model, one has to look for reasons whether and why organizational costs were not minimized with respect to some welfare objective. The general methodological discussion by Hart and Honoré (1959) on the useful specification of causation, highlighting the complexity of imputing causality, points to the need to form some understanding of what are considered 'normal' conditions of an economy, so one can look for departures from these normal states in discerning why organizational costs have not been further minimized.

Having considered the problems of characterizing externality, I turned my attention to finding the sources of the many meanings of externality throughout the varied literature, in order to offer an overview of the many approaches, and to evaluate the relevance and reach of the distinctions and motivations underscoring the many approaches. Two generic senses of external and internal seem to be involved in most characterizations of externality. In one sense, external (internal) refers to activity that is beyond (within) the control of some unit of account. Some kind of interdependence is implied without reference to consequences of action in terms of inefficiency. In the other sense, external (internal) refers to activity that has not been properly 'accounted' for by some unit of account. Activity was not 'efficiently' controlled.[1]

---

[1] Notice that the word 'control' can refer to the degree of power of the decision-maker (as in the first generic sense), or it can refer to the degree of attaining some objective. I may only have partial control over some outcome, yet my

Attempts to characterize externality stumbled over attempts to find a good criterion demarcating 'external' from 'internal'. Characterizations that tried to specify some special kind of interdependence by reference to the degree of control, degree of excludability, degree of interdependence, or kind of consent, or nature of utility functions, were all plagued by the arbitrariness of choosing a cut-off point. Likewise, characterizations that used the existence, or not, of some institution ('external' to private exchange, 'external' to market exchange) as the line of demarcation between external and internal activity, were faced with the problem of giving a clear definition of the relevant institution, or if that problem could be surmounted, of justifying the need for such a distinction. Hilary Putnam (1988: 27) says that 'philosophers often take perfectly sensible continua and get in trouble by trying to convert them into dichotomies'.[2] Something similar seems to be happening with economists trying to forge a dichotomy between external and internal activity without reference to consequences in terms of inefficiency. This problem is avoided when 'external' is used so broadly that there is no cut-off point, e.g. general interdependence or inefficiency. But then there seems little need for a special denomination. Finally, difficulties crop up when we treat externality mainly as inefficiency, but also try to forge a one-to-one correspondence between underlying kinds of interdependence and inefficiency.

Despite the questionable value of externality as a classificatory principle, there are important motivations that underscore the many attempts to characterize externality. These are reflected in the two generic senses and need to be separated and respectively investigated. The consequentialist concern draws from the view of externality as activity not properly 'accounted for'. By extending the reasoning that led Arrow (1970), and Heller and Starrett (1976), to gradually transform the notion of market failure, it arrives at a broader notion of inefficiency than market failure. Institutions become endogenous variables in the analysis to be evaluated according to their effectiveness in helping to attain some social-welfare objective. A consequentialist concern treats institutions as instruments guiding action and evaluates them

interaction with others may be 'controlled' through some entitlement structure so that the outcome of our interaction is efficient.

[2] Hilary Putnam credits Chomsky with having suggested this idea to him.

according to the outcomes they are associated with. It requires that we better understand the links between norms, institutions, behaviour, and technology, in order to find why certain activities or consequences may have escaped our purview.

The intrinsic-feature approach offers a possible motivation behind attempts to separate out special kinds of interdependence (from general interdependence). Institutions or entitlements are not valued just for their instrumental function of advancing efficiency, but are seen to have some intrinsic value, such as the libertarian one of protecting an individual's private domain. 'External' activity may be seen to violate some rule or some kinds of interaction which have intrinsic value and therefore are of special concern.

I did not pursue the intrinsic-feature approach which would rely more heavily on moral and legal philosophy than economic reasoning. Giving a non-consequentialist justification of alternative modes of organizing economic activity (consent-based interaction, importance of private property, or market, the 'coercive' nature of certain kinds of activity), requires a much deeper philosophical investigation than is often afforded by economists. Since economists are trained as consequentialists, I turned my attention to this concern in the second part of my book. An important element in understanding and evaluating institutions is to consider how they may be formed as a function of individual interaction. In Chapter 8, I critically examined a few theories of institution formation. I tried to dispel the view that the mere possibility of cooperative gains in institution formation would ensure that institutions evolve optimally as the result of interaction among self-centred individuals. In a pre-market or pre-institution environment there is no structure that will align individual and social benefits and costs.

An endogenous view of institutions raises the quesiton of how to define efficient institutions and what action authorities should take in order to form such institutions. In Chapter 9, I offered a critique of one of the commonly used principles of efficient institution formation in the Law and Economics literature known as 'wealth-maximization.' I argue that wealth-maximization is indeterminate when the scope of entitlement formation is large and therefore offers no guide to action, and when entitlements are changed locally, wealth-maximization affords far too much legitimacy to agents' willingness to pay, being insensitive to distributional concerns and the lessons of second-best theory.

Finally, in Chapter 10, I turned to the notion of optimality as it emerges in models that treat institutions endogenously. Its merit lies in that organizational costs, as users of resources, are fully taken into account in evaluating institutions. A serious problem, however, arises in that by treating all institutions endogenously one arrives at the disheartening conclusion that there is no room for improving on the institutions that exist. If the notion of optimality is to be given content in models that incorporate organizational costs, some way of introducing a reasonable set of counterfactuals is called for.

In this book I have tried to clarify the plural concepts that underlie the apparently homogeneous notion of externality. In answer to the question What is externality?, or, What is a good characterization of externality?, I say that there cannot be a unique good characterization of externality. Externality has come to denote many things, none of which separately, or in combination, seem to justify the apellation 'externality', and more importantly, none of which do full justice to the important issues underlying this notion. I have tried to show that an understanding of the complex notion of externality will help clarify several central methodological issues and notions of economic theory, e.g. optimality, market failure, causality of failure, non-convexity, etc., and place at centre stage institutional and behavioural choices for resource allocation.

BIBLIOGRAPHY

AKERLOF, G. A. (1984), 'The Economics of Caste and of the Rat Race and other Woeful Tales', in *An Economic Theorists Book of Tales* (Cambridge: Cambridge University Press).

ALCHIAN, A. A., and ALLEN, W. R. (1969), *Exchange and Production, Theory in Use* (1st edn. Belmont: Wadsworth Publishing Co., Inc.)

—— and DEMSETZ, H. (1972), 'Production, Information Costs, and Economic Organization', *American Economic Review*, 62: 777–95.

ANDERSON, L. G. (1986), *The Economics of Fisheries Management* (rev. edn. Baltimore: Johns Hopkins University Press).

ANDERSON, T. L., and HILL, A. J. (1975), 'The Evolution of Property Rights: A Study of the American West', *Journal of Law and Economics*, 18/1: 163–79.

ARCHIBALD, G. C., and DONALDSON, D. (1976), 'Non-paternalism and the Basic Theorem of Welfare Economics', *Canadian Journal of Economics*, 991/3: 492–507.

ARROW, K. J. (1951), *Soical Choice and Individual Values* (New Haven, Conn.: Yale University Press).

—— (1963), *Social Choice and Individual Value* (rev. edn., New York: John Wiley & Sons).

—— (1970), 'The Organization of Economic Activity: Issues Pertinent to the Choice of Market Versus Non-market Allocation', in R. H. Haveman and J. Margolis (eds.), *Public Expenditures and Policy Analysis* (Chicago: Markham).

—— (1972), 'Gifts and Exchanges', *Philosophy and Public Affairs*, 1/1.

BAIRD, R. M., and ROSENBAUM, S. E. (1988) (eds.), *Philosophy of Punishment* (New York: Prometheus Books).

BATES, R. H. (1983), *Essays on the Political Economy of Rural Africa* (Cambridge: Cambridge University Press).

BATOR, F. M. (1958), 'The Anatomy of Market Failure', *Quarterly Journal of Economics*, 72: 351–79.

BAUMOL, W. J. (1952), *Welfare Economics and the Theory of the State* (Cambridge, Mass.: Harvard University Press).

—— and BRADFORD, D. F. (1972), 'Detrimental Externalities and Non-convexity of the Production Set', *Economica*, 39: 160–76.

—— and OATES, W. E. (1975), *The Theory of Environmental Policy* (NJ: Prentice-Hall).

BECKER, G. S. (1968), 'Crime and Punishment: An Economic Approach', *Journal of Political Economy*, 76/2: 169–217.

BECKER, G. S. (1975) (ed.), *Economics of the Family: Marriage, Children, and Human Capital* (Chicago: University of Chicago Press).

—— and MURPHY, K. M. (1988), 'A Theory of Rational Addiction', *Journal of Political Economy*, 964: 675–700.

BERGSON, A. (1938), 'A Reformulation of Certain Aspects of Welfare Economics', *Quarterly Journal of Economics*, 52: 314–44.

BLAUG, M. (1980), *The Methodology of Economics* (Cambridge: Cambridge University Press).

BOWEN, H. R. (1943), 'The Interpretation of Voting in the Allocation of Economic Resources', *Quarterly Journal of Economics*, 58: 27–49.

BOWLES, S., and GINTIS, H. (1988), 'Contested Exchange: Political Economy and Modern Economic Theory', *American Economic Review*, 78/2: 145–50.

BRENNAN, G., and BUCHANAN, J. (1985), *The Reason of Rules* (Cambridge: Cambridge University Press).

BROMLEY, D. W. (1989), *Economic Interests and Institutions* (Oxford: Basil Blackwell).

BUCHANAN, A. E. (1985), *Ethics, Efficiency and the Market* (Totown, NJ: Rowman & Allanheed).

BUCHANAN, J. M., and FAITH, R. L. (1981), 'Entrepreneurship and the Internalization of Externalities', *Journal of Law and Economics*, 24/1: 95–111.

—— and STUBBLEBINE, W. E. (1962), 'Externality', *Economica*, 29 (Nov.), 371–84.

—— and TULLOCK, G. (1962), *The Calculus of Consent* (Ann Arbor, Mich.: University of Michigan Press).

BUSH, W. C., and MAYER, L. S. (1974), 'Some Implications of Anarchy for the Distribution of Property Rights', *Journal of Economic Theory*, 8: 401–12.

CALABRESI, G. (1968), 'Transaction Costs, Resource Allocation and Liability Rules—A Comment', *Journal of Law and Economics*, 11: 67–73.

—— and MELAMED, A. D. (1972), 'Property Rules, Liability Rules, and Inalienability: One View of the Cathedral', *Harvard Law Review*, 85: 1089.

CHEUNG, S. N. S. (1970), 'The Structure of a Contract and the Theory of a Non-exclusive Resource', *Journal of Law and Economics*, 13 (Apr.), 49–70.

—— (1974), 'A Theory of Price Control', *Journal of Law and Economics*, 17 (Oct.), 124–38.

—— (1983), 'The Contractual Nature of the Firm', *Journal of Law and Economics*, 26 (Apr.), 1–21.

CHIPMAN, J. S. (1970), 'External Economies of Scale and Competitive Equilibrium', *Quarterly Journal of Economics*, 84: 347–85.

CLAPHAM, J. H. (1922), 'On Empty Economic Boxes', *Economic Journal*, 32: 305–14; repr. in Stigler and Boulding (1953).

CLARK, C. W. (1985), *Bioeconomic Modelling and Fisheries Management* (New York: Wiley-Interscience).

COASE, R. H. (1937), 'The Nature of the Firm', *Economica*, 4: 386–405.

—— (1960), 'The Problem of Social Cost', *Journal of Law and Economics*, 3: 1–44.

COLEMAN, JAMES (1990), *Foundations of Social Theory* (Belkanp Press of Harvard University Press).

COLEMAN, JULES L. (1988), *Markets, Morals and the Law* (Cambridge: Cambridge University Press).

COOTER, R. (1982), 'The Cost of Coase', *Journal of Legal Studies*, 11: 1–33.

CORNES, R., and SANDLER, T. (1986), *The Theory of Externalities, Public Goods, and Club Goods* (Cambridge: Cambridge University Press).

COWEN, T. (1988), 'Public Goods Definitions and their Institutional Context: A Critique of Public Goods Theory', *Review of Social Economy*, 53–63.

DAHLMAN, C. J. (1979), 'The Problem of Externality', *Journal of Law and Economics*, 22: 141–62.

—— (1980), *The Open Field System and Beyond: A Property Rights Analysis of an Economic Institution* (Cambridge: Cambridge University Press).

DASGUPTA, P. S., and HEAL, G. M. (1979), *Economic Theory and Exhaustible Resources* (Cambridge: Cambridge University Press).

DAVIS, L. E., and NORTH, D. C. (1970), 'Insitutional Change and American Economic Growth: A First Step Towards a Theory of Institutional Innovation', *Journal of Economic History*, 30: 131–49.

DEALESSI, L. (1980), 'The Economics of Property Rights: A Survey of the Literature', *Research in Law and Economics*, 2: 1–47.

DEMSETZ, H. (1967), 'Towards a Theory of Property Rights', *American Economic Review*, 57: 347–59.

—— (1969), 'Information and Efficiency: Another Viewpoint', *Journal of Law and Economics*, 12: 1–22.

DORE, R. (1987), *Taking Japan Seriously* (Stanford: Stanford University Press).

DWORKIN, R. M. (1980), 'Is Wealth Value?', *Journal of Legal Studies*, 9: 191.

EGGERTSSON, T. (1990), *Economic Behaviour and Institutions* (Cambridge: Cambridge University Press).

ELLIS, H., and FELLNER, W. (1943), 'External Economies and Diseconomies', *American Economic Review*, 23/3: 493–511; repr. in Stigler and Boulding (1953).

ELSTER, J. (1986) (ed.), *The Multiple Self* (Cambridge: Cambridge University Press).

—— (1989), *The Cement of Society: A Study of Social Order* (Cambridge: Cambridge University Press).

FENOALTEA, S. (1986), 'The Economics of the Common Fields: The State of the Debate' (Upsulu, International Symposium on Property Rights, Organizational Forms and Economic Behavior).

FIELD, A. J. (1984), 'Microeconomics, Norms and Rationality', *Economic Development and Cultural Change*, 32: 683–711.

FIELD, B. C. (1986), 'Induced Changes in Property Rights Institutions', Research paper (Amherst, Mass.: University of Massachusetts, Department of Agricultural and Resource Economics).

FISCHER, J. M. (1986), *Moral Responsibility* (Ithaca, NY: Cornell University Press).

FOLEY, D. (1970), 'Economic Equilibrium with Costly Marketing', *Journal of Economic Theory*, 2: 276–91.

FRANK, R. (1986), *Choosing the Right Pond: Human Behavior in the Quest for Status* (New York: Oxford University Press).

—— (1989), *Passions within Reason: The Strategic Role of Emotions* (New York: Norton).

FRANKFURT, H. (1969), 'Alternative Possibilities and Moral Responsibility', *Journal of Philosophy*, 66: 828–39.

FURUBOTN, E. G., and PEJOVICH, S. (1974) (eds.), *The Economics of Property Rights* (Cambridge, Mass.: Ballinger).

GAUTHIER, D. (1986), *Morals by Agreement* (Oxford: Clarendon Press).

GORDON, H. S. (1954), 'The Economic Theory of a Common Property Resource: The Fishery', *Journal of Political Economy*, 62 (Apr.), 124–42.

GREEN, E. D. (1982), 'Equilibrium and Efficiency under Pure Entitlement Systems', *Public Choice*, 39: 185–212.

HAMLIN, A. P. (1986), *Ethics, Economics and the State* (New York: St Martin's Press).

HARE, R. M. (1979), 'What is Wrong with Slavery?', *Philosophy and Public Affairs*, 8.

HART, H. L. A., and HONORÉ, T. (1959), *Causation in the Law* (1st edn., Oxford: Clarendon Press).

—— (1985), *Causation in the Law* (2nd edn., Oxford: Clarendon Press).

HARTWICK, J. M., and OLEWILER, N. D. (1986), *The Economics of Natural Resource Use* (New York: Harper & Row, Publishers).

HEAL, G. M. (1973), *The Theory of Economic Planning* (Amsterdam: North Holland).

HECHTER, M. (1990), 'Comment: On the Inadequacy of Game Theory for the Solution of Real-World Collective Action Problems', in K. S.

Cook and M. Levi (eds.), *The Limits of Rationality* (Chicago: University of Chicago Press).

HELLER, W. P., and STARRETT, D. A. (1976), 'On the Nature of Externalities', in S. A. Y. Lin (ed.), *Theory and Measurement of Economic Externalities* (New York: Academic Press).

HIRSCH, F. (1977), *Social Limits to Growth* (London: Routledge & Kegan Paul).

HODGSON, G. M. (1988), *Economics and Institutions* (Philadelphia: University of Pennsylvania Press).

KNIGHT, F. H. (1924), 'Some Fallacies in the Interpretation of Social Cost', *Quarterly Journal of Economics*, 37 (Aug.), 582–606.

KOOPMANS, T. C. (1957), *Three Essays on the State of Economic Science* (New York: McGraw-Hill).

KRONMAN, A. T. (1980), 'Wealth Maximization as a Normative Principle', *Journal of Legal Studies*, 9: 227–42.

LACEY, A. R. (1986), *A Dictionary of Philosophy* (London: Routledge & Kegan Paul).

LAFFONT, J. (1988), *Fundamentals of Public Economics* (Cambridge, Mass.: MIT Press).

LANGE, O. (1936), 'On the Economic Theory of Socialism', *Review of Economic Studies*, 4: 53–71; repr. in O. Lange and F. M. Taylor (eds.), *On the Economic Theory of Socialism* (Minneapolis: University of Minnesota Press).

LANGLOIS, R. N. (1986*a*) (ed.), *Economics as a Process: Essays in the New Institutional Economics* (Cambridge: Cambridge University Press).

—— (1986*b*), 'Coherence and Flexibility: Social Institutions in a World of Radical Uncertainty', in I. M. Kirzner (ed.), *Subjectivism, Intelligibility and Economic Understanding* (New York: New York University Press).

LEDYARD, J. O. (1976), 'Discussion', in S. A. Y. Lin (ed.), *Theory and Measurement of Economic Externalities* (New York: Academic Press).

LEWIS, D. (1981), 'Are We Free to Break the Laws', *Theoria*, 47: 112–21.

LINDAHL, E. (1919), 'Just Taxation—A Positive Solution'; in Peacock and Musgrave (1958).

MARGOLIS, H. (1982), *Selfishness, Altruism and Rationality* (Chicago: The University of Chicago Press).

MARGOLIS, S. E. (1987), 'Two Definitions of Efficiency in Law and Economics', *Journal of Legal Studies*, 16 (June): 471–82.

MARSHALL, A. (1890), *Principles of Economics* (1st edn., London: Macmillan).

—— (1919), *Industry and Trade* (London: Macmillan).

—— (1920), *Principles of Economics* (8th edn., London: Macmillan).

McCLOSKEY, D. N. (1972), 'The Enclosure of Open Fields: Preface to a Study of Its Impact on the Efficiency of English Agriculture in the Eighteenth Century', *Journal of Economic History*, 32 (Mar.), 15–35.

MEADE, J. (1952), 'External Economies and Diseconomies in a Competitive Situation', *Economic Journal*, 62: 54–67.

—— (1973), *The Theory of Economic Externalities: The Control of Environmental Pollution and Similar Costs* (Geneva: A. W. Sijhoff-Leiden).

MILL, J. S. (1985), *On Liberty* (London: Penguin Classics).

MISHAN, E. J. (1969), 'The Relationship Between Joint Products, Collective Goods, and Externalities', *Journal of Political Economy*, 72/3: 329–48.

—— (1971), 'The Postwar Literature on Externalities: An Interpretive Essay', *Journal of Economic Literature*, 9: 1–28.

—— (1981), *Introduction to Normative Economics* (New York: Oxford University Press).

MONTIAS, J. M. (1976), *Structure of Economic Systems* (New Haven, Conn.: Yale University Press).

MORISHIMA, M. (1982), *Why Has Japan 'Succeeded'?* (Cambridge: Cambridge University Press).

MUELLER, D. C. (1989), *Public Choice II: A Revised Edition of Public Choice* (Cambridge: Cambridge University Press).

MUSGRAVE, R. A. (1939), 'The Voluntary Exchange Theory of Public Economy', *Quarterly Journal of Economics*, 53: 213–38.

NAGEL, T. (1986), *The View from Nowhere* (New York: Oxford University Press).

NELSON, R. (1981), 'Assessing Private Enterprise: An Exegisis of Tangled Doctrine', *Bell Journal of Economics*, 12: 93–111.

NG, Y. K. (1973), 'Income Distribution as a Peculiar Public Good: The Paradox of Redistribution and the Paradox of Universal Externality', *Public Finance/Finance Publiques*, 28/1: 1–10.

NORTH, D. (1981), *Structure and Change in Economic History* (New York: Norton).

NOVE, A. (1983), *The Economics of Feasible Socialism* (London: Allen & Unwin).

NOZICK, R. (1974), *Anarchy, State and Utopia* (Oxford: Basil Blackwell).

O'DRISCOLL (1986), 'Competition as a Process: A Law and Economics Perspective', in Langlois (1986*a*).

OATES, W. (1983), 'The Regulation of Externalities: Efficient Behavior by Sources and Victims', *Public Finance/Finance Publiques*, 38: 362–75.

PEACOCK, A. T., and MUSGRAVE, R. A. (1958) (eds.), *Classics in the Theory of Public Finance* (London: Macmillan).

PERRINGS, C. (1987), *Economy and Environment* (Cambridge: Cambridge University Press).

PIGOU, A. C. (1924), *The Economics of Welfare* (2nd edn., London: Macmillan).

—— (1962), *The Economics of Welfare* (repr. of 1932 4th edn., London: Macmillan).

POLINSKY, A. M. (1983), *An Introduction to Law and Economics* (Boston, Mass.: Little Brown & Company).

POSNER, R. (1977), *Economic Analysis of Law* (2nd edn., Cambridge, Mass.: Harvard University Press).

—— (1980), 'The Value of Wealth: A Comment on Dworkin and Kronman', *Journal of Legal Studies*, 9: 243–52.

—— (1983), *The Economics of Justice* (Cambridge, Mass.: Harvard University Press).

—— (1986), *Economic Analysis of Law* (3rd edn., Cambridge: Cambridge University Press).

PUTNAM, H. (1988), *The Many Faces of Realism* (La Salle: Open Court).

QUINE, W. V. (1987), *Quiddities: An Intermittently Philosophical Dictionary* (Cambridge, Mass.: The Belkanp Press of Harvard University Press).

RILEY, J. (1988), *Liberal Utilitarianism* (Cambridge: Cambridge University Press).

ROBERTSON, D. H. (1924), 'Those Empty Boxes', *Economic Journal*, 36: 16–30; repr. in Stigler and Boulding (1953).

ROBINSON, J. (1941), 'The Rising Supply Price', *Economica*, 8: 1–8; repr. in Stigler and Boulding (1953).

RUTTAN, V. W., and HAYAMI, Y. (1984), 'Towards a Theory of Induced Insitutional Innovation', *Journal of Development Studies*, 20: 203–23.

SAMUELS, W. J. (1972), 'Welfare Economics, Power, and Property', in G. Wunderlich and W. L. Gibson (eds.), *Perspectives of Property* (Pennsylvania State University).

—— (1988) (ed.), *Institutional Economics* (Brookfield, Vt.: Gower Pub. Co).

SAMUELSON, P. A. (1947), *Foundations of Economic Analysis* (Cambridge, Mass.: Harvard University Press).

—— (1954), 'The Pure Theory of Public Expenditure', *Review of Economics and Statistics*, 36: 387–9.

—— (1955), 'Diagramatic Exposition of a Theory of Public Expenditure', *Review of Economics and Statistics*, 37: 350–6.

—— (1958), 'Aspects of Public Expenditure Theories', *Review of Economics and Statistics*, 40: 332–8.

SCHELLING, T. C. (1960), *The Strategy of Conflict* (Cambridge, Mass.: Harvard University Press).

SCHELLING, T. C. (1984), *Choice and Consequence* (Cambridge, Mass.: Harvard University Press).

SCHMID, A. A. (1987), *Property, Power, and Public Choice* (2nd edn., New York: Praeger).

SCHOTTER, A. (1981), *The Economic Theory of Social Institutions* (Cambridge: Cambridge University Press).

SCHUMPETER, J. A. (1954), *History of Economic Analysis* (London: Allen & Unwin).

SCITOVSKY, T. (1954), 'Two Concepts of External Economies', *Journal of Political Economy*, 62: 70–82.

—— (1976), *The Joyless Economy* (Oxford: Oxford University Press).

SEN, A. K. (1970), 'The Impossibility of a Paretian Liberal', *Journal of Political Economy*, 78: 152–7.

—— (1973), 'Behavior and the Concept of Preference', *Economica*, 40: 241–59.

—— (1977), 'Rational Fools: A Critique of the Behavioural Foundations of Economic Theory', *Philosophy and Public Affairs*, 6: 317–44.

—— (1985), 'Goals, Commitment and Identity', *Journal of Law, Economics, and Organization*, 1: 341–55.

SHIBATA, H., and WINRICH, J. S. (1983), 'Control of Pollution when the Offended Defend Themselves', *Economica*, 50: 425–38.

SIDGWICK, H. (1883), *The Principles of Political Economy* (1st edn. London: Macmillan and Co. and New York).

—— (1901), *The Principles of Political Economy* (3rd edn.).

SIMON, H. A. (1982), *Models of Bounded Rationality*, 2 vols. (Cambridge, Mass.: MIT Press).

—— (1983) *Reason in Human Affairs* (Stanford: Stanford University Press).

SRAFFA, P. (1926), 'The Laws of Return Under Competitive Conditions', *Economic Journal*, 36; repr. in Stigler and Boulding (1953).

STARRETT, D. A. (1971), Identifying Production and Cost Relationships in the Presence of Externalities, Hier Discussion Paper No. 186, Harvard University, Cambridge Mass.

—— (1972) 'Fundamental Non-Convexities in the Theory of Externalities', *Journal of Economic Theory*, 4: 180–99.

STATEN, M., and UMBECK, J. (1986), 'Economic Inefficiency of Law: A Logical and Empirical Impossibility', Working Paper (Department of Economics, University of Delaware, and Department of Economics, Purdue University).

STIGLER, G. J., and BOULDING, K. E. (1953) (eds.), *Readings in Price Theory* (London: George Allen & Unwin).

SUZUMURA, K. (1983), *Rational Choice, Collective Decisions, and Social Welfare* (Cambridge: Cambridge University Press).

TAYLOR, M. (1976), *Anarchy and Cooperation* (New York: Wiley).

—— (1990), 'Cooperation and Rationality: Notes on the Collective Action Problem and Its Solutions', in K. S. Cook and M. Levi (eds.), *The Limits of Rationality* (Chicago: University of Chicago Press).

UMBECK, J. (1981), 'Might Makes Right—A Theory of the Formation and Initial Distribution of Property Rights', *Economic Inquiry*, 19/1: 38–59.

VARIAN, H. (1989), 'A Solution to the Problem of Externalities when Agents are Well-Informed', Technical report (University of Michigan, Ann Arbor).

VINER, J. (1931), 'Cost Curves and Supply Curves', *Zeitschrift fur Nationalokonomie*; repr. in Stigler and Boulding (1953).

WICKSELL, K. (1958), 'New Principle of Just Taxation', in Peacock and Musgrave (1958) (1st pub. 1896 as 'Ein Neus Prinzip der gerechten Besteuerung').

WINTER, S. G. (1969), 'A Simple Remark on the Second Optimality Theorem of Welfare Economics', *Journal of Economic Theory*, 1: 99–103.

—— (1986), 'Comments on Arrow and on Lucas', in R. M. Hogarth and M. W. Reder (eds.), *Rational Choice: The Contrast between Economics and Psychology* (Chicago: The University of Chicago Press).

WRIGLESWORTH, J. L. (1985), *Libertarian Conflicts in Social Choice* (Cambridge: Cambridge University Press).

YOUNG, A. A. (1913), 'Pigou's Wealth and Welfare', *Quarterly Journal of Economics*, 27: 672–86.

ZERBE, R. O. (1976), 'The Problem of Social Cost: Fifteen Years Later', in S. A. Y. Lin (ed.), *Theory and Measurement of Economic Externalities* (New York: Academic Press).

INDEX